D1172854

LARRY BOWA
"I Still Hate to Lose"

Barry M. Bloom

Sports Publishing L.L.C.

www.sportspublishingllc.com

A. Bartlett Giamatti's "The Green Fields of the Mind" is
reprinted from *A Great and Glorious Game* by permission of
Algonquin Books of Chapel Hill.

Excerpts from Chapter 10 are based on an article that appeared
in the *San Diego Tribune*.

Director of production: Susan M. Moyer
Project manager: Tracy Gaudreau
Developmental editor: Elisa Bock Laird
Copy editor: Cynthia L. McNew
Dust jacket design: Christine Mohrbacher
Photo editor: Erin Linden-Levy

ISBN: 1-58261-788-0

Printed in the United States

Sports Publishing L.L.C.
www.sportspublishingllc.com

To Alicia with love...

It breaks your heart.
It is designed to break your heart.
The game begins in the spring,
And it blossoms in the summer,
Filling the afternoons and evenings,
And then,
As soon as the chill rains come,
It stops,
And leaves you to face the fall alone.
—A. Bartlett Giamatti, "The Green Fields of the Mind"

Monday we watch-a Firefly's house, but he no come out. He wasn't home.
Tuesday we go to the ballgame, but he fool us. He no show up.
Wednesday he go to the ballgame, and we fool him. We no show up.
Thursday was a doubleheader. Nobody show up.
Friday it rained all day. There was no ballgame, so we stayed home
and we listened to it on-a the radio.
—Chico Marx as Chicolini, *Duck Soup*

We have two lives—the one we learn with and the life we live after that.
—Bernard Malamud, *The Natural*

Take me where you're going,
Where I see those waters flow.
Past the wheat fields and the valleys
And those mountains tipped with snow.
Take me where you're going,
Where I've often wished to be.
Take me ever gently to the sea.
—Written on the banks of the Mississippi, 1974, revised, 2004, the author

—Contents—

Bloom's Take: Bowa Lived to Win Another Day

I was asleep in my New York hotel room early in the morning of Saturday, May 28, 1988, when the telephone rang. A quick check of the digital clock said it was 4:30 a.m. The voice on the other end of the line told me that Jack McKeon, the Padres' general manager, and his sidekick, Bill "Boomer" Beck, had checked into the Grand Hyatt that evening. That could only mean one thing: Larry Bowa's days of managing the Padres were over. The rumors of Bowa's demise had been building all week through the first four games of a nine-game road trip across the East. Each day brought a new drumbeat. First, Charles "Chub" Feeney, the team's venerable club president, had joined the Padres the night before at Shea Stadium. He was uncharacteristically mum and wouldn't talk to reporters. Now this. I knew I wasn't going to get any more sleep that night. McKeon was supposed to be on a scouting trip. Instead, he would take over as manager.

At that time, I was in my fifth full year of covering the Padres for the old *San Diego Tribune*, a newspaper distributed in the afternoon that would eventually go the way of all evening editions. The paper, with its late afternoon green-sheet sports section, was folded into what now is the *San Diego Union-Tribune* in 1992. But in 1988, I knew I had the break on the story. The *Union* would hit the streets that morning only with speculation that Bowa was at his end days. The *Tribune* would hit the streets soon after with the news that Bowa had been terminated.

By then, Bowa and I had developed a close personal relationship that was unusual in the give and take between reporter and manager. We had spent the 1987 season putting together a book—*Bleep! Larry Bowa Manages.* That account chronicled the ups and downs of his first season as a major league manager and was sprinkled with stories and anecdotes from his 16-year playing career as one of the National League's most prolific shortstops with the Phillies, Cubs and Mets.

As a novice baseball writer, I had a casual relationship with Bowa that began when he played for those great Phillies teams of the late 1970s and on to the Cubs who ingloriously lost to the Padres in the 1984 National League Championship Series. Those Phillies teams were rough and tumble. Hall of Fame pitcher Steve Carlton didn't talk to the media. Hall of Fame third baseman Mike Schmidt could snarl at you with the best of them. Under mild-mannered manager Danny Ozark, the clubhouse on most days was a mine field of contemptuous baseball players not unlike other championship-caliber teams of that era. The Phillies then added the two elements that catapulted them to the 1980 World Series championship. They signed Pete Rose as a free agent and replaced Ozark with the cantankerous Dallas Green as manager.

Despite his well documented gambling problems as a manager, there were few players who could combine the candor, availability and will to win exhibited by Pete Rose, baseball's all-time leader with 4,256 hits. As a reporter, if you didn't walk away from one interview session with your notebook filed with Rose quotes, then you might as well have gone into another business. Rose's infectious attitude changed the culture of the clubhouse just enough to put the Phillies over the top. And Green's penchant for honesty and not taking any crap from the players was the perfect counterbalance. Rose and Green changed the "I" attitude of those Phillies into "we."

Bowa was always in the center of the storm, the team's unacknowledged leader and chief internal instigator. What I remember most about Bowa, the player, was that he was almost always at his locker, win or lose, to answer questions after the game. That said, he could cut right through a reporter with his unbridled sarcasm if he didn't like the question asked. Many a scribe, radio or TV personality withered away from the onslaught. The Phillies, in general, and Bowa, in particular, were not for the faint of heart. Let me be clear that at this juncture I really had no relationship with Bowa beyond the give and take in front of his locker. I was around his team so infrequently, save for the seemingly annual postseason runs, that I'm not sure he even knew my name. If he did, he never addressed me that way. He usually just raised his head from a postgame paper plate of food and answered the questions in a "why are you bothering me in between bites" kind of manner. It was worse after a defeat.

"As far back as I can remember, I always hated to lose," Bowa said.

Our relationship changed for the better after McKeon brought in Bowa to manage the Padres.

I was hired at the *Tribune* in 1982 as part of the wave in San Diego that brought tough-minded reporters such as Tom Cushman, Bud Shaw, T. R. Reinman and Clark Judge to the National League's furthest western outpost. As such, we wrote what we saw and heard, took no prisoners and offered management no favors whether it was Cushman writing columns, Judge covering the Chargers or me staying on top of the Padres. Before the advent of cable television and the internet made information almost instantaneous, the *Tribune* had to give its readers stories with bite that went beyond the news of the day. That was the way we competed with the morning *Union* and perhaps extended the life of the *Tribune* by a decade in the process. Thus we had players carping at the manager, the manager carping at the players and everyone usually angry with us.

By the time of Bowa's promotion from managing the Padres' Triple-A affiliate in Las Vegas, I had experienced numerous battles with McKeon, club president Ballard Smith, former manager Dick Williams and even the owner, the late Joan Kroc. In 1984, the players tried to ban me from the clubhouse, and Williams did banish me for a month from his office, telling the other writers who regularly covered the team that if any of his quotes turned up in my stories, they would be banished, too. And that was during a season in which the Padres were winning! Particularly in McKeon's case, it was a tug of immovable objects. The more irascible he became, the more obstinate I was in print. It was a love-hate relationship that never changed until he was fired during the 1990 season, my next to last full year covering the team. In retrospect, a lot of the animosity was petty and didn't serve either of us very well. In my mind, we've ironed all of that out now, and it was an experience to cover his unexpected run as manager of the Florida Marlins to the 2003 World Series championship over the Yankees for MLB.com. As with Bowa, you have to admire McKeon's will to win and the will to persevere beyond all odds. No matter what anyone thinks, writes or says, don't ever count those two guys out.

So it must have been good timing and fate that brought all three of us together during the off season of 1986. It was McKeon's idea to take me along on a January 1987 scouting trip to Puerto Rico. Bowa flew down from his home in Philadelphia and met us in San Juan. We hopped to ballparks from San Juan to Caguas to Ponce watching Padres prospects perform in the Puerto Rican Winter League. And McKeon had assembled a wealth of them, who all went on to great careers in the major leagues: Joey Cora, the brothers Alomar (Roberto and Sandy), Carlos Baerga, and Benito Santiago, who would be the National League Rookie of the Year under Bowa and end the 1987 season with a 34-game hitting streak. Before the native sons of Puerto Rico were included in Major League Baseball's June draft of amateur players, McKeon was a genius at mining that area of Latin America for the Padres.

The trip gave me a brief respite of goodwill with McKeon and helped me forge my relationship with Bowa, which couldn't hurt going into another baseball season. About a month later, just before the start of spring training, I was back in San Diego and received a telephone call from Bowa, asking me to co-author his first book. A publishing company, Bonus Books in Chicago, had queried him about doing a diary of his first season managing in the big leagues.

"We got along well in San Juan, and I need a guy who is just as big an asshole as I am to hang with me all season to write it," Bowa said. "I asked around, and everyone told me that asshole is you."

Enough background. Let's now spin the clock forward to that early May morning in 1988. The Padres were 16-30 and had defeated the Mets the previous night, 2-0, at Shea Stadium behind the pitching of Mark Grant and Mark Davis. They had been swept in a three-game series at Montreal during the first leg of the trip but were not on a particularly odious losing streak. They had lost 97 games under Bowa in 1987, though, and the mutinous feeling among the players was pretty palpable. Immediately after receiving the call that McKeon and Beck were in the house, I called the front desk to confirm. The two had indeed checked in and were listed under their own names.

I waited until about 6:00 a.m. before calling them. McKeon was not in his room. I woke up Beck, the Padres' director of publicity, who would neither confirm nor deny Bowa's ousting but simply called it "a probability."

"There's only one person who can substantiate that," said Beck, who is the traveling secretary for the Marlins and who got back together again with McKeon when he was hired to manage the team on May 11, 2003.

That person was Chub Feeney, who was making all the crucial Padres decisions at that point. It was only 3:00 a.m. in the West, so I had plenty of time to verify and prepare the story. I let Feeney sleep and called Bowa. By this time it was about 6:30 a.m. He was awake.

"Larry, have you heard from Chub this morning?" I asked.

"No," Bowa said.

"Do you know that Jack and Boomer are in the hotel?"

"That means I'm boxed," Bowa said.

"Yeah, Larry," I told him. "I'm sorry. Do you have any comment? I'm writing it."

I had just informed a major league manager and a man who had become a close friend and confidante that he had been fired. I was an emotional wreck, but I had to write the story.

"Well, if that's the case [McKeon and Beck being there], you know they're going to do something," Bowa said for the first edition of my story. "If that's what they think is wrong, it's up to them. You would have thought, though, that they might have had the decency to let me know first. I'm not calling anybody. If they want to call me, it's up to them. You've got to have some dignity."

Before I filed the story, I called Feeney. By then it was 8:30 a.m., and Bowa and I had had numerous conversations. But Feeney had yet to call Bowa. Feeney was once president of the New York/San Francisco Giants and president of the National League from 1970 to 1986. He had joined the Padres midway through the 1987 season and wasn't particularly enamored of Bowa's trashy on-field outbursts. Still, he gave him a contract to return in 1988 with numerous admonitions to clean up his act. Larry tried—how he tried—but that old Bowa family temper handed down to him by his late father, Paul, often got the best of him.

"I remember Chub calling me in at the beginning of the season and telling me not to worry about wins and losses," Bowa said recently. "We had a young team. Let the kids keep maturing and keep playing them. And I was fine with that. But a month later, he called me back in and told me we've got to win some games. He wouldn't define for me which way he wanted me to go. I didn't care as long as I had his support. He said I was the manager. So I just kept playing the kids. We knew we weren't going to win the pennant or anything."

Feeney confirmed Bowa's firing and that it would be announced at an upcoming press conference.

"We'll have something for you sometime this morning," Feeney said. "I've got to talk to Larry. That's my only reason for being here."

Then, as almost an off-the-record aside, he asked me not to call Larry and give him the news. It was way too late for that. Chub had no way of knowing what had happened during the previous few hours.

When Feeney finally called Bowa, he asked him to come up to his room. Bowa exploded and turned him down flat.

"I asked him, 'For what?'" Bowa said. "'For you to tell me I'm fired? I knew about that at seven o'clock. Barry Bloom already told me.'"

Bowa then said he added: "Hey, Chub, first of all I don't want to come up there. And second of all I already heard this from a writer. You talk about professionalism, this is the lowest I've ever seen in my life."

This is the way it happened, so let me clear up a misconception that seems to have proliferated over the years and reared its ugly head again late in the 2003 season when McKeon's Marlins were battling Bowa's Phillies for the National League's wild-card berth: Jack McKeon didn't fire Larry Bowa; Chub Feeney fired Larry Bowa. It was Chub's decision solely. McKeon simply stepped into the breach and took over managing the team.

"Why would I fire Larry?" McKeon said in 2003. "I hired the guy. Larry was my friend. Still is."

Let me add this qualifier, though: The Feeney era was not McKeon's happiest of his long tenure with the Padres, which lasted more than a decade. Feeney fancied himself a general manager and usurped McKeon's ability to make trades and sign contracts. Feeney's biggest deal as president of the Padres, not unexpectedly with his old friends the Giants, was a big bust for San Diego in 1987. It was a July 4 surprise: Kevin Mitchell, Dave Dravecky and Craig Lefferts to San Francisco for Chris Brown, Mark Grant, Keith Comstock and Mark Davis. The three former Padres helped the Giants win the National League West title and took them to the seventh game of the NLCS before losing the pennant to St. Louis.

Davis, a left-handed reliever, was ultimately a good catch for the Padres. As a closer, he had 44 saves for the team in 1989 and won the Cy Young Award in the National League. After that, Davis became a free agent and was mired in a bitter contract dispute with the Padres, who broke off negotiations. He signed with the Kansas City Royals and never again enjoyed the same success. Brown, a talented third baseman with gobs of potential, was hit in the head by a pitch while he was with the Giants and never got over the fear of standing in again at home plate. Brown turned into a hypochondriac and even missed a game when he claimed that he slept badly on one eye.

Brown, who batted .232 for the Padres in 1987, was the kind of player who drives Bowa crazy. Only days before he was fired, Bowa assessed the team while standing around the batting cage in Montreal's Olympic Stadium. When reporters got to Chris Brown, Bowa said:

"He'll be an eight-to-fiver. He won't be playing this game very long."

Brown had missed 21 games and hadn't played in the nearly three weeks before Bowa was fired. In one of his parting shots, Bowa said this about Brown:

"Chris Brown is a dog, and you can write that. If I'm getting fired because of him, you can be my guest."

Brown and Feeney were gone at the end of the 1988 season, following Bowa out the door by only about four months. Feeney never again worked in Major League Baseball and died of a heart attack in 1994. At the age of 28, Brown was out of baseball completely by the end of 1989 season.

But I digress. McKeon was in a vise that he didn't create between Feeney and Bowa, the manager he hired. He was now Traderless Jack because Feeney had taken away all of his organizational powers, and he was watching games being frittered away while Bowa festered and exploded. McKeon, who had built the Padres' 1984 pennant winner, had little impact. For example, both Bowa and McKeon wanted to make the rookie Roberto Alomar the starting second baseman after Alomar had excelled during spring training. Feeney nixed the idea, sending Alomar to the minor leagues in an attempt to extend his ineligibility to file for salary arbitration. Feeney finally relented on April 20 after the Padres had limped off to a 4-9 start. Alomar turned out to be a 12-time All-Star. Things might have worked out differently for Bowa had Alomar been with the team from the beginning of that season.

Feeney never really fancied working with Bowa or McKeon, the two men he inherited in the top two positions when Kroc decided to abort the sale of the team and hired him to replace Ballard Smith on June 10, 1987. At the time, Kroc gave Feeney the option to fire McKeon, but he chose instead to let Jack languish in the front office. Nearly a year later, in one fell swoop, Feeney figured that he had solved two problems: He got rid of Bowa and moved McKeon out from under foot and onto the field.

McKeon, now 72 years old, said recently that Feeney told him about the impending switch a few days before the debacle of May 28. He gave McKeon only a few hours to take the job. Jack didn't have any choice. It was manna from heaven and another new lease on his now seemingly endless baseball life. Bowa, of course, knew he was hung out to dry.

"All the baseball people are laughing at this organization," Bowa said the morning he was fired.

Feeney, though, wasn't laughing. He wasn't happy with me for my part in breaking the news to Bowa, and he tried to put a brave face on what was nothing short of a fiasco.

"We tried to do it the right way," Feeney said that day. "We just screwed it up. I didn't want to fire him before the game [on the previous Friday night] and put the whole thing into a tizzy. I thought [Saturday] morning was the proper time to do it. I'm sorry Larry is upset about that. It's one of those things that happens. It's very difficult to keep a secret."

Bowa will always wonder if his reactions that day, so honest, so off the cuff and so reminiscent of his departure from Philadelphia as a player in 1981, had cost him. When backed into a corner, Bowa always came out swinging. Had Feeney put the word out on him around baseball that he couldn't manage? That was the rumor behind the scenes. Feeney was well respected until the day he died. He was really old school long before the term old school ever existed. Bowa will never know.

"He said he liked the way I managed but didn't like my antics on the field," Bowa recalled.

Otherwise, Bowa never discussed the matter with Feeney. And Feeney never told me.

"If it happened now, I'd handle it differently," Bowa said recently. "I'd want to talk with the boss and discuss the conditions that existed that led to the decision. Everybody feels like they got fired because of the job that they did. But management doesn't look at the meetings you had: If I asked to have an Alomar up with the team and didn't get him. How did that affect the situation? If you don't get what you want, you can't blast your boss in the paper. You have to live with it, and nobody really knows except you what happened behind the scenes. You can't just rip, because it makes the organization look bad.

"Looking back on it now, you understand the dynamics of it. The first time you lose a job, you take it personal. You should always take it personal, but when you watch the way stuff evolves now, a lot of it is out of your hands. You just have to go with it. Nobody said it was going to be fair. Nobody. Ever."

By August 11, 1988, Bowa was back with the Phillies as third base coach and would remain there in that capacity until the end of the 1996 season. Coaching stints with the Angels and Mariners would follow. One thing Bowa does know: He didn't get a chance to manage again until the Phillies finally hired him for the 2001 season. In Philadelphia, where the organization has a plan and vision heading into its first season in a new stadium—Citizens Bank Park— Bowa obviously has the support of management. The Phillies, who haven't made the playoffs since 1993, have been adding players and payroll under Bowa's watch with a serious intent to win.

And here we are back together writing again.

"One thing hasn't changed," Bowa said. "I still hate to lose."

— Acknowledgments —

It's not often that an author gets a chance to revisit a project, to take a second look at a work that was researched and written 18 years ago. In this case, Larry Bowa and I have grown up and matured together. Although we have taken different roads, we have developed parallel careers that support each other: baseball manager and sportswriter, subject and biographer. We have built our relationship through trials and tribulations and retained the bond as friends. In the end, this book is as much about my journey as it is about his, and I thank him profusely for giving me that chance to take it. Just like Larry, I have learned along the way how to soften my rough edges, and I'd like to thank some of the people who helped me evolve.

Tom Cushman, Bud Poliquin and Bill Pinella were my editors at the old *San Diego Tribune* and gave me the chance to cover the Padres and meet Mr. Bowa. Karin Winner is still the editor in chief at the combined *San Diego Union-Tribune*, and she put me into the position to hone my skills as a news and sports business writer. Jay "Just Make the Calls" Beberman, the editor at Bloomberg News, plucked me out of San Diego and gave me a national profile. Bob DuPuy, the president and chief operating officer of Major League Baseball, encouraged me to move to MLB.com, where I began covering the labor negotiations during the summer of 2002 and developed into a national reporter under the guidance of Bob Bowman, our chief executive, and Dinn Mann, our editor in chief—special thanks to Dinn for recognizing the value of writing this book. Thanks too, to Geoff Grant, our managing editor, with whom I work on a daily basis, carving out a schedule and producing some very high-profile stories.

This book wouldn't even have been published if not for the dogged persistence of my agent, Jay Acton, who wouldn't take no for an answer and spent the summer of 2003 selling the project. Thanks as well to Elisa Bock Laird, the developmental editor at Sports Publishing L.L.C., who helped give the project focus and followed the course of this manuscript every step along the way.

I have known Bowa so long and so well that interviews contained in our first book—*Bleep! Larry Bowa Manages*—were conducted decades ago. I cherish my relationships with Chub Feeney, Joan Kroc, Paul and Mary Bowa, and Eric Show, who all died before their time, but whose words were preserved earlier for eternity. I miss them all.

Thanks, as well, to scout Eddie Bockman, manager Frank Lucchesi, coach Billy DeMars, Hall of Famer Mike Schmidt, and manager/general manager Jim Frey, who gave their time to the first book and whose words are memorialized here. Thanks go to Bill Giles, Eddie Wade, Dave Montgomery, and John Kruk of the Phillies, Lou Piniella of the Devil Rays, Terry Collins of the Dodgers, Tony Tavares of the Expos, Jim Fregosi of the Braves, the retired Joe Carter, and Bill Conlin of the *Philadelphia Daily News* for allowing me to partake of their insights. Thanks to Leigh Tobin of the Phillies, Rick Vaughn of the Devil Rays, Josh Rawitch of the Dodgers, and Steve Copses of the Marlins for helping to facilitate many of these interviews, sometimes on very short notice.

Thanks, in particular, to Jack McKeon, who gave me initial access to Bowa and through some rocky times is the one baseball personality who serves as a string connecting almost my entire writing career. Jack was a main contributor to the first work and gave me his time and insight, reflecting back on those events in the months before this manuscript was complete.

And finally, thanks so much to my wife, Alicia, who has been there since 1984, who has supported me through the ups and downs, the good times and the bad, through the raising of our children—Joanna and Raphael—who are now off creating their own lives. Without your love there would no story, no happy beginning or happy ending.

−1−

IT ALL BEGAN
IN SACRAMENTO

Eddie Bockman sat in front of the Bowa household on the south side of Sacramento in his late-model car. He held a copy of the contract that Paul Bowa and his son, Larry, were studying inside the bright ranch-style house. To Larry Bowa, the important matter was the contract. To his father, the numbers that jumped off the page in black and white were even more significant: Two thousand dollars. A scout for the Philadelphia Phillies wanted to sign his son for a measly $2,000. Larry was ready to go.

To his chagrin, Larry had not been selected in baseball's first draft of amateur players. Not even in the last round. The contract meant redemption, a chance at the big leagues. All Bowa wanted was a chance. He'd take it from there. Paul was counseling him to hold out for more money. Paul had talked to some friends involved in American Legion ball in the city, and they had told him that there were other major league teams interested. That Bowa was worth more.

"I didn't want him to sign," Paul, who has passed away since these interviews, said more than a decade ago. "I think he could have gotten more. But if he didn't, I didn't want to be the one to kill Larry's chances of playing in the major leagues."

Recalled Bowa: "I didn't care about the money. All I wanted to do was play ball. That's all I had wanted to do for as long as I can remember."

That insatiable desire was what Bockman had counted on. The Northern California scout for the Phillies had seen the wiry kid play on a consistent basis. Once, he had journeyed the 90 miles from his home on the San Francisco Peninsula to Sacramento to watch Bowa play shortstop for Sacramento City College. But Bowa was ejected during the first inning of each game of a doubleheader.

In the first game, Bowa walked to lead off the inning and tried to steal second. When the second base umpire called him out, he came up jawing and was immediately sent to the bench.

"In junior college games they only use two umpires," Bockman recalled. "I don't think Larry realized that the umpire who had thrown him out of the first game was behind the plate in the second game."

Bowa led off and was rung up by the same umpire on four pitches. Before he knew it, he was thrown out again.

"I'm sure I deserved to be kicked out, but he carried a grudge into the second game," Bowa said. "And I was boxed in that game, too."

So much for Bockman's scouting trip.

"I caught him as he was going over to the bus," Bockman said. "He was still upset. You know him—throwing helmets, trashing bats. I told him, 'I'll be back to see you. You'll be a pretty good player if you can stay in the game.' He asked me who I was. When I told him, that pretty much quieted him down."

In so many ways, one couldn't help but be taken aback by Paul's resemblance to his son. He was a craggy version of Larry, who was 26 years his junior. Similar in size: five feet, 10 inches, 160 pounds. He had the same protruding jaw that seemed to beckon all challengers. He had those same squinty eyes.

"We were clones," Bowa said.

They also were as one in personality. If anyone was seeking clues about the genesis of Bowa's infamous explosive streak, one needed to go no further than his father. Paul and his wife, Mary, who also has passed away since these interviews, were Sacramento natives.

Their heritage dated back to the days of the great gold rush when fortune seekers and frontiersmen panned the basins of Northern California's Delta region. Like his son a generation later, Paul was the type of gritty baseball player who would just as soon run over you as around you.

Paul's temper was the scourge of the minor leagues—a trait he handed over to his son along with dogged determination. "There was nothing I wanted to do more when I was a kid than play major league baseball," Paul said.

He never earned the chance. Paul, a scrappy third baseman, found himself bouncing around the St. Louis Cardinals organization. During the 1940s he was the player-manager of a low-level minor league club in Duluth, Minnesota. Little did he know at the time that he had embarked on his final professional baseball season. Just having recovered from the sudden debilitation of an appendectomy, Paul dug in at home plate. In a micro-second he was slammed in the head by a fastball. Paul was protected only by his woolen baseball cap—in effect, no protection at all. When he awoke three days later, Mary was standing by his side. A priest had read Paul his last rites.

"I can remember some of it," Larry said. "I remember riding a train with my mom. That's how they used to travel. And all the players who played for my dad used to come and pick me up and take me down through the cars and all that. I remember all that stuff. I remember him going on a road trip in Duluth. Poor old mom was holding me. We were looking out the window. Talk about a blizzard. And my mom was depressed. I remember things like that. I don't remember him getting hit in the head. I know they brought a priest. He'd have stayed in baseball somewhere if it wasn't for my mom. She was just tired of all the travel, being away from home."

Mary was also scared. The beaning incident was more than she could handle. "I didn't think I could go through something like that again," Mary said.

It was then that Paul came to the crossroads faced by so many professional players who are not able to make the grade after an extended period of time—go back for another season in the bushes or return home for good. Mary pushed hard for the return to Sacramento, even threatening what remained of their matrimonial bliss. She was tired of boarding houses, cheap hotels and long periods alone in strange little towns, caring for her young child. So Paul left his baseball dream behind, a decision he lamented until the end of his life. Mary gave birth to a daughter named Paula shortly thereafter.

"I wanted to go back for one more season on my own. Give it one more shot as a manager. Leave them at home," Paul recalled.

"I think what's in his mind is, if he wasn't pushed out by mom, could he have been a successful manager in the big leagues? He loved it. He knew the game of baseball," Bowa said. "They finally got cable while I was still playing with the Phillies, and he watched our games. He used to call me up sometimes and ask me why I did things. He tried to watch all the games. He was from that old school: Don't take anything from anybody. If they don't like it, forget about it."

And so Bowa was left as the standard bearer of the dream. Paul drove a beer truck, ran a bar, and worked on a printing press. He eventually retired with emphysema, caused by, he believed, working continuously with certain chemicals. He continued to manage and play American Legion ball on weekends, becoming a local legend because of his confrontations with umpires and other managers. Paul believed that Larry was short-changed at McClatchy High School because of a longtime feud between Paul and Bill Whiteneck, then the baseball coach.

Bowa never played high school baseball, ostensibly, Whiteneck told him, because it conflicted with his position on the basketball team. How would you like to be remembered for having made that decision? Compare Whiteneck to those numerous editors and publishers who once said that this Harry Potter thing would never make it. Of course, there are different versions of what happened in Bowa's sticky high school situation.

Paul: "We had gotten into some arguments when we were managing against each other, so he took it out on Larry."

Larry: "I don't know if they feuded. That might have been the reason. But in my mind, I really believe he thought I was too small. He was a big guy. He was one of those guys who lifted weights. He was a pretty good physical specimen. That's my opinion. My dad probably had his own opinion. I mean, I was cut three years in a row. That was the worst. I don't know, I can't tell you what death is like, but I didn't feel like doing anything. I was so depressed. I got home that day, I mean the first time I was cut, and I was so embarrassed I didn't even tell my dad. Every day, they would pick me up at 5:30 p.m., or something. So for two days, I would just hang around school and pretend that I practiced.

"And then, a friend of my dad, who knew the coach, saw my dad at the park and said, 'It's a shame Larry got cut.' He said, 'He what?' 'Yeah, he got cut a couple of days ago.' So I went home that night and my dad says to me, 'Sit down, I want to talk to you. How's practice going?' I went, 'It's going all right.' He says, 'Why are you lying to me? You got cut, didn't you?' And it was just like ... I said, 'Yeah, I got cut.' He said, 'That doesn't mean anything. You got cut? So you got cut. It's just one man's opinion. What was the reason he gave you?' I said, 'Well, he said I was too small. The guy they were going with, they felt he was going to be a better player.' So my dad says, 'Well, you can go do one of two things: You can quit, or you can go out for the Legion team.'"

On his father's advice, Bowa played Legion ball and eventually made his college team. According to Bowa, he was named All-Conference both years he played at Sacramento City College.

Despite his size, peewee at that time, Bowa also was a pretty fair basketball player in high school, attacking that sport with the same zeal with which he attacked baseball. "I played basketball for the B team because I was too small," he said. "I averaged 20 points a game. I could shoot. I'd go out in the back yard at home. My dad put up a basket. During the basketball season, I'd shoot until 9:30, 10 o'clock every night. We'd have a big spotlight on the basket."

Paul would take Larry out to Land Park during his Little League days and stress baseball fundamentals. When his father was at work and there was no one around for a game, Bowa used to bounce a hardball off the whitewashed wall of Holy Spirit Catholic School close to home until his father would fetch him and bring his boy home for dinner. "He'd just play there all day with a hardball and a glove," Paul recalled, allowing the memory to stream through his mind. "The cover would come off the old ball and he'd tape it up and go out there the very next day."

Bowa is clear about who had the greatest influence on the early stages of his life: his father.

"See, even then, I did the little things," he said. "We went out and bunted. You know how your dad goes out and throws to you and you hit? We bunted for a half hour. He'd throw them, and then we'd pick them all up. Then he'd say, 'Now we're going to hit,' just him and me. Then we'd go out and pick up everything. It was unbelievable. But the one thing my dad never did: He never said, 'You're going to the park.' I always had to say to him, 'Come on. I want to work on a couple of things.' Even though there were balls and things around, he never said, 'You have to play baseball.' In fact, he tried to talk me out of playing baseball because I was too small. He thought I'd be in the minors for 10 years.

"Even late in his life he was still hyper. He still had to get up and go. I think his proudest moment was at the World Series in 1980. That was the ultimate for him. He came down to the locker room when we were celebrating. He was in hog heaven. He was a ballplayer who knew how tough it was to get a job. He always preached getting a college degree and all that. I used to say, 'Yeah, okay, Dad,' because I hated school. I kept telling him, 'I'm going to make it. I'm going to make it.' He said, 'I'm telling you, the odds are against you.'"

By the time Bowa went out for Legion ball, a full-grown rivalry had developed between the two men. The young Bowa, maniacal on the one hand—"I was obsessed with it"—and the elder

Bowa, still charged with that incredible will to win. Bowa had become so much like his father in on-field temperament that his parents ultimately decided to watch the ballgames from beyond right field. Both parents, of course, had their different reasons. Mary didn't like to hear her son's gutter language. "The Larry who comes home is not the same person I read about in the papers," she once said. "I've never heard a foul word out of his mouth in this home." Paul didn't want his presence to influence the umpires against Larry, who had learned to create enough trouble for himself.

"When I started to play winter ball, there were the same umpires as when he played," Bowa said. "He got kicked out of so many games. They started baiting me. My dad sitting there would probably infuriate the umpire even more. My mom would get embarrassed."

But when the two men were on the field at the same time, it became even more heated.

"It became so bad in American Legion," Bowa said. "He was manager of a team called Fort Sutter, and I played for Post 61. You talk about tension at the breakfast table and before we'd go to the park ... My mom hated it. It was unbelievable. We didn't talk. They'd beat us, and we'd come back and beat them. That particular year, his team won it. But when they played us, I tried to do anything to beat his butt. Mom was like the mediator. The first thing we used to do when we sat down at the table, and I'm talking about from Little League on, was to establish one rule—no baseball talk at the dinner table. But inevitably, it seemed like every single night there would be a fight at the dinner table. I mean, people would get up without finishing their meal. To the end of her life, my mom was obsessed with sitting down because something would always happen. He'd say something about baseball. I'd say, 'No, that's not right. I didn't do that.' Before you know it, he's yelling at me. I'm jumping up. I'm walking off to my room. My mom's leaping up. She's just cooked a meal. It would happen every day.

"I always felt sorry for my mom and younger sister. My sister, all the way through high school until I signed, she thought she was left out. I used to get all the headlines playing ball. She says she felt like the outsider, which was understandable. She was raised around sports, and she loves sports. Even when they were kids, her two boys, Joe and Nick, looked like they were going to be pretty good athletes. My nephew, Nick Johnson, in fact, played first base in the [2003] World Series for the Yankees and was then traded to the Montreal Expos. We always got along great because of our ages. She's six years younger than me. There was no problem with her. But when we set up vacations during the summer, it was always around me. As you look back on it, it probably wasn't fair.

"One thing that stands out in my mind as I look back on my teenage years: Guys used to always go out and get drunk. The big thing in high school then was to go out and get a six-pack of beer. I never did that. It wasn't that I was afraid of my mom or dad, although I always was told that you were not supposed to do that stuff. When I see kids now who drink or do drugs and say it's because of peer pressure, it's hard for me to relate to that. There was plenty of peer pressure when I was in high school. It was just as prevalent then as it is now. When guys do cocaine now and blame it on their buddies for doing it, that's hard for me to relate to.

"That's personal makeup, I guess. I've never had trouble disciplining myself. Maybe it was because of the army. But even before I went in the reserves, I had a schedule I used to adhere to. If I told the guys I would meet them at the park at 8:30 in the morning, I'd be there at 8:30. I know I got that from my dad. He hated being late. I can't tell you how much I respected him.

"You know, we were never what you'd call well off. But my sister and I always had what we wanted. He found a way by working hard, by getting extra jobs. At Christmas time, you know, kids rattle off about eight or nine things they want. We used to get everything we wanted. As I look back now, I know that they couldn't afford a lot. He just found a way to provide. Yeah, my dad taught me how to play the game. How you were supposed to play it. When you're in the field, don't worry about hitting. When you're hitting, don't worry about the field. Never quit. No matter how tough things go. Never quit."

That last piece of advice, whether it was in Bowa's genes or drummed in by his father, was perhaps the single reason why he was able to carve a professional baseball career—that, and the ability finally to control the legendary Bowa temper. In college and Legion ball, Bowa developed such bad blood between himself and the umpires that he was consistently ejected from ballgames. His father began to realize that Bowa needed another venue. He had to whisk Bowa out of the area.

"If I didn't do that, Larry would've never made it," Paul said. "The kid had to get a chance to play."

That's when Eddie Bockman stepped in. After Bockman's promise at the doubleheader debacle—"I'll be back to see you"— months went by. The scout, who is retired now, never made it back to the Delta. As fortune would have it, though, in 1965 Bowa was invited to a Phillies tryout camp, where he impressed Bockman with his pugnacious play. Bockman managed a Winter League team that the Phillies sponsored on the San Francisco Bay Peninsula. Bowa was invited to play shortstop on that team with one stipulation:

"If he started throwing any helmets and bats or abused any umpires, he was through," said Bockman.

"Every weekend we got up at seven o'clock in the morning and drove to San Francisco or San Mateo, all those small towns in the Peninsula League," Bowa said.

Added Bockman: "He behaved himself. and he played like hell."

It just so happened that the World Series that year featured the Minnesota Twins and the Los Angeles Dodgers. Bockman was scheduled to join the Phillies' brass for an organizational meeting when the series shifted from Minneapolis to L.A. for Game 3. Among the treasures Bockman took with him on the one-hour flight south from the Bay Area was an eight-millimeter film documenting the talents of one 19-year-old named Lawrence Robert Bowa.

"The team was in the rebuilding process," Bockman said. "It was just after that disaster of 1964. You remember when the Phillies blew a six and a half game lead with 12 games left to play? We were looking at everybody. I was talking to Paul Owens, who was the player personnel director at the time, and I brought up Larry. I asked him if he was interested in taking a look at the film. He said, 'Sure.'"

And so in a major hotel in Los Angeles, where the movie industry may be second only to the used car business, Owens and Bockman set out to find an eight-millimeter motion picture camera—a relic of another time now. A bellman located one in storage and set it up in Owens's room.

"Paul jerked the sheet off the bed, hung it up on the wall, and we watched the film," Bockman said. "It was a little fuzzy, but you could get the picture. Larry was a speedy kid at the time with good instincts in the field. The question was whether or not he could hit."

Owens had this reaction to Bowa's speed: "Slow the film down," he told Bockman. "It looks like a silent movie." Bockman informed his boss that the film was running at the right speed.

"Paul asked me how much money he wanted," Bockman recalled. "'Money?' I said. 'He doesn't want any money. All he wants is a chance to play.' So Paul told me to sign him if it didn't cost too much. I gave him $2,000, but I didn't have to give him anything. After that, it was up to Larry. He made himself into everything he is today."

PLAYER DEVELOPMENT

Frank Lucchesi and Billy DeMars were the most influential baseball people during the formative stages of Larry Bowa's career. Lucchesi, a longtime manager, coach and scout, was the man who nurtured Bowa through much of the Philadelphia Phillies' farm system. As the big club's new manager, Lucchesi was responsible for keeping Bowa in the lineup early in the 1970 season, Bowa's first in the major leagues. DeMars, a batting coach with a long, successful career, was the man who taught Bowa how to hit big-league pitching.

"I'd have to say it's pretty true. I made Larry into a hitter," said the 78-year-old DeMars, who is retired and living in Florida. "If you asked him, he'd probably say the same thing."

DeMars was like an on-field father to Bowa, picking up where his real dad left off. Lucchesi was like a mentor. If it hadn't been for Lucchesi's stubbornness against growing local media pressure, Bowa would have been demoted to Class AAA Eugene not even two months into the 1970 season.

"I'll tell you, if it wasn't for Frank Lucchesi, I don't know what would have happened to Bowa," DeMars said. "He let him play every day. At the beginning, he played him every day even though the guy was only hitting .130. If it was some other manager, he might not have given him that chance."

Bowa came along in the Phillies program at absolutely the perfect time. The team that had lost 99 games in 1969 under Bob Skinner and George Myatt and was in another rebuilding phase. The Phillies hadn't won a National League pennant since the "Whiz Kids" era of 20 years past and were the last of the original 16 major league teams to still not have won a world championship during the 20th century. Talk about embarrassing ... Bowa had been force-fed through the minor leagues—a $2,000 bonus baby.

How bad was the neophyte Bowa as a hitter? During his first visit to Phillies camp in Florida, Bowa stepped into the batting cage under the watchful eyes of Gene Mauch, who was still the big-league manager. Recalls Bill Conlin, who covered the team at the time for the *Philadelphia Daily News*:

"It was one of the worst at-bats anyone had ever seen. It looked like he was flailing at baseballs with a rolled-up newspaper."

After Bowa had limped out of the box, Mauch turned to nobody in particular and said, "I couldn't hear him swing."

Said Conlin: "He was gone the next day."

Several years later, Bowa had already been labeled by the organization as simply a spunky utility player who was capable of ascending to the major leagues under Skinner in 1969.

"I didn't want to make the big club that soon," Bowa recalled. "They wanted me there as a utility player. I wanted to play everyday. At the end, there were 26 guys left in camp. Skinner said, 'I want Bowa here to be a utility player.' I just went up to him. I told him, 'I don't want to play in the big leagues yet. I want to play every day. I want to be a regular.' He said, 'Well, if you feel like that, then let me suggest one thing.' It was the last day of spring training. 'I want you to go to Eugene and learn how to switch hit. That's the only way you're going to make the big leagues as a regular. Hitting only from the right side, you can play utility right now.'

"So that's what I did. I mean, you ever do something with one hand for 20 years and now they say do it with the other hand? It was the worst feeling I've ever had in my life. You talk about a hopeless feeling. But I kept battling. I just wish that, as good a baseball man as my dad was, I wish he made me switch hit as far back as the Little League. But it never came up. We never even talked about it. Later on, my dad said, 'If there was one thing I could do over again, I wish I had started you out switch hitting.' When my sister's two boys were little, my dad already had them switch hitting.

"In '69, Frank was the manager at Eugene. We went out every day and we hit, hit, hit. All of a sudden, toward the middle of the year, I started getting into a groove. I ended up hitting .287 overall."

Woody Allen once said about guys like DeMars: "Those who can't do, teach. Those who can't teach, teach gym." DeMars couldn't do. He batted .237 and had 50 hits in 80 big-league games from 1948 to 1951 playing for the Philadelphia Athletics and the St. Louis Browns. But he could teach. Under DeMars's watchful eye, Bowa was able to leap to the big leagues after one season as a switch hitter.

Said DeMars: "That's hard. All of a sudden you find yourself in the major leagues, and you've only been a switch hitter for one season in the minors. He was a lot weaker from the left side, but we worked so much on the left side that eventually he became a better hitter on that side than he was on the right."

But not during the early phase of that first season. Bowa was the opening-day shortstop that year at Connie Mack Stadium, the last year for the Phillies in their ancient ballpark in North Philly before they moved far south to Veterans Stadium. The way Bowa played during his first few months in the majors, who could have foreseen that he would be an opening-day fixture with the Phillies lineup for the next 12 years? Only the dogged Lucchesi seemed to have any foresight.

"I've been very flattered over the years," recalled Lucchesi, who is 76 now and retired in Texas. "All over the country, the press has always written nice things: 'Frank Lucchesi made Larry Bowa.' And I'll say it again. Larry Bowa made himself.

"I will say this: Of course 1970 was the big key for Bowa. He was a rookie and he started out pretty rough as far as his hitting goes, and he wasn't making all the plays in the field either. I recall by mid-May, the Philly press was all over him. One Philly columnist said, 'How long can Lucchesi go with Bowa?' And then another one said, 'Is Bowa's locker all ready at Eugene?' Then there was another line or two that Bowa hits like a Little Leaguer. That's when I called him in.

"He had his head down because he thought he was being shipped out. I was sitting down behind my desk. I stood up, walked over to him, put my hand on his shoulder, and I said, 'Larry, forget what's in the paper. You're my shortstop tonight, you're my shortstop tomorrow, and you're my shortstop next week. You're going to be my shortstop all year. Someday, you're going to prove me right that you're going to be one hell of a shortstop. Just remember that. Now get out of here.'

"The reason I stuck with him is that I knew what was inside of him. I knew he had guts. I've never seen a kid with that much heart. It didn't happen right away, but in a few weeks, he started to turn it around."

What happened was that Bowa discovered the resource of Billy DeMars.

Bowa: "There we were at Connie Mack Stadium, Billy De-Mars and me at every home game. We'd be out there at two o'clock. He'd pitch them, the whole bag. I'd hit them and go get them. We did it every single day. And in Philadelphia during the summer, you know how humid it gets. I must have weighed about 145 pounds at the end of the year. I'd like to have a dollar for every ball I hit extra. And then everything started happening on a positive note. It took me four, five years to really feel comfortable hitting left-handed."

DeMars: "We started that first year, I wasn't even the hitting coach. He was hitting .185 the latter part of May. I said, 'If you want to come out, I'll throw to you every day.' So we'd go out there on the field. What we started working on was hitting down into the ball because he had a terrible habit of pulling away and swinging up.

That's what we did every day while we were home, and at the end of the season, he wound up hitting .250.

"Once he had the success the first year, he and I would stick together. We would work almost every day from spring training on. Once we got in the batting cage, that helped a lot. And then during the winter of 1974, I was going down to Florida on vacation, and he lived down there. And we went out every day there, too. I had a batting tee. He'd hit a couple of hundred balls off the batting tee. I'd throw a couple of hundred balls to him, and I'd make him bunt a hundred balls. We did that every day until spring training started. We did that from 1974 all the way until I left in 1981. That very first year, 1974, I think he hit .275. The next year he hit .305. If you look at his stats from '74 to '81, his average is right around .285.

"It was just a case where I had the knowledge on the hitting, but he put in the time. I didn't have to go looking for Larry. We put in a lot of time. That was his approach. I was willing to work at it and he was willing to put the time in every day. He was already a great fielder, he could run, and he had a great arm. And he hustled like hell. Once he started to improve his bat, Frank's opinion of him was borne out."

Lucchesi: "I knew him pretty well. I had Bowa for a couple of years at Reading in the Eastern Pennsylvania League. I also had him at Eugene in the Pacific Coast League and then three years in Philadelphia. He was a kid that had a lot of get up and go. He worked hard at the game. He didn't go through the motions. If there was something he had a weakness in, he would try to improve it. I remember, during infield, Bowa would take his ground balls like he was in a ballgame. I never tried to take the aggressiveness away from him. I recall, it might have been Opening Day his rookie year at Connie Mack Stadium. He got thrown out trying to steal. He was a little down, so I called him in the office and he thought I was going to say something negative, but it was positive. I said, 'Bowa, don't stop. Stay aggressive. I don't care if you got thrown out. Keep doing it.'

"Going way back to 1966, the Phillies brought him up from Spartanburg for the last week in San Diego, which was still Triple-A at the time. I remember when he joined the ball club, we started him in a ballgame, and you know, he was only about 150 pounds at the time; he wasn't too big a guy. We didn't have a uniform to fit him. They were all big. When he went out on the field it was kind of funny. The uniform was baggy. It was long. But I don't think size had anything to do with it. The kid just wanted to play."

Dave Montgomery, who began his career in ticket sales for the Phillies only a year after Bowa came up to the big leagues and would become the team's general partner, president, and chief executive officer, said the shortstop had an immediate impact on the team's culture.

"You couldn't help but to be impressed by his passion for the game and the incredible way he had to maximize his skills," Montgomery said. "I watched him in his early stages learn to hit left-handed, which was a huge adjustment. I will never see another short-stop that had Bowa's throwing accuracy. It was amazing. The first baseman's shirt was as far as his throws would stray. He made himself the excellent player he became."

Perhaps that work ethic is the reason that Bowa gives back the same way. As a player late in his career he'd take a young kid and work with him for hours on his fielding and hitting. The same thing is true about his stints managing in San Diego and Philadelphia. If a player wants to hit early, Bowa will be out at the ballpark six hours before a night game to throw batting practice.

For example, it's only a snapshot, but early in the 2003 season, the Phillies had optional batting practice hours before a night game at Dodger Stadium. Pat Burrell and Jim Thome, the fourth and fifth hitters in the batting order, were the first ones into the cage against the offerings of Bowa.

Both players had asked for the extra work. The fact that a high-priced star like Thome would seek extra hitting is one of the reasons why Bowa's job managing the team was more tenable in 2003.

"What is intriguing to me about Bowa is that his intensity level is so unique," said Thome, a big free agent signee for the Phillies, who ultimately led the National League with 47 homers and added 131 runs batted in. "You can't teach that. He loves the game. That's what he stands for. As a player, you want a manager who loves it as much as you do."

And Bowa need not forget that it all began with the confidence of Frank Lucchesi and the work habits of Billy DeMars.

3

SCHMIDT ON BOWA, BOWA ON SCHMIDT

Larry Bowa still had one more obstacle to overcome early in his career: the emergence of Michael Jack Schmidt. The two would anchor the left side of the Phillies' infield for nearly a decade, Schmidt at third base with his power and Gold Glove and Bowa with his wide range at shortstop and his relentless pursuit of improvement at the plate. The two had polar personalities. Bowa often needled his teammates and never stopped chirping. Schmidt was the strong, silent type who always seemed to be uncomfortable carrying his burden. Bowa worked incessantly to get the most out of his limited talents, an outgrowth of the classic small-man, I-can-make-myself-better-than-you syndrome. Schmidt, at least in the early phase of his Hall of Fame career, took his vast talents for granted. Schmidt was a bruiser—six foot, two inches and 205 pounds. Bowa was a wharf rat—five foot 10 and 155 pounds. Bowa couldn't resist trying to get under Schmidt's somewhat thin skin, often succeeding. Schmidt just wanted to be left alone.

It was like trying to mix oil and water.

"Larry was a great clubhouse needler, but Larry didn't have great timing," said Schmidt, who was invited by Bowa to be a special instructor for the Phillies for Bowa's first three spring trainings as manager and is now managing the Phillies' Single-A team at Clearwater, Florida. "There were times when he didn't needle people, and I think he should have. There were times when he did needle me that I thought it would be best to lay off. One time, I got so angry in a clubhouse in Houston that I almost wanted to kill him. I probably would have if there weren't four other players there. I'd probably be in prison right now."

The relationship jumped off to a competitive start before the two even met—after Schmidt, then a shortstop, was selected by the Phillies in the second round of the 1971 June draft of amateur players.

"When they signed Schmitty, this is what the scout told him: 'The shortstop there isn't going to be there very long, and you're going to be the shortstop,'" recalled Bowa, who was the shortstop Schmidt was told he would replace.

"Right away, I've got a chip on my shoulder," Bowa said. "So they flew him into Philly. I said, 'Forget this guy Mike Schmidt, big deal.' So he comes in, and he's styling. He's a college kid. Everything's cool. He takes ground balls with me and everything.

"I remember a comment he made: 'I plan on playing shortstop in Philadelphia.' And my reply was, 'Not as long as I'm here.'"

Bowa had established himself by the time Schmidt emerged on the scene. Bowa had been groomed by Frank Lucchesi, who managed him for three seasons, both in the minors and major leagues. It was Lucchesi who had stuck with Bowa at shortstop when Bowa wasn't pulling his weight in the batter's box during that trying rookie 1970 season.

"Because I knew what he was made of," Lucchesi said, recalling the criticism that mounted at the time in the Philly papers.

Lucchesi continued to stick with Bowa at shortstop as both men emerged as players, Bowa in the majors and Schmidt in the minors.

"They sent him to Reading—Double-A," Bowa remembers about Schmidt. "And he tore it up. He hit a lot of home runs. I was having my good years then … So I kept going, and the more I read about Mike Schmidt, the harder I worked. And you know the rest of it. He ended up playing third."

It didn't begin well for Schmidt, who batted .196 with 18 homers and 52 runs batted in during the 1973 season, his first full season in the big leagues.

And for the first decade of his career, Schmidt's every misstep was lustily jeered by the rabid Philly fans, who once booed Santa at an Eagles game and so infuriated hometown and home-grown basketball hero Kobe Bryant of the Los Angeles Lakers during the 2002 NBA All-Star Game that he went on that day to an MVP performance.

Bowa, in contrast, took his share of razzing. But he was Everyman to the fans of Philadelphia, that guy who made it to the major leagues on spit and guts.

"In his early career, I think he let the fans really get to him in Philly," Bowa said about Schmidt. "Eventually, he dealt with it about as well as anybody. I think he put so much pressure on himself when he came up. He was a top pick. Anything he does, he does great. He could play golf with you, and he'd shoot par. You could play basketball with him, and he'd shoot the eyes out of it. You could bowl with him, and he'd bowl 200. He's a great athlete. I think one of the reasons why he wasn't successful early in his career was that everything came easy to him.

"He'd never really gone through any adversity. In that first year he went through a lot of crap."

Schmidt said it took years for his relationship with Bowa to thaw. "It took me probably five or six years to get into good graces with Larry Bowa as an individual," Schmidt said. "I think there was a great deal of jealousy evident in our relationship. I don't know what it was, but I think Larry harbored some inner jealousy toward me. That's just what I sensed. I think after, say, 1976, he got a little older and I got a little more mature and I had proven worthy of his respect, I think he sort of changed. He looked at me more in terms of a potentially great player.

"I think when Pete Rose came to the Phillies in 1979, Larry's relationship with me changed greatly because he sensed the way Pete and I got along. He sensed the respect with which Pete and I treated each other."

Schmidt and Bowa were always at opposite ends of the spectrum. When Schmidt slumped, he would turn his rage inward and become sullen. When Bowa slumped, he'd snap and turn the page the next day.

"That was the one thing I didn't like about him," Bowa said. "I knew it was killing him inside. I'd say, 'Why don't you show some emotion? Hit something. Get mad. Go berserk.'

"Oh yeah, I did a good job. I'd get on players. But I'd know who to get on. I got on Greg 'The Bull' Luzinski a lot more than I ever got on Schmidt. He was probably my biggest sounding board. He'd locker next to me, and I would get all over him. If he wasn't hitting good, I'd say, 'Well, why don't you do something, you big hog?' And everyone would look at him like, 'Why don't you just knock the hell out of this guy?' But Greg knew me...

"Bull took a lot of crap from the fans and in my opinion, not deservedly. I thought he was a much better clutch hitter than Schmidt. Schmidt eventually turned into a good clutch hitter, but in those early days when we were behind, Bull would come up and hit one. Schmitty would always hit his when the score was 7-1, 7-2. But Schmitty eventually had gone into that mold where he'd break a game open for you."

Bowa wanted Schmidt to be more expressive, but it just wasn't going to happen. Bowa had already become infamous for his snaps. One day in Houston after a particularly bad plate appearance, Bowa climbed the stairs through the winding walkway that connected the visitors' clubhouse and dugout in the old Astrodome and shattered all of the light bulbs with his bat. His teammates weren't too happy about groping back to the locker room in the dark. One night in the midst of a slump, Bowa, who is not much of a drinker, was drowning his sorrows at the hotel bar when he joined a group of players for a stroll. They encountered a thick glass fire door that Bowa decided to open with the butt end of a fire extinguisher. That's the way Bowa has always vented his anger.

Their polar attitudes also extended to their philosophy on the field. In Schmidt's opinion, Bowa's basic tenet as a manager—team over the individual—was not the way Bowa acted as a player. "Except for when we won the championship in 1980, I don't think Larry Bowa as a regular player ever came to grips with the value of team success over individual success," Schmidt said. "Now that's not a rip. What I'm saying is that some people need to have that kind of focus to succeed. Some people really have to care extra how they're doing individually. To be honest with you, I guess there were times when I was no different than that."

Bowa never brought home the hardware that Schmidt collected in his career. He led the National League with 13 triples in 1972 and finished as high as third in the league MVP voting only once. Bowa won two Gold Gloves for his play at short—in 1972 and 1978 and was an All-Star five times. He had 15 homers in his 16-year career.

With 548 lifetime homers, Schmidt established his path to the Hall of Fame and was elected in 1995. During his 18 years in a local uniform, in Philly, he clearly established himself as the man. His 48 homers in 1980 are the most ever in a single season by a third baseman and is a Phillies record. A three-time National League Most Valuable Player, he was a 12-time All-Star and won 10 Gold Gloves for his spectacular play at third base.

But Bowa's grit was as essential to the Phillies' success as Schmidt's ability to steal games with one swing of the bat, like he did one memorable day at Montreal near the end of the 1980 season to win the National League East title for the Phillies.

Schmidt wasn't the only observer of the Phillies scene whom Larry Bowa disturbed. In 1978, when Bowa batted .294 and came in third to Dave Parker in the National League MVP balloting, Bowa was blasted for his clubhouse and playing style by a beat writer, Ray "Buzzy" Kelly, Jr., who covered the team for the *Camden Courier Post*. The next day, Bowa set up Kelly by having him paged for a phone call in a nearly empty Veterans Stadium locker room.

Bowa and Kelly railed against each other until the argument became so heated that the two men had to be separated by pitcher Ron Reed. In the brief scuffle, Kelly came away with a small mark on his cheek that was treated by physicians.

The incident blew over quickly with Kelly and Bowa resolving their differences. As usual, Bowa did not allow the harsh words to carry over. Bowa insists that he never hit Kelly. "The entire incident was blown out of proportion," Bowa says.

Still, Schmidt's characterization of Bowa as a hard-nosed individualist may not be so out of place. Bowa worked so hard and so long to develop that he was always leery of other players who could just skate in and operate on natural ability, like Schmidt. In the end, though, Bowa's nails-on-the-blackboard verbal style seemed to have a positive effect on Schmidt's work habits and his development as a leader.

"Larry was always quick to criticize other people's work habits," Schmidt said. "There's an average type of worker, a guy with poor habits, and there's the hard worker. And hard-working people, the people who are consumed by their profession, always seem to feel they should get more out of it because they put more into it. Sometimes, a guy comes along who gets a lot more out of it than he puts into it. To be honest with you, I probably put a hell of a lot more into it at the end of my career than I did in my first four or five years. All of a sudden, I started setting standards as a player that I eventually understood couldn't be kept up without hard work.

"I don't think I ever had the kind of work habits that Bowa had. Bowa hit endlessly, endlessly, extra hitting, trying to make himself into a good switch hitter. And he became a .300 hitter. He got the most of his talent. I don't have to tell you that. Those are all things you've heard players say before. He got the maximum out of the talent he had. He came to an organization that was really hurting as a young player. He was forced into the big leagues and had to learn to play and to win at the big-league level. I think the same thing is true about Pete Rose. Whatever he lacked in ability he made up for in desire and hard work.

"Bowa made himself a great shortstop. We jelled. We were as good a left side of the infield as there was at the time. He never did anything really, really fluidly. He just caught everything. He caught everything and everything got to first base. It never looked real fluid and pretty and graceful, but it always got done."

The two were never really close friends as teammates, either. But together, as tough competitors, Bowa and Schmidt ultimately formed a bond at the core of the team that defeated the Kansas City Royals to win the 1980 World Series.

4

A New Era of Phillies Baseball

The 1970s began for the Phillies much the way the new millennium opened—with a plan in place to build the ball club into a championship team as it moved into a new ballpark. The team needed to exorcise the ghosts that had plagued them since the 1964 National League pennant race, and a more modern ballpark than the outdated Connie Mack Stadium was a symbol the fans could rally around.

Old Shibe Park—renamed in 1953 after Connie Mack, the intrepid former owner and manager of the Philadelphia Athletics—was home to the A's from 1909 to 1954, when the team left for Kansas City. The Phillies abandoned the crumbling Baker Bowl in 1937 and played in the old yard on 22nd and Leigh from 1938 to 1970. Certainly, by the time the Phillies fled Connie Mack after Bowa's first year in the major leagues, the little park tucked within a neighborhood of decaying row houses had outlived its usefulness.

"Connie Mack was falling apart at the seams," said Bill Giles, the vice president of marketing and promotions back then. "It was really a physical disaster waiting to happen. Once you got into the ballpark, it was a great place to watch the game because you were so close to the action. They had a bunch of beams and pillars that blocked the view from some seats, but it was a great ballpark. The thing that ruined it was that you couldn't park, and the neighborhood was very dangerous. People were afraid to go to the area."

Veterans Stadium, a new multipurpose facility in South Philly, was the impetus that created the excitement and expectation surrounding the Phillies in 1971. The Phillies were simply trying to jump-start interest in the franchise and break the curse that had haunted Connie Mack since 1964. Any Phillies fan with any mettle remembers what happened in the last weeks of the 1964 National League pennant race. The Phillies returned from Los Angeles after a 3-2 victory over the Dodgers on September 20, 1964, with a six and a half game lead and only 12 games to play. In those days, there were no playoffs. The winner in each league would simply play in the World Series.

All the Phillies, who were 90-60, had to do was play .500 ball (6-6) until the season ended, and they would have met the New York Yankees in that October's Fall Classic. What followed, though, was a collapse for the ages. The Phillies lost 10 in a row as manager Gene Mauch lined up his top two starters—Jim Bunning and Chris Short—seemingly every other day until the end of the season. The strategy turned out to be disastrous. The last three losses in the streak were to the eventual pennant- and World Series-winning St. Louis Cardinals. By the time the Phillies defeated the Reds in their last two games of the season at Cincinnati's Crosley Field, it was too late. The Phillies finished one game out. Later Phillies teams would never hear the end of it. They were dogged by the great collapse of 1964.

"I have no idea what happened in 1964, I wasn't there, but I know that story by heart," Bowa said. "Everybody in Philly who puts on a uniform knows it by heart... Every year we'd go through a losing streak we'd read about it. In 1980 when things got hairy we'd read about it. In all fairness to the guys on our team, nobody knew about '64. But by the time we got to the World Series, we all knew about the collapse of that team. It was a constant. They would not let people forget. Even today, when you go a little bad, memories of '64 creep back into our heads. It's our curse. That's something they're going to live with in Philadelphia forever. No matter how well the teams do in Philly, that's the mindset of the fans—something bad is going to happen."

The Vet opened on April 10, 1971, for a game on a chilly afternoon against the Montreal Expos, the team that had closed Connie Mack Stadium against the Phillies on October 1, 1970. Bowa had the first hit—a single to right field in the first inning. It came off Montreal right-hander Bill Stoneman, who had previously no-hit the Phillies at Connie Mack Stadium. Ironically, the Expos' manager was the dreaded Gene Mauch, who proclaimed the Vet "the best new park in baseball." The Phillies won 4-1 in front of 55,352—the largest crowd at the time to ever see a baseball game in Pennsylvania. (The year before, the Phillies had drawn only 708,247 for the entire season to Connie Mack. In the first season at the Vet, attendance more than doubled, to 1,511,223.)

Although the fans showed up to watch their team, the 1970s seemed to collapse as the curse followed the Phillies to the Vet. The 1971-1973 seasons wouldn't be kind on the field to the Phillies, who averaged 94 losses over the course of those three seasons.

"We got the heck knocked out of us," said Bowa, who really didn't emerge as an offensive force until he hit .275 in 1974—a turn-around from his career-low .211 during the previous season. "We weren't good, except in '72 we were good every fifth day. It was almost like Steve Carlton scared us to be good."

The trade for the left-handed Carlton, an eventual Hall of Famer, before the 1972 season was one of the building blocks of the 1980 World Series champions. General manager Paul Owens picked up Carlton from the St. Louis Cardinals for Rick Wise, and he had an immediate impact on the moribund Phillies. In 1972, Carlton won 27 games; the Phillies only won 59.

Danny Ozark was brought in to manage the Phillies in 1973, and after one last 91-loss season, the transition from bad to good began to happen.

"He was a laid-back guy," Bowa said about the soft-spoken man who managed the Phillies from 1973 to 1979. "He didn't demand that much from you. He knew he had guys who policed themselves. We didn't come late. We worked hard. Some guys thought he was too aloof and too laid back, but Danny basically let us play. I thought he was good for our team."

Bowa kept improving. No one argued with his defensive skills. But by 1975, he hit .305, his career high and the only season he batted over .300. After an off year of .248 in 1976, Bowa excelled again to .280 in 1977 and .294 in 1978 when the team was starting to jell into a champion.

"Bowa never cheated on effort," Giles said. "As a player he was always very determined and energetic. He played hard."

The Phillies continued to mold and shape the players on their team. Before the advent of free agency, there were only three ways to build and improve a team: develop a player, trade for a player or purchase a player. The 1976 Phillies, who finished 101-61 and along with the 1977 team own the best record in club history, were built in just such a fashion. At the time, owners felt they held all of the cards due to the reserve clause, a stipulation in the basic agreement that bound each player to his own club in perpetuity. Owens kept adding significant players to the core product, such as reliever Tug McGraw from the New York Mets and center fielder Garry Maddox from the San Francisco Giants in 1975, second baseman Ted Sizemore from the Dodgers and right fielder Bake McBride from the Cardinals in 1977, just to name a few.

Then in one fell swoop, an arbitrator shot down the reserve clause, and in 1977 players gained some freedom of choice and movement. An owner of one team could outbid the owner of another for a prime player's services. That decision would have a profound effect on the evolution of the Phillies.

The 1976 Phillies were defeated in the National League Championship Series, swept by the Cincinnati Reds, a great team that would be shattered by free agency. Few fans in Philadelphia could quite quibble with the outcome. But the expectations were much higher when the Phillies won 101 games again in 1977 and faced the Dodgers in the playoffs.

"We got beat by some pretty good teams," Bowa said. "The Dodgers, the Big Red Machine—they were nasty, and they were deep. These weren't lousy teams. There were no holes in those teams."

Perhaps Game 3 of the 1977 National League Championship Series best illustrates the pathos of that particular Phillies era.

On October 7, 1977, the Phillies, tied one game apiece with the Dodgers in the old best-of-five championship series, carried a 5-3 lead into the ninth inning at Veterans Stadium. They had gone ahead in the second inning, when, trailing that Dodgers team of Steve Garvey, Ron Cey, Davey Lopes and Billy Russell by a score of 2-0, pitcher Burt Hooton blew up. As 63,719 in the Vet pounded their feet, shaking the stadium to its rafters, Hooton walked four straight men with the bases loaded to allow three Phillies runs. Bowa had drawn the final walk to give the Phillies the lead.

In the ninth inning, behind their ace reliever Gene Garber, the Phillies recorded the first two outs and with no Dodgers on base were just one out away from taking the series lead. Vic Davalillo pinch hit and beat out a drag bunt to second baseman Sizemore. The knowledgeable but not always charitable Phillies fans held their collective breath as Manny Mota pinch hit. Mota hit a very catchable drive toward the warning track in the left field corner. It probably would have been caught had Ozark not left the lumbering Luzinski in left field.

"I never understood that," Bowa recalled. "All year long Danny is taking Bull out for a defensive replacement late in the game. Sure as hell, a fly ball goes out there that Jerry Martin just sucks up. If he's out there, we win that game. Danny had some excuse about getting Bull another at-bat in the ninth inning. But we weren't even going to bat in the ninth inning if we won."

It was a formidable mistake. Luzinski missed the ball. Mota had a double, and Davalillo scored when the relay skipped through Sizemore for an error. Mota went to third. It was now 5-4 with Lopes coming to the plate. The next play was the season's pivotal one. Lopes smashed a grounder toward Schmidt at third, which apparently hit a seam in the artificial surface and kicked up off Schmidt's glove. Bowa was right behind him in the hole to grab it with his bare hand, a remarkable heads-up play. In one fluid motion, Bowa caught the ball and threw it to first baseman Richie Hebner. First base umpire Bruce Froemming spread his arms wide to signal Lopes safe in a call that seemed to be countered by every television replay angle. A huge argument ensued.

"I'll never forget that," Bowa said. "Man, Froemming anticipated that just because Schmitty didn't catch the ball, I couldn't throw Lopes out. I went crazy. That was the game. We win that game, we win that series."

"I'll never forget the reaction Bowa made and the great throw he made. It was unbelievable," Giles recalled. "And the guy was out."

As it turned out, the Dodgers won the game when Lopes went to second on Garber's errant pickoff throw and scored on Russell's single. They won the series when Tommy John threw a seven-hitter in the pouring rain the very next night. The elements, a manager's decision and an umpire's call turned that series around. "That was the best team we had there," Bowa said. "It was better than the team we won with in '80. But in those years, it always seemed like we were one hit away. A guy busting it open. We couldn't get a big hit at a crucial time."

The Phillies slipped to 90-72 in 1978 and won the National League East title for the third straight time. But when they dropped the opening two games of the series at the Vet to the Dodgers and again lost to them in the playoffs, it was obvious that something needed to change. Game 4 and the NLCS ended at Dodger Stadium when the usually unflappable Maddox dropped a routine liner to center field just before Russell won it 4-3 with a two-out, 10th-inning single. For three straight years the Phillies had lived up to the curse of their 1964 predecessors and lost.

"You go so long, and you don't win," Bowa said. "Then you fall short in the playoffs three years in a row. You go from saying, 'We're just glad to be here,' to saying, 'This group can't win.' The more you read about it, you start thinking maybe we aren't good enough to win. Maybe we do lack one or two things. Things just always seemed to happen. The ball Maddox dropped obviously was huge. He was as good as I'd seen when I played. But he just flat-out missed it."

The Phillies needed a big free agent catalyst, and that catalyst came in a package named Pete Rose, who was one of the mainstays of the Big Red Machine that dominated the National League in the 1970s and won back-to-back World Series in 1975 and 1976.

It's hard to imagine that Bowa respected any single player more than Rose—who, like Bowa, was the epitome of the blue-collar, working-class player, a guy who got the most out of his skills, who came out to play hard every day and could overcome any lack of skill with sheer burning intensity. Rose's all-time career record 4,256 hits is enough to attest to that. Rose was simply a winner, the ultimate team player. In his illustrious 24-year playing career, which ended in 1986, Rose set all kinds of records, but his most significant accomplishment may be that he played with seven division-winning teams—five of them for Cincinnati before he signed with Philadelphia in 1979.

"Playing with Rose was great," Bowa said. "He's unbelievable. His intensity... He had a way of just putting everything out of his mind when he plays the game. That's how he released all his anxiety and whatever was built up inside him. That's how he released it. He concentrated better than any human being I've ever seen on every pitch. And he literally loved the game. He put us over the hump. We kept coming close before he got there. But he put us over it. When you played against him, you hated him. When you played with him, you loved him."

It took a little time. Even with Rose at first base instead of Hebner, the Phillies finished fourth in 1979, and Ozark was replaced by the grumpy, stick-it-in-your-ear Dallas Green as manager.

"There was Pete, of course, but the big difference was the manager as far as demeanor," Bowa said. "Dallas wasn't afraid to step on anyone's toes. He let us know throughout the year that we weren't as good as we thought we were. At the time, we said, 'Who's he?' But looking back on it, he was right. We read too many clippings that we were better than we were."

The Phillies, who had evolved into a cantankerous bunch, were told time and again all season that the team would be broken up if 1980 didn't provide the ultimate success, a World Series championship.

"We had ultimatums given to us all during 1980: 'If you don't win, we're tearing this team apart.' It was constantly being written all year. It was like we were on a mission," Bowa said.

In that atmosphere, the 1980 team had more guts than any of the earlier teams, which was illustrated in the Phillies' one-game victory in the National League East over Montreal when Schmidt homered in the 11th inning off Stan Bahnsen on the next to the last day of the season at Olympic Stadium.

But the 91-71 flash finish in the division race was merely the appetizer for the next round, the Phillies' stunning playoff comeback in Houston to win their first pennant in 30 years. Trailing two games to one, the Phillies came from behind to win both Games 4 and 5 in 10 innings at the Astrodome. The last four games of the best-of-five series were decided in extra innings. The Astros had defeated the Dodgers in a one-game playoff for the National League West title. Game 163 came after the Astros lost three in a row at Dodger Stadium to squander a three-game lead with just three games to go. It was the first time Houston had ascended to the playoffs since joining the National League as an expansion team in 1962.

The Phillies-Astros playoff series was a battle of immovable objects that seemed to have slipped away from Philadelphia after winning Game 1.

"I'll never forget the final game," Bowa said. "We were down against Nolan Ryan, who never used to lose a lead in the late innings. Especially at home. Pete Rose came up to me and he said, 'If you get on, we're going to win this damn game.' And I didn't have much success against Ryan.

"My first game in pro ball, the Phillies send me to Spartanburg. The first damn game, we're playin' in Greenville against the New York Mets' team. I had had a real good spring training, and I felt like a stud. The line on me was—this guy came from nowhere, he got $2,000, he's a prospect. First game, we faced Nolan Ryan. Four punchouts. I had no prayer. I figured if this is what professional ball was going to be like, I had no chance.

"So here we are and Pete wants me to get on against Ryan in the eighth inning of the fifth game of the playoffs. I got a base hit over short. The next hitter was Bob Boone. He hits a ball to Ryan that goes off his glove. It would have been a sure double-play ball. That's first and second, and it's all happening on first pitches. The next guy up, Greg Gross, drops a perfect bunt. We have the bases loaded with nobody out. They start warming somebody up. Pete ends up walking. That brought in a run. Before they could even get their relievers up, Ryan was on the ropes."

The Phillies won 8-7 in the 10th inning on a double by Maddox, atoning for his error of two years earlier, and they were on to the World Series for only the third time in club history. It was their first victory ever in a postseason series.

"The Houston LCS was the greatest baseball confrontation I've ever seen," Giles said. "All five games were just nail biters and had everything in the world baseball could provide. It was an unbelievable series."

The Phillies and Royals—the World Series participants in 1980—provided neat mirror images. The Phillies had never won a World Series, and the Royals were in it for the first time. The Phillies were National League East champs in 1976, 1977 and 1978 and lost each time in the playoffs. Likewise, the Royals won the American League West in 1976, 1977 and 1978, only to lose each time in the playoffs to the New York Yankees. In 1980, the Royals finally vanquished the hated Yankees to go to the World Series. The Phillies lifted the burden of 1964 and had battled just to get there against the Royals.

The Royals also were the expansion team that replaced the vagabond Athletics in Kansas City after the A's—the same team that shared Shibe Park for 16 years with the Phillies before moving to Kansas City—went to Oakland in 1968. These were the burdens carried by both teams as the series opened at Veterans Stadium on October 14, 1980.

"Those playoffs and the World Series were amazing. The World Series, though, was the best. I had more fun in the World Series than I ever had playing baseball," Bowa recalled. "The Houston series was draining. We played our butts off. It was like it didn't matter what we did in the World Series. We just went out and had fun. There was more pressure in the Houston series than the World Series. It wasn't even close. I really felt that we weren't going to be denied in the World Series. We had worked too hard."

But the 1980 Phillies team never did anything easily, and it looked like the 1964 curse had followed them into the World Series. Game 1 opened with Bob Walk on the mound for the Phillies, a rookie right-hander who was 11-7 with a 4.57 earned run average in 27 starts. He was opposed by Dennis Leonard, a right-hander who was a longtime ace for the Royals, winning 144 games in his 12-year major league career, all in Kansas City.

It wasn't a dream matchup for Dallas Green, but the Phillies had drained their pitching staff just trying to get past the Astros. So to no one's surprise, the Royals jumped all over Walk.

"First game, we were behind Kansas City 4-0 in the third inning," said Bowa, who had a tremendous series with nine hits. "We were dead. We were just drained. We weren't doing anything. So I got a base hit off Leonard. I'll never forget the scenario. I have the tape at home. They're saying on TV that Bowa isn't going to run here. 'They're down four runs, and Bowa has to play it safe.'

"First pitch. I'm gone. I'm on my own, but Dallas gave me a hold sign because we were down four runs. I thought, forget that. I could get a jump. I had a great jump, but it was a bang-bang play. I mean, boom-boom. I said to myself, 'If I'm out, I might as well keep running.' There was no way I wanted to go back to the dugout to face him. But I was safe. Boonie gets a double and knocks me in. We scored five runs and wound up winning 7-6. That turned the game around, being aggressive. Dallas didn't say a word to me, but I knew he was ticked. He was relieved that I made it, but I looked in the dugout. He had his arms folded, and he gives you that look."

The next night, behind Carlton, the Phillies came from behind with four runs in the bottom of the eighth to erase a 4-2 deficit and win 5-4. It was the game that George Brett, one of baseball's best hitters, had to leave in the sixth inning with the raging hemorrhoids heard 'round the world. Brett, an eventual Hall of Famer, flirted with the magic .400 figure during the 1980 regular season, finishing at .390 to win his second of three American League batting titles.

The Phillies were leading two games to none, and Brett was doubtful for Game 3 when the series shifted to Kansas City for the next three games. Everything was in Philadelphia's favor: The championship was in sight, and the Phillies were prepared make the curse of 1964 a ghost story of the past.

But the ghosts came back to haunt the Phillies. Even though the team had just won four postseason games in a row in stunning fashion, for a few days they ran out of magic. Only hours after leaving a Kansas City hospital, Brett stepped up in the bottom of the first inning and homered. The two teams battled for nine innings, tied 3-3, but Willie Mays Aikens singled home Willie Wilson with the deciding run in the bottom of the 10th. The next night, Aikens hit a pair of homers, and the Royals jumped off to a 5-1 lead. They held on to win 5-3, and suddenly the series was tied.

In the pivotal Game 5, Schmidt hit a two-run homer early, but again the Phillies had to come back with two runs in the ninth to win. McGraw didn't make it easy in the bottom of the ninth; he walked the bases loaded with two out before Jose Cardenal struck out to save the Phillies' 4-3 victory.

Now it was back to the Vet for Game 6 on October 21, 1980, with a chance for the Phillies to clinch the World Series for the first time in their history. In 1915, the Phillies lost in five games to Boston, with the Red Sox winning the final three games, and in 1950, the Yankees swept the Phillies' "Whiz Kids."

"I never, ever would say anything is a lock, but when I went out the door that day I told my wife, Sheena, that we were going to win," Bowa said. "Carlton was going. The crowd had been waiting for hundreds of years. The day before you could feel it. You go to the store. You go driving around. People would be waving at you. I had never had a feeling like that in my life. This is over."

It was an uncommon night at the Vet. Policemen mounted on horses were on hand to guard the field, hoping to ward off overzealous revelers if the Phillies won it. Carlton was again on the mound, and this time the Royals were really never in the game. The Phillies had a 4-0 lead after five innings. Schmidt set the offense in motion with a two-run single in the third inning. McGraw replaced Carlton in the eighth and took a 4-1 lead into the ninth. At that point, the crowd of 65,838 was in a frenzy, and the mounted police had circled the field.

"I'll never forget how the sixth game ended. We're winning 4-1. They load the bases in the ninth inning with one out. Frank White is at bat. Around the rim of the field are all those mounted horsemen and guard dogs, and the people in the Vet are going crazy. It was some scene. White pops it up foul over near our dugout. Boonie and Pete converge. The ball pops out of Boonie's glove, and Pete grabs it. That's when you knew we were going to win. Willie Wilson struck out to end it."

In any other Phillies era, that ball would've popped loose and the Phillies might have found a way to lose the game. But in this case, the will of Pete Rose to win overcame the ghosts of 1964. Instead, Wilson whiffed with runners on second and third to end it.

It was Wilson's 12th strikeout of that series. McGraw leapt off the mound with his arms raised skyward. It became his signature moment with the Phillies.

"Tug came in, and he was on empty," Bowa said. "He was just going on guts. We were just very, very lucky that Willie Wilson had a terrible World Series. He had 230 hits during the regular season. Going in we said he was the guy we had to keep off base, and he wasn't even a factor."

The victory unlocked a torrent of emotions in Philadelphia that lasted for days. That night, the fans trashed Broad Street all the way from the Vet downtown to City Hall. Late at night, after they had exhausted themselves, shattered glass was everywhere and newspaper boxes were overturned. It led to perhaps the biggest party in the history of Philadelphia sports the following day, October 22, 1980.

"The unbelievable thing was going down Broad Street in the motorcade the next day," Bowa said. "We must have had two million people at the parade. That place was packed. I've never seen so many older people crying. I mean, lined up the street past the Vet, the Spectrum and to John F. Kennedy Stadium. That's where we ended the parade. The place looked like the Army–Navy game was there. You never forget something like that. You look back on your career in baseball and through all of the ups and downs, that's something that will never be replaced. It might be replaced if I ever got into the World Series as a manager. But as a player, it'll never be replaced."

Bowa's maturation as a player undoubtedly reached its zenith in 1980 during the Phillies' run to that always elusive world championship. He batted .316 in the thrilling five-game playoff series in which the Phillies came from behind to beat Houston for the pennant. Then he really excelled. He batted .375 against Kansas City as the Phillies finally brought the world championship trophy home to Philadelphia. In the six-game series, he set what was then a World Series record by starting seven double plays.

"Larry had an outstanding World Series that year. He could easily have been named the MVP," recalled Schmidt, who hit .381 with two homers and seven RBIs and was voted the MVP of that series. "They chose me maybe because of a little more notoriety during the regular season. I had the RBIs. Larry might have had more hits [Bowa had nine, Schmidt had seven]. He was exceptional in the field. Like I said, he could very easily have been chosen the MVP."

For Bowa, though, winning the World Series was special enough. It was the peak of his tenure in Philadelphia. And as it turned out, it was the peak of his career.

"It was more than winning a World Series," Bowa said. "It was that we'd gone through everything together. We'd gone through the downs. We'd gone through the mediocre seasons. We'd gone through the just-misses. It was really something special."

But this Phillies era would be over in less than a year.

The Phillies fell prey, in part, to the escalation of salaries wrought by the same free agent market that netted them Rose and undoubtedly the World Series championship. The owners and players were girding up for their first real economic battle. In essence, the old group was becoming a little gray around the edges, but when the players struck during the season for the first time after the games of June 10, 1981, it signaled the end of the most joyous of all Phillies eras. That day, Rose singled off Houston's Ryan at the Vet. It was his 3,630th hit, tying him with Cardinals great Stan Musial for the all-time hits lead in the National League. Rose would have to wait more than two months to pass Musial.

"Pete joked that it was the longest slump he'd ever had in his life," Bowa said. "He said, 'You never see me go that long without a hit.'"

The Phillies, in first place in the NL East with a 31-24 record at the time of the strike, were given an automatic spot in a playoff format that was expanded by an extra round. They would play the team that finished atop the East in the second half. The season didn't resume until August 10, and that team turned out to be the Montreal Expos.

"If we didn't have a split season, we would've won that thing," Bowa said. "We dominated the first half. We would've just rolled. And they told us, 'If you win the second half it doesn't matter, we're going to take the second place team.' And that's when everyone said, 'What are we playing for?'"

That feeling evidently extended into the first round of the play-offs, which the Phillies lost to the Expos in five games. Midnight struck for those Phillies on October 11, 1981, after a 3-0 loss at the Vet. On October 15, Green left to become general manager of the Chicago Cubs. Two weeks later, Giles headed the group that purchased the Phillies for $30 million from Ruly Carpenter, ending the stewardship of the Carpenter family after 38 years.

It was the beginning of the end for Bowa in Philly, too. His days as a Phillies player were over, but the acrimony was just beginning.

5

So Long Phillies: Bowa on Giles, Giles on Bowa

The wheels of Bowa's Philadelphia departure actually began to spin late in the 1981 season. As usual, he sat down to negotiate an extension of his contract directly with owner Ruly Carpenter. This time Bowa, then 36 years old, was looking for one last three-year contract extension to carry him through to the end of his career. He had a strong season for the Phillies, batting .283 in 1981, his best season at the plate since 1978. The last thing he envisioned at the time was what eventually happened: a trade to the Chicago Cubs.

Before Carpenter sold the Phillies to the group headed by Bill Giles, he and Bowa met to talk contract. Bowa said he always did his contracts face to face with Carpenter, whose family owned the Phillies from 1943 to 1981. Ruly's father, Bob, purchased the Phillies on November 23, 1943, for $400,000 and was president of the club until handing over the reins to his son in 1972. At the time of the meeting, Bowa didn't even have an agent. Bowa's business philosophy was still rooted in baseball's pre-free agency days when, in Philadelphia at least, the owner's handshake was as good as his word. Ruly was firm, but he'd always listen. Bowa would make a proposal, and Carpenter would try to play hardball. The two were used to going back and forth.

"Sometimes it would go on for a couple of months," Bowa said. "Then he'd call my wife. He'd say, 'Sheena, why don't you come up here for lunch and we'll get this contract hammered out?' I'd get on the line and laugh, 'Sheena's not negotiating this contract.' He'd say, 'If I can get your wife in here, we'll have this thing settled in a second.'

"I mean, he would always work it out with me. Once, I had a contract where on paper it showed I was making $200,000, but he paid for a $250,000 house in cash. He did things like that. He'd say I was asking for too much money. And I'd say, 'Well, let's do it another way. Buy my house for me.' He was loaded. It was nothing to him. He used to have parties. I mean, you never see owners having parties. He was the most down-to-earth person I've ever seen in my life. Always talked to the wives, to the kids. He kept everything in proper perspective. If you looked at him walking through a hotel lobby, you'd say, 'I wonder who he is? He must be a salesman for some men's store or something.' That's how down to earth the man was."

Carpenter sold the club to the Giles group for $30 million, the highest price ever paid for a Major League Baseball team at the time and a tidy $29.6 million more than what his dad had paid for it 38 years earlier. Bowa said that a three-year contract was on the table.

"If I don't sign you, you can ask to be traded," Bowa said, recalling Carpenter's words during that meeting. "So I told Ruly, 'That's fair.'" Bowa was a five- and 10-year player, with five consecutive years on one team and 10 years service in the major leagues. By rights granted to the players in the basic agreement negotiated in collective bargaining between MLB and the MLB Players Association, Bowa had the right to turn down a trade to any team. That rule was memorialized in bargaining decades ago and still stands.

Under the Giles group, the Phillies had a more bottom-line feeling, Bowa said. Giles has been with the team since 1969. As vice president of promotions, he invented that crazy green blob mascot called the Phanatic, who teased players and umpires and entertained fans while scooting around the artificial turf field of Veterans Stadium for the last 25 years. He brought in the Great Wallenda to traverse a high wire that was stretched from the Vet's left field foul pole to the right field foul pole. At the same time in the 1970s when the Phillies began improving on the field, their marketing under Giles began catching up with the baseball operations run by general manager Paul Owens. Home attendance went from 519,414 in 1969 at deteriorating Connie Mack Stadium to a then-peak of 2,700,070 in 1977 as the Phillies became competitive in the Vet.

"In the old days the Phillies were like a big family," Bowa recalled. "We did everything on trust and a handshake. I found out pretty quickly that times had certainly changed when Giles took over. I was devastated after we won the World Series in 1980. It was the opening of our next spring training, and Ruly called everybody together and said, 'We're putting the team up for sale.' I said, 'Oh no, what's he doing?' The straw that broke the camel's back is when Claudell Washington—a journeyman who played for seven teams in his 17-year career and hit .278—signed that big contract with the Atlanta Braves. Ruly said, 'This is it. He's coming off all those mediocre years. That's an unbelievable amount of money [then Braves owner] Ted Turner gave him.' He said, 'I'm out of here.'"

Carpenter exited baseball at his pinnacle. By 1976, the moribund franchise had appeared in the postseason only twice in its history when Carpenter's Phillies began a run of five playoff appearances in six years that was capped by the 1980 World Series championship. The championship team was going to be costly to keep together in the relatively new free agent market, which had opened for good after the 1976 season. At that point, Carpenter determined that he had nothing more to gain and a lot more to lose, particularly his money, and opted out. At the same time, the mom-and-pop baseball owners, the pioneer entrepreneurs like the O'Malley family in Los Angeles, Gussie Busch in St. Louis and the Galbreaths in Pittsburgh, began to fade away like dinosaurs, making way for the corporate groups that dominate the sports landscape today.

"Ruly got out of baseball because of free agency and everything going to court," Bowa said. "Afterward he said he still loved the game, watched the game. He'd go watch minor league games. But he also said, 'When you start dealing with lawyers and agents instead of balls and strikes, I don't need it.' I spoke to him not long after he got out. I asked him, 'Do you miss it?' He said, 'Not one bit. I still see my baseball.'"

Bowa was personally feeling the effects of Carpenter's departure and the advent of Giles as his big boss. Plus, the Giles group had to scatter around for funding just to pull the purchase deal together. The group was probably underfunded, certainly by baseball standards today, and each financial decision became an essential one, including signing Bowa to a new contract. When the Giles group got in, Bowa said he was offered a one-year contract.

"I said, 'No way. The deal was, I get a three-year contract or you trade me.'

"Giles said, 'We're not trading you.'

"I said, 'That's the deal. You guys are trying to renege on the deal.' I didn't realize then that a new ownership group really doesn't have to acknowledge what the previous owners had promised, particularly when the deal wasn't even in writing. But I had to get in touch with Ruly, who was out of it. And after I did, Ruly explained to Giles that that was the agreement."

Giles, of course, has a different opinion.

"Larry felt that Ruly Carpenter had promised him a three-year extension on his contract," said Giles. "And Larry thought I would honor what he had talked to Ruly about. But I talked to Ruly and Ruly said, 'I told him that I would extend his contract if I owned the team.' And Ruly knew pretty well at the time that he wasn't going to own the team."

Carpenter might have been telling Bowa one thing and Giles another. But that's when Bowa decided to take the dispute public.

It was early 1982, and the headlines read, "Bowa Calls Giles Liar."

"I told the press, 'They're going to have to trade me, or there is going to be a problem here,'" Bowa said. "Because it was a verbal commitment that Ruly Carpenter gave me. In fact, everything I did with him was verbal. I mean, he'd say, 'You're going to sign a two-year contract a month from now. Let's do it.' And it was always done. He was always fair with me. I was coming off a five-year contract. And he paid me $500,000, the most I ever made in baseball for one year. He was as good an owner as I've ever met in my life. But he was from that old owners' school where it was family. Now it's corporations and conglomerates. You're not going to get that feeling."

Recalls Giles: "He and I definitely got into a fight through the newspapers. Larry called me a liar and a few other things in the papers. Ultimately I felt it was best that we trade him. That was the infamous trade that helped us for one or two years, and Ryne Sandberg became a possible Hall of Famer."

"I think Giles wanted to prove to everybody how strong he was going to be as the new owner," Bowa said. "You know, 'I'm going to stick to my guns. I'm going to do it my way.' We bantered back and forth in the papers for a month. He'd say, 'He can't play any more. He's at the end of his career.' So finally, Lee Elia, who used to be a coach for us when Dallas Green was the manager, got the job as Cubs manager under Dallas. It was kind of funny in a way. The Phillies were knocked out of the playoffs by Montreal in 1981. And it seemed like the very next day, Dallas quit as manager and took over as general manager of the Cubs. I know Dallas wanted to be the Phillies' general manager bad. But the way they were set up and the way it turned out with Ruly leaving anyway, it never would have happened. So, of course, he takes Elia with him. So Lee and I are playing golf together, and I said, 'Why don't you talk to Dallas and get me out of here, man? I can help you guys out.'

"He said, 'They aren't going to give you up.'

"I said, 'Hey, they've got to give me up. They've got to trade me or they've got to give me three more years. And they're not going to give me a three-year deal.'"

Bowa felt he had no alternative. He wasn't a free agent. He was under contract for one more season, and he didn't want to play for the Phillies under the circumstances. As a veteran of 12 years in the organization, who had worked hard to get every ounce out of his talent, he thought he deserved more respect than that.

"It was getting close to spring training and I still hadn't signed. I was ticked," Bowa explained. "I'd had it up to here. So I ripped Giles. And that's the way it came out in the paper. They asked me about all this stuff and I said, 'Well, Bill Giles isn't actually being very truthful about this.' When I think on it now, I kind of have to scratch my head and wonder what I was thinking back then. Bill and I are all patched up. We're good friends."

Bowa said he kept up the assault on Giles in newspapers until Green called and asked him if was interested in coming to Chicago.

"I said, 'Yeah. But I want a three-year contract,'" Bowa said.

"He says, 'I've got no problem with that.'"

Then Bowa said he helped engineer the trade. The Phillies wanted Ivan DeJesus from the Cubs, an infielder who would replace Bowa at shortstop and play alongside second baseman Joe Morgan in the 1983 World Series. But Bowa suggested to Elia that the Cubs get Sandberg with him in the deal. Elia, who managed Sandberg in the Phillies' minor leagues, wasn't sold on the idea.

"I told him, 'I know his work habits at that time were considered lazy. Very, very low key. But I'm telling you, he's going to be a player,'" Bowa said.

"So they finally put the deal together. The Chicago writers call me up. And I didn't know the final trade yet. So I asked, 'Who's the guy they threw in?' When they said Sandberg, I told them, 'Well then, I was the guy they threw in because Sandberg is going to be a great player.' And the guy says, 'Come on.' I said, 'I'm telling you. He's going to be an unbelievable player.' Of course, I was proven right on that one. He turned out to be a spectacular second baseman for the Cubs, and he is on the Hall of Fame ballot.

"They traded Sandberg and me for Ivan DeJesus. That has to be one of the all-timers. Bill just wanted to show people, 'I'm the new owner and this is the way it's going to be.' And I guess I was the guy he wanted to set the example with. I had been in the organization a long time, and I was the outspoken guy on the ball club."

Bowa said he'd gotten the inklings of all this from Giles years earlier when they went to a banquet together in New Jersey. Bowa was still playing for the Phillies. Giles was in community relations, in charge of putting people in the ballpark, ticket sales and promotions. It was one of those raw winter nights. Giles picked up Bowa at his house and the two ventured into the evening.

"It was that night that I realized how far Bill wanted to go in baseball and with the Phillies in particular," Bowa said. "We started talking and this sticks out in my mind: I said, 'What would you like to do, Bill?' And he said, 'I'd really like to own a baseball team. That's my long-range goal.'

"I asked, 'What intrigues you about that?'

"He said, 'I'd just like the feeling of being able to trade somebody any time I wanted to. I'd like to have the power to get rid of people if I didn't think they were doing the job.'

"As I look back on that conversation, it stands out so clear. And when it happened to me, I said, 'He got his wish.' But I give him a lot of credit for pursuing his dreams and making sure they came true."

In hindsight only now, Bowa can look back and question some of the ways he handled things as a player. At 57 years old, he has a management point of view after years of being around the business on all sides, as a player, coach and manager.

"I don't want to say that I was naïve when I stopped playing and went into managing, but I guess I was," Bowa said recently. "Some of my own players in my own Philadelphia clubhouse probably think I dropped off the moon or something. That I never had to deal with the same things they do. The money is a lot greater today, but the business is very much the same."

Bowa knows now that he could have finished his career in Philadelphia and signed a series of one-year contracts to get him through to the end, but he wanted the protection of a three-year extension. He didn't realize it at the time, but it was a big mistake.

"I had no problem keeping him. He could have retired with us," Giles said. "I just didn't want to guarantee him the three-year deal, because his skills were starting to deteriorate a little bit."

Years later, Bowa would apologize for the way he handled the situation and reconcile with Giles.

"I understand now that Bill was just representing the new Phillies ownership, that I was getting up in years as a player and that he had to be fiscally responsible," Bowa said. "As a player, you don't worry about those things. You don't look at the big picture. You just worry about yourself. It was a lesson learned."

—6—

THE
1984 PLAYOFFS

It is the seventh inning of Game 5 of the National League Championship Series, and San Diego's Jack Murphy Stadium is absolute pandemonium. It is a sunny Sunday afternoon—October 7, 1984—and a packed house—58,359. The Chicago Cubs, once leading 3-0 in the game and once leading 2-0 in the series, are about to watch the pennant slip away. It is 3-2 as Chicago's big right-hander, Rick Sutcliffe, faces Carmelo Martinez to open the inning. Ball one. Sutcliffe drops behind the mound in a crouch to catch his breath as the noise swells. Ball two. He bends over and ties his shoes. He adjusts his cap and looks in to catcher Jody Davis for the sign. Ball three. Relievers are warming up feverishly in the bullpen. Larry Bowa sprints over from his position at shortstop to calm Sutcliffe down.

"I couldn't believe it," Bowa recalled later about the decision by manager Jim Frey to leave Sutcliffe in the game. "Sutcliffe was all but telling him he was through. He's doing a hell of a job, but he's tiring. He's tying his shoes. He's doing everything. I go to the mound and I say, 'How are you doing, Rick?' He's such a competitor, but I can see he's dead. And all the relievers are up. We've got them all going and ready. Damn if he doesn't leave him in there. He was tired. He was trying to give somebody a sign.

"No pitcher who is as competitive as he is is going to say he's tired. You can go out there and ask him how he feels. He'll tell you, 'I feel great.' No way he's going to say he's tired. You've got to know as a manager that he's had it. He did everything but send up a flag. When I went to the mound, I could tell he was done. There's a look in a guy's eyes. You can look right through him and say, 'You've had it.'

"Did anybody ever ask Frey about it? Oh, he had an answer, I'm sure."

Frey's answer: "When people say I screwed it up by leaving Sutcliffe in too long, I think they're jerks. Anybody who would suggest that, I think is a jerk. You're telling me that Sutcliffe was tired. How do you know Sutcliffe was tired? You mean when people walk hitters, they're tired? Is that what you're saying? I didn't think he was.

"Every time I let him fight his way out of a jam in June and July and August and September, it was great. But in this particular instance... And who knows? If the ball was caught at first, maybe we would have still won."

Sutcliffe, who is now a baseball analyst for the Padres and ESPN, didn't pitch out of this particular jam, and Tim Flannery's grounder did indeed shoot through first baseman Leon Durham's legs for the error that tied the score. What appeared to be a routine double-play grounder hit by Tony Gwynn took a bad hop and skipped over second baseman Ryne Sandberg's shoulder for the double that gave the Padres enough runs to win the series. What happened in one short weekend to the 1984 Cubs is still a matter of debate years later, particularly in light of their 2003 collapse against the Florida Marlins in the NLCS.

In both cases—1984 and 2003—the Cubs were one win away from going to the World Series and had three shots at winning that game. In both cases, Jack McKeon was involved—as the general manager of the Padres in 1984 and as the manager of the Florida Marlins in 2003. In both cases, the Cubs had their best pitcher of that era on the mound—Sutcliffe in 1984 and Mark Prior in 2003. In both cases there were fateful plays that sent the Cubs on to their demise. In 1984, it was the balls that shot through Durham's legs and bounced over Sandberg's shoulder. In 2003 against the eventual

World Series-champion Marlins in the eighth inning of Game 6 at Wrigley Field, it was the pop foul deflected by a fan in the left field corner and away from Moises Alou followed by the bobble by short-stop Alex Gonzalez on an apparent double-play grounder.

The Cubs were leading 3-0 and were five outs away from winning the pennant against the Marlins. But they still haven't been to the World Series since 1945. And definitely each generation of fans has endured some scars. But for Bowa, it's still the bad taste of 1984 that lingers.

Bowa: "I knew we were in trouble after we won two straight in Chicago. I mean, we're flying from Chicago to San Diego, and there are wives on the flight. And the majority of the wives are along with the players who have never been in the playoffs. They're there. And they're drinking champagne and wine. I'm sitting next to Gary Matthews, and I'm saying, 'You've got to be kidding me. We haven't done anything yet. We've still got to win the last game in San Diego.' Sure as hell, man. Just a little thing like that can change everything. Momentum plays such a big part in it. Mentally, your mind relaxes a little bit. When Steve Garvey hit that home run to win Game 4, I said, 'We're in trouble.' I knew we were in trouble."

Frey already had history with Bowa, as the losing manager when Bowa's Phillies defeated Frey's Kansas City Royals in the 1980 World Series. Four years later, the two were together on the north side of Chicago trying to beat back the fate of the Billy Goat curse and a history of failure that stretches back to the 1908 World Series—the last one the Cubs won.

"What I remember most about '84 is coming to Chicago and managing a team that hadn't won in a while and winning a division," Frey said. "I remember the excitement that was created and the fans and the attendance. That was an exciting and very interesting experience. And nobody is going to make me feel bad about it because a couple of balls went into the outfield. No one. There isn't anybody in the world who is going to make me think we didn't do a good job with that team."

Bowa: "We screwed up not pitching Sutcliffe in Game 4. When we scored those five runs? We win that with Sutcliffe on the mound. Frey's setting up his rotation so Sutcliffe can face Detroit in the first game of the World Series if we win it in four. You see what happens? You don't do that. You let the guy pitch when he's supposed to pitch. If he pitches that night, we win. They don't get six runs off Sutcliffe in a night game. I'm telling you, we would have won that game. But we're going to set it up. We're going to have Sutcliffe ready to open the World Series in Detroit. We don't even get to Detroit."

Frey: "I said at the moment that the fourth game was more important than the fifth. We had three leads, but Steve Garvey, three times with two out, gets base hits to get them back in the game. And then he hits that home run. Those hits he got in the middle of the game, getting them back into it when it appeared we were putting them away, that was the difference. We had a lot of scoring opportunities. Some of my ballplayers came up in situations where another base hit would have put them away. All of those things to me, when I go over that series, are more important than the fifth game. We really should have won the fourth game. But Garvey was the big man."

Of course it all depends on your perspective. For Padres fans up to that point in the team's history, that weekend of baseball was undoubtedly the most electrifying anyone in San Diego had ever witnessed. For Chicago fans, it simply fulfilled a legacy.

"Obviously things could have worked out better for the Chicago ball club and the Chicago fans and Jim Frey," Frey said. "Most importantly to me at that time, we had players who had played very well for six months and within a few minutes we let it all get away. Everything we had done was forgotten because of a couple of ground balls. It doesn't seem right, to me, if you put things in proper perspective, that for six or seven months everybody's jumping up and down and screaming about how great the Cubs are and what a wonderful year we're having, and 15 minutes later someone tells you that you blew it.

"The '84 playoffs is something I don't dwell on. I don't have any big, strong second guesses about what I did. A lot more disappointing things have happened to me since that day. Getting fired is a lot worse than losing the playoffs, believe me. Some of those moments are more dramatic and have a more lasting effect on you than a game or a series."

The 1984 playoffs began on October 2, 1984, with a blast for the Cubs, who tortured the Padres and starter Eric Show with a 13-0 blitz in Game 1. Show looked up at the flags on the roof behind home plate at Wrigley Field prior to the game. They were blowing straight out. It was a death knell. Bob Dernier and Gary Matthews hit homers off Show in the first inning. And when Sutcliffe planted one out on Sheffield Avenue, the carnage was complete. The Cubs hit five homers in Game 1 and played a good, solid second game to win 4-2 and take a 2-0 lead in the last of the best-of-five League Championship Series. In 1985, that would change to a best-of-seven format, but a year too late for the Cubs.

The Padres' obit was being written. Cubs World Series tickets were being scalped. But that ending was far too pat, too contrived and too conservative. Three games were left to be played in California, and the San Diego fans, stirred up by a Mike Royko column, wouldn't let the Padres die. The late Chicago journalist alleged that San Diego didn't deserve a pennant winner because it was stocked with surfers and white wine drinkers. Fans came out in the thousands to the stadium parking lot to welcome the weary Padres home from Chicago the night of that Game 2 defeat.

"We were so down, we didn't know what hit us," said Dave Dravecky, a Padres relief pitcher on that team who would later lose his left arm to cancer. "We take the buses back from the airport to get our cars back at the stadium, and there was something like 4,000 people waiting for us. That got us going. It meant we weren't alone and that people really cared."

The next night, October 4, 1984, the stadium was bonkers. During pregame introductions, shortstop Garry Templeton stepped out of character and waved a towel over his head to further incite a mob that didn't need inciting. The comeback was on. "I think Garry Templeton had more of an effect on the fans than they did on him," said Frey. "He did something that was so unnatural for Garry Templeton to do at that particular time. It kind of aroused the fans, I thought. The waving of the towel when the players were introduced. Otherwise, I have no idea what got anything started. I don't know anything more about it. I don't give a darn about psychology or anything like that. And I don't think any of this means a damn anyway. This absolutely doesn't mean anything to me. It's not an important issue to me."

Perhaps not now. In Game 3 Templeton did more than towel-wave. He snared a Leon Durham line drive to blunt a first-inning Cubs rally. And his fifth-inning double knocked in two runs and gave the Padres their first lead of the series. Ed Whitson finally offered the Padres some decent front-line pitching. It all added up to a 7-1 win.

Two nights later came that miraculous Game 4. Garvey's two-out double in the third inning gave the Padres a 2-0 lead off starter Scott Sanderson. Jody Davis and Durham hit back-to-back homers off Tim Lollar in the fourth to hoist the Cubs ahead 3-2. Garvey's two-out single in the fifth made it 3-3. In the seventh, another two-out Garvey single made it San Diego 5, Chicago 3. The Cubs tied it with two runs off Goose Gossage in the eighth. That set up Garvey's incredible heroics in the home half of the ninth. Lee Smith opened the inning by striking out Alan Wiggins. Tony Gwynn singled to center. That brought up Garvey. To cap an almost superhuman performance, Garvey lined a two-run homer over the right center field fence to tie the series at two games apiece.

Garvey had dislocated a thumb in 1983 and never regained the same power, hitting only eight homers during the 1984 season. He was so sick to his stomach in the hours before the game that he had to drag himself off a training table just to play. But that single swing, met with explosive delirium, is still remembered as the greatest moment in San Diego sports history 20 years later. Garvey had four clutch hits worth five RBIs and was ultimately named MVP of the series. Immediately afterward, while being congratulated on nation-wide TV by Tim McCarver, Garvey told the country, "It was my pleasure."

That brought the series down to a one-game playoff on Sunday afternoon with Sutcliffe going against Show in a Game 1 rematch. There was no wind, but for Show, the results were the same. Durham homered in the first. Davis homered in the second. Before manager Dick Williams could go out and get Show, the Cubs were leading 3-0. Show, in almost a gesture of defiance, tossed Williams the ball before he could reach the mound. The Cubs never scored another run and had only five hits in the game. Sitting above the fray in the owner's box at what was then lovingly called "The Murph," Trader Jack McKeon could sense the inevitable. Only two years later, McKeon would give Bowa his first job as a manager—at Triple A Las Vegas in the Padres organization.

"We were down in the game, and I'll never forget being in the box with [then president] Ballard [Smith] and he said it didn't look too good," McKeon recalled. "And I said: 'Don't worry about it, if we score a run here, we can make it interesting.'"

The Padres chewed back to make it 3-2 after six innings and then pounced for four more runs in the seventh to win the game 6-3 and their first National League pennant. There was the ball that inexplicably bounced through Durham's legs. There was the ball that skipped by Sandberg. Was it a century's worth of Cubs pathos coming home to roost? Or was it simply fate?

"I couldn't believe it," said Bowa, who was really a nonfactor with just three hits in the series. "I had never seen a ball go through Durham's legs. I'd seen some ground balls bounce off him, but he's a pretty good first baseman. And the one that went over Sandberg, he didn't miss a ball like that either. Gwynn's ball, it came up, but I've seen him catch it. He got a double out of it, but it should have been a double play. It was one of those where you're looking for the ball low, and it comes right up. It was a bad hop, but the kind of athlete he is, I never expect him to miss any ball."

That game set in motion some life-altering changes for a number of key Chicago Cubs characters. Bowa, who would openly feud with Frey, would not make it through the 1985 season in Chicago. Frey would be fired as manager in June 1986. Frey's buddy and coach, Don Zimmer, would be shown the gate along with the manager. Dallas Green, the club's president, would fall out with management of the Tribune Company (which still owns the Cubs) and resign after the 1987 season, despite two years remaining on his contract.

The ironies? Frey, who was signed by WGN to do color commentary on Cubs broadcasts in 1987, would replace Green, the man who fired him, as general manager at the end of that season. Zimmer would be brought back to manage the team in 1988. Bowa would be hired to manage the Padres a little more than two years after those chilling playoffs.

Frey left no doubt that his 1984 experience with the Cubs was well behind him. "If people think I'm going to my grave blaming myself for that, they've got another thing coming," Frey said. "I thought we did a great job with a team that wasn't supposed to win."

Bowa's feud with Frey began in the spring of 1985 when he arrived at camp in Mesa, Arizona, to find a rookie named Shawon Dunston about to take over his job. Bowa, at 39, felt that Frey was treating him with disrespect by offering his position to an untested rookie without at least a competition. "My feeling was, we won in '84," Bowa said. "Now in '85, unless Dunston had an outstanding spring training, which he did not, my feeling was that I should have that job. We won. Now if I lose it, great. But that wasn't the case. He called me in, but all spring he kept saying to the press, 'I'm not telling you who my shortstop is.' Finally, near the end, I went in and said, 'Look, you don't have to tell the writers, but how about telling me? Who's the shortstop?' When I went in there, that's when he said that Dunston was the shortstop. I said, 'Good. I'll just be the utility player, then.' That's the only season in 16 years I didn't start on Opening Day. I thought that was weak."

Frey's version?

"What happened between us?" he said. "Ask him. He's the guy who's been doing all the talking. I never said one word about Larry Bowa. I spent six weeks of spring training, once a week, reading what Bowa said about Jim Frey. You've never read anything about Jim Frey saying anything about Bowa. When I took Larry Bowa out of the lineup, he complained. That's all there is to it. There's no more to it. I didn't say anything. When he went to the press, and said, 'How can he take me out of the lineup?' they'd come to me, I'd say, 'Because I'm going to play somebody else today.' I never said anything else.

"Let me tell you this: I'm going to tell you this one time and you're only going to choose what you want to write anyway. And if you don't do this one right, don't ask me any more questions. The first thing I did in the spring of '85, the very first thing I did, was to call Larry Bowa in my office and explain to him that there was a good chance that he wasn't going to play every day on the ball club. He might play part-time. I am going to see if Dunston has a chance to be a major league baseball player. That was the very first thing I did on the very first morning. The rest of the spring he said, 'The man has never told me what the situation is.' This is the first time I'm telling anyone this. I never answered the question before because I didn't think I had to."

Bowa's blitz in the Chicago papers so rankled Frey that he finally sent out Don Zimmer with a written statement attacking the veteran player. Only days before the Cubs were scheduled to break camp, Zimmer summoned *Chicago Tribune* beat writer Fred Mitchell into the Cubs dugout for a solo press conference. Mitchell recorded the entire diatribe on tape.

This Bowa comment about Frey is what started it all: "I have no dialogue with the man. None. I just come in every day and read the board to see if I'm playing. I wish I knew how he was thinking. How he planned to use me. I want him to be honest with me, not try to pull the wool over my eyes. The bottom line is that Dunston really didn't do that well in Triple A. If he tore up Triple A, I'd say there's no doubt he should be up here."

Zimmer, who resigned as bench coach of the New York Yankees after the 2003 World Series and signed as a senior adviser with the Tampa Bay Devil Rays, put on his reading specs and let fly:

"Larry Bowa is the most selfish player I have ever known. He is not a team player, and he cares for no one but himself. If I were Jody Davis, I might have choked him. On throws to second that should have been stopped, Bowa made no attempt. Do you know that Captain Bowa did not speak to Ryne Sandberg for a week to 10 days during the season last year? Well, I know it and other guys on the team know it. Sandberg must have been going too good. If you can't get along with Sandberg, you can't get along with your wife.

"He has now taken off on the manager for about the fourth time in the press. One time last year, his name wasn't on the lineup card. He didn't come on the field. He didn't come in the dugout. He hid. Captain Bowa. I thought the captain was supposed to help the manager keep things together. His locker was behind mine. When he was going good, he couldn't wait for you guys to come in the locker room for some more of his bull. When things went bad for him, like the day he made two or three errors and we lost the game, he hid from you guys. You find him: Larry Bowa-style."

Years later, Bowa countered Zimmer by saying, "I've never shied away from any questions, whether I've done bad or good. And I've never made three errors in a game. I don't know what he was talking about."

As far as the Sandberg falling out goes, the National League's Most Valuable Player in 1984 tells a somewhat different story.

"When I was traded over to the Cubs with him from the Phillies in 1982, I was just out of Triple A," Sandberg said. "I remember that first spring training. He just showed a lot of support for me. Not only on the field, but also off the field. That year, I played third base next to him all year. We just had pretty good communications between each other. I learned a lot of the basic fundamentals of playing infield from him. The next year, they had said I was moving to second base, so he suggested we both show up to spring training in Mesa about two weeks early. He showed up. It was no big deal for me because I lived down there.

"I thought it was neat that a veteran guy, who knows his position so well, would show up early with somebody else. He had incredible work habits as a player. They rubbed off on me. Definitely. He's a firm believer of getting into a routine during the season. He worked extra hard in spring training. He'd stay after workouts to take ground balls. He showed up early before workouts and took grounders. I just kind of followed him. He was one of the biggest early influences on my career. It was a big disappointment the day they finally released him.

"They didn't want Shawon to feel like he was being pressured to play outstanding because if Larry was on the bench, he'd go in and replace him. That was the main reason. It wasn't that he was a bad influence on the team or anything. Larry even worked with Shawon during spring training. I don't think it was a big bitter thing between the two of them."

About Sandberg, Bowa said: "I worked his butt off. I told him, 'You've got to work hard if you want to get up in this game. You can do it. You've got great tools.' We worked, we worked, and we worked. They didn't know where he was going to play. The harder he worked, the more you could see that, hey, this guy was going to be a stud. He was still skinny. He didn't lift weights or anything.

"I remember one year in Philly, he got called up in September. Sandberg is standing behind me while I'm taking my ground balls. This guy is not saying anything. I'm waiting for him to say, 'Can I take some with you?' So I keep taking them. Finally, I say, 'Do you want some ground balls? Well, just jump in here. Let's go.' He was so shy. But he turned into a gamer and eventually taught all the other guys. He had great work habits. But the rap on him in Philly was that he was lazy. They didn't think he'd be anything but a utility player."

Dunston did open the season at short, but when he bombed out and was sent back to the minors, Frey reluctantly had to go back to Bowa. It was a safe bet that Frey had no further use for Bowa. His days with the Cubs were numbered. Frey was so incensed at Bowa that he even ridiculed certain people in the organization who he felt were siding with Bowa. Frey was livid at the public relations department for trying to find a positive in a season going down the drain. Bowa was batting about .150, but each day the press notes would indicate that the Cubs were far better than a .500 team with Bowa in the lineup. Frey eventually exploded at the public relations director, Bob Ibach. The Cubs were on a midsummer road trip to Philadelphia when the 1985 season began to unravel. After a game at the Vet, the late broadcaster Harry Caray set up a dinner at a local establishment named Morton's for the upper brass. Frey was not in a sociable mood when Ibach joined the party. Out of nowhere, Frey pointedly growled at him, "Everywhere we go on this road trip, everyone wants to know why we keep winning with Larry Bowa in the lineup. That's the question I most often have to answer. And you know why? Because they read about it every day in your press notes." The loud diatribe caused such a stir that the Ibach had to leave the restaurant.

When Bowa surpassed Rabbit Maranville for the most games played by a shortstop in National League history, the Cubs' promotion department considered holding a ceremony for Bowa at home plate in Wrigley Field. But it never happened, allegedly because Frey stopped it. That's how badly the relationship between player and manager had deteriorated. Along the way, Bowa kept reiterating that there were no open lines of communication between the shortstop and the manager.

"You'd go into his office and ask him something, and he'd hit you with his favorite line," Bowa said. "'I have the only pencil in town.' He makes out the lineup. Big deal. He says that instead of saying, 'You have some merit. I have some merit. Let me toss it around.' Instead he says, 'I have the only pencil in town.' What are you supposed to say to that?"

Bowa felt that his ace in the hole against Frey in the organization was Dallas Green, his former Phillies manager and the guy who brought him to Chicago from Philadelphia. But eventually, even that card was played out. When Dunston was recalled from the minors, Frey pushed Green into releasing Bowa six weeks before the end of the season. At a tearful press conference, Bowa said goodbye to the Windy City for good. The parting of the ways came little more than 10 months from the day the Cubs lost the pennant in San Diego. And the falling out between the player and manager was just a precursor to what Bowa would experience as a manager with such players as Joey Cora and Stanley Jefferson in his tenure with the Padres and guys like Scott Rolen with the Phillies. Eventually, Bowa would find the proverbial shoe on the other foot.

7

A PLAYING CAREER ENDS

Bowa knew that his playing career was coming to an end. There were six weeks to go in the 1985 season. He was batting .246, but worst of all he mostly had been relegated to the bench and had only played in 72 games. Even at 40, for a guy who was used to starting almost every day for his entire career, the situation didn't sit very well in Bowa's stomach. Still the call and then the subsequent meeting with general manager Dallas Green in his office at Wrigley Field came as a shock. It was August 13, 1985, and Bowa was out as a member of the Cubs. His playing days ended at the conclusion of that season with the New York Mets.

Bowa had decided during spring training that 1985 was going to be his last active year under almost any circumstances. "I didn't want to hang around as a reserve player," he said. "You get to a point where you have to say to yourself, 'I've done what I can do.' And I had done what I could do on the field."

Still, Bowa wanted to go out on his own terms.

But that grim August day, Green called Bowa in and told him, "I've got to do the toughest thing I've ever had to do in my baseball career. I've got to release you."

Bowa was stunned. There were only two weeks to go before major league rosters expanded to 40 players to accommodate top minor-leaguers whose regular season ends around August 31. And a year after going to the playoffs, the Cubs were on their way to finishing with a 77-84 record and in fourth place. They were going nowhere, with or without Bowa.

"You've got to do what?" Bowa said incredulously.

"I've got to release you. We want to bring up Shawon Dunston," Green reiterated.

Bowa suggested that Green put him on the disabled list. "Let him play," Bowa said about Dunston. "Then put me back on the 40-man roster, and I'm out of here anyway."

"Nope," Green said. "Jim Frey doesn't want you around while Dunston is playing."

No matter what Bowa said, there was no turning back.

Bowa learned when he left Philadelphia in 1982 to not burn bridges. He had ripped the new owner Bill Giles back then, forcing the trade that sent him from the Phillies to the Cubs. This time, he accepted it. For the first time in his life, he didn't go out screaming.

"I didn't rip anybody, really. It was probably the most emotional I've ever been as a player, getting released," Bowa recalled. "The next day I came in for a news conference, to face the Chicago press for the last time, and I just broke down. I couldn't believe it. I cried openly. It was a blow. Not to my ego. I had a lot of pride, and I thought I was doing a good job. I had just played the game of the week [on August 10]. I made about four plays in the hole. I got two hits off that young Mets right-hander Dwight Gooden, who was just coming into his own, throwing all that heat and going 24-4 that season.

"Dallas just kept saying, 'I'll explain it all to you one day when we're both away from this game.'

"I told him, 'You don't have to explain anything. I know exactly what's coming down.'

"It was all between the manager and me, Jim Frey and me."

Frey was always an offensive-oriented manager and proponent of the big bang theory. He didn't like singles hitters, although Frey knew they had their place in the game. Frey never played in the big leagues. Ironically, he was a career minor-leaguer who capitalized on little ball himself. From 1950 to 1963, Frey batted .302 with only 95 homers and 728 RBIs in 1,206 games. But Frey's managerial philosophy was carved out during his 15 years working as a coach—among other things—in the Baltimore Orioles organization under manager Earl Weaver. Weaver created pennant-winning teams by shunning time-honored tactics such as the hit-and-run and stolen bases for station-to-station (base-to-base) baseball followed by the big extra-base hit or home run. Weaver hated giving up outs. Making a batter lay down a bunt to move a runner into scoring position wasn't his idea of a good time.

It was the way the tactics of baseball had evolved in the American League after the designated hitter was adopted in 1973. Since then, American League pitchers haven't hit in regular-season games between American League foes. Theoretically, an American League batting order can be built with nine tough hitters in the line-up. To this day, most pitchers aren't adept at hitting and are perhaps even less adept than they were 30 years ago. The designated hitter is utilized at most levels of high school, college and minor league ball. Only the National League strictly uses the old rule when NL foes play each other during the regular season. Pitchers hit, meaning that some old-school, fundamentally sound baseball—like moving runners around the bases and sacrificing outs—is still in vogue to create runs.

That was Frey's mindset, through his Baltimore years and through one year-plus managing the Kansas City Royals. It may have been no coincidence that Frey was the manager in 1980 when Bowa's Phillies defeated the Royals in the World Series. Sometimes old animosities die hard in baseball. Bowa, the needler, and Frey were cut somewhat from the same cloth. Both are small men who had to make the most of their abilities to succeed. Both, obviously, had authority issues. Frey, of course, didn't have the playing success Bowa had in his career. He was even fired as Royals manager late in the 1981 season less than a month after managing the American League in the All-Star Game.

And Frey inherited Bowa at shortstop when he took over as Cubs manager in 1984. Bowa was the product of the Phillies cabal that moved in to run the Cubs organization in 1982—Green, his old Phillies manager, was named Cubs general manager, and Lee Elia, his old Phillies coach, was named the new Cubs manager. Bowa, then in a contract dispute with Giles, was reunited with his old partners. But Elia played himself out quickly in Chicago. When a fifth-place finish in 1982 was followed by a 5-14 start to the 1983 season, the boobirds filled Wrigley, taunted the players, and began calling for Elia's ouster. A legendary profanity-filled postgame explosion set the stage for Elia's demise. Here's a segment of the cleaned-up version of Elia's tirade:

"They're really, really behind you around here," Elia said on April 29, 1983. "What am I supposed to do, go out there and let my players get destroyed every day and be quiet about it? For the nickel-and-dime people who turn up? These fans don't even work. That's why they're out at the game. They ought to go out and get a job and find out what it's like to go out and earn a living. Eighty-five percent of the world is working. The other 15 percent come out here and boo my team."

(Keep in mind that the Cubs still played all their home games during the day because the lights at Wrigley Field were still a few years away.)

The Cubs hadn't been to the World Series since 1945 and hadn't won one since 1908. It was frustrating for all concerned, but the invective eventually led to Elia's firing. Charlie Fox, a baseball lifer, came down from the front office to manage the final 39 games of the 1983 season. Frey was looking for a job. Green hired him despite the fact that Frey had a reputation for alienating many of his players during his short tenure with Kansas City. Bowa had a .267 season at the plate in 1983, but he committed only 11 errors and led all National League shortstops with a .984 fielding percentage. Fox named Bowa team captain during the waning days of the 1983 season. The setup for a Frey and Bowa collision was there.

"I never really fit into his plans. Not even from the very start," Bowa said. "The guy was very critical of my offensive performance.

It stood out in my mind because he never played in the big leagues. I mean, if this guy was a great player, you could say he wants me to be like him. You know, he was a minor league bum, basically. But talking to him, you'd think he had played 30 years in the big leagues.

"So basically right from the start, he disliked the way I played. I was a singles-type hitter who did little things. He was for that big swing, baby. Let it go. It's not that I don't have respect for him. I just think he has a chip on his shoulder because he never played in the big leagues.

"I think there is merit to having done something in the big leagues when you're a manager. I've found that out in my two major league jobs since then. I'm not saying that just because a guy played big-league ball he knows more. I'm just talking about how the team views it. I can sit there all day and say to the Phillies, 'I think you ought to do it this way.' And if they say to me, 'What do you know about it?' I can say, 'I've got a World Series ring. I've been in six play-offs. I've been in five All-Star games. That's what I know about it. What have you done?'

"But you go up to a guy who has never played, what's he going to say? I've managed 20 years in the minor leagues? The players don't listen. That's just the way the big-league players operate. I'm not saying it is right, because I know some guys in the minor leagues who have never played a day of big-league ball that are more knowledgeable than guys who have played in the majors for 20 years. That's just the way the system is."

Bowa batted .200 and had only three hits in the Cubs' five-game loss to the Padres in the 1984 National League Championship Series. But by the following spring training, Frey had already started paving the way for a rookie named Shawon Dunston to replace Bowa at shortstop. Even though Dunston had struggled, hitting .233 in 61 games for the Cubs' Triple A affiliate at Des Moines, Iowa, after being moved up from lower level Midland the previous season, Frey wanted Dunston.

Dunston would ultimately have a nice 18-year career—his first 11 seasons with the Cubs—that included two All-Star berths, but he was a green rookie in 1985. Like the young Mike Schmidt coming in as a shortstop more than a decade earlier in Philadelphia, Bowa was going to tussle with anyone to remain the starting shortstop. It didn't matter. It could have been the acrobatic Ozzie Smith trying to take Bowa's job.

"Frey wanted the kid to take the job, but he was a rookie and just wasn't ready," Bowa said. "But Frey would sit me down three or four days at a time and then all of a sudden he would say, 'OK, now you're playing.' I'd come into the locker room that day mentally not ready to play. As a player, every morning I used to get up and I knew what I was going to do. I knew what pitcher I was facing. I had everything down. I'm not blaming that all on him. That was probably a tough adjustment for me. I had been a regular for 15 years. I should have adjusted better mentally.

"Frey said I made Dunston nervous, that Dunston could not play to his capabilities with me watching his every move. It was a joke. We were 25 games out at the time. There was no reason to release me except that Frey wanted me out. It shows how intimidated Frey was. That's what it says to me. Dallas caved in to him because Dallas is a man who in the end can say: 'You did it your way, and it was lousy. So get out!' You know what I'm saying? And that's exactly what happened to Frey early in 1986, anyway. He followed me out the door as manager by only a few months.

"You know, Frey could have come back to him and said, 'I wanted Bowa out of here. He caused a lot of problems. That's why Dunston didn't play.' But Dallas wasn't going to give him that."

The days of sitting behind Dunston didn't last. Despite Frey backing him to the hilt, Dunston was batting .125 with just three hits for the month of May when cooler heads prevailed. On May 15, Dunston was sent back to the minor leagues, where he batted .268 in 73 games. For two months, Bowa was again the starting shortstop.

The Cubs could have waited until the minor league season ended to bring Dunston up. But true to Green's word, on August 13—the day Bowa was released—Dunston was recalled from Iowa.

Bowa trusted Green. He had developed that give and take with Dallas when they were together for two seasons as player and manager in Philadelphia.

"One thing about Dallas to me, and I know this as a fact, Dallas does not like yes men," Bowa said. "When you sit down and talk to Dallas, he sort of likes you to disagree with him. He likes to argue, which is one reason I think we got along. We respect each other. We've had our arguments."

Green, like Bowa as a manager later, had a way of sending the players messages through the newspapers. In 1980, for instance, the Phillies were floundering and Green ripped the team to the beat reporters. The stories the next day all quoted the manager saying that the Phillies didn't know how to play or how to win.

A one-day story like that can easily be built into a two- or three-day story if reporters can get some one to respond to the original comments. Knowing Bowa's nature, reporters went right to him and rehashed Green's remarks

"We were going badly, and they caught me at a bad time. A reporter asked me, "Man, did you hear what Dallas said? He said you guys don't know how to win. You're selfish. All you do is think of yourselves, not of the team.'"

Bowa bit. "I said, 'Go ask Dallas what he ever did in the big leagues?' It was the headline story the next day: 'Bowa to Green: What Have You Done in the Big Leagues!'

"So we happened to be going on a road trip the day the story came out. And we were in the airport at the gate, waiting for the plane. Dallas was on one side reading the paper, and I was standing on the other side with Greg Luzinski. Dallas looks over at me, and I'm waiting to be taken apart. But he smiles and says, 'Hey Bo—touché.'

"That's the kind of relationship we had."

That's the kind of relationship Bowa didn't have with Frey, who in 1985 began to bristle at even the mere mention of Bowa's name.

"With [Green], you would go in and he would say, 'OK, let me hear you out.' And then he would tell you his viewpoint and that would be it," Bowa said. "With Frey, he wouldn't say jack to you. You'd come in, and you wouldn't know whether you were playing or sitting. I can understand it being like that with guys who are just coming up. But a guy, who has played 15, 16, 17 years, I think you owe it to him to say, 'Hey, Larry, tomorrow you're not playing' or, 'Tomorrow you are playing.' I think you owe the guy at least that much respect.

"That's why when Dallas called me into his Wrigley Field office that day, I was stunned. I looked at him like, 'I can't believe this is happening.'

"But he said, 'You know what's going on down there.'"

Bowa said that the fans and writers in Chicago "treated me great."

"I had a good time there," he said. "It was a real change. I wouldn't have wanted to play there my entire career because I think it would have taken three or four years off my career. Playing mostly during the day. No doubt in my mind. I mean, at the end of your career, I think it's a great change. You're used to playing all night games. Now you go there. You play so many day games. You live a normal life. You get up at eight a.m. and eat breakfast. You come home at night, barbecue. I mean, it was like a regular eight-to-five job. But playing under the sun almost every day, if you're a regular player, it would kill you.

"Dallas even asked me if I wanted to stay in the organization as a manager. And I appreciated it. I liked playing for him. But I wasn't ready to make that decision."

In about a month he was. After the Cubs released him, Bowa went home and told his wife, Sheena, that he probably wasn't going to play again.

"I told her, 'The only way I'd play is if the Mets call. They're in first place. They've got a shot.' I knew their backup shortstop was just put on the disabled list and they needed another one. Davey Johnson, the manager of the Mets, called on August 20.

"So I went there and they came up short. The Mets finished three games behind St. Louis in the National League East. That was it."

Bowa hit .105 in 14 games (19 at-bats) after the Mets picked him up. He finished with a lifetime batting average of .260 and a .980 fielding percentage—the best in history among all National League shortstops.

But just as one phase of Bowa's career was over, another was about to begin.

8

BOWA:
"I HATE TO LOSE!"

T he klieg lights were set up in a horseshoe-shaped room called the Stadium Club—a utilitarian space in San Diego Jack Murphy Stadium where the Padres used to hold important media conferences. The television cameras and tape recorders were ready to roll.

For weeks it had been rumored that Lawrence Robert Bowa, the then-41-year-old spark plug from Sacramento, would become the 11th manager in the short, chaotic history of a Padres franchise that had joined the National League as an expansion team in time for the 1969 season. On October 28, 1986, it finally became a reality.

Only days before, Padres president Ballard Smith, disillusioned by the club's 74-88, fourth-place finish in the National League's Western Division and only two years removed from its first pennant, had disposed of then-manager Steve Boros. Bowa would become the Padres' third manager in eight months, or since that spring day—February 24, 1986—when Dick Williams stunned everyone by resigning his post on the opening day of spring training after four winning seasons.

Williams's resignation was only part of a tale, which involved a power struggle, cross accusations and recriminations. In the end, that struggle nearly toppled the organization that the late Ray Kroc saved for the city back in 1974. Smith, who would resign as club president midway through the 1987 season, also divorced his wife, Linda, the daughter of the late hamburger empress and Padres owner, Joan Kroc.

Kroc inherited the club when her husband, Ray, the founder of McDonald's, passed away in January 1984. She hung on to it until 1990 when it was sold to a group of 15 investors led by television mogul Tom Werner. After that Joan disappeared from public life, choosing instead to grant large financial gifts of charity to needy organizations and municipalities until the day she died in October 2003 of brain cancer. Her death ironically came only days after the Padres played their last game at the stadium in Mission Valley they had called home for 35 years and months before the opening of new PETCO Park in downtown San Diego.

But it was safe to say that the Padres were no happy family when Bowa, capitalizing on one successful season as a minor league manager at Triple A Las Vegas, faced the local media with all his usual bravado.

"I'll tell you this," Bowa said at the press conference. "I played for a long time in the big leagues, and I hate to lose. And I want that attitude to spread among our players. I'll also say this: There's no doubt in my mind that I can run a baseball team. No doubt. I'll make some mistakes. This team is going to let it all hang out. I can't guarantee that we'll win X amount of games. But I guarantee that this team will give 100 percent every day. If a guy doesn't give 100 percent, he won't play. It's as simple as that. Really, is it too much to ask for a guy to give his best for 27 outs?"

Bowa, who was allowed to add only one coach, Greg Riddoch, to a veteran staff, would find out that managing in the big leagues was nothing like managing in Vegas. Long after Bowa was gone, Riddoch would have a stint managing the Padres and suffer the same ignominious fate.

"In the Coast League, it was basically self-motivated because players hadn't reached their goal," Bowa said. "They knew they had to go out and bust their butts. They knew that I turned in a report every day to Jack McKeon and the front office. If a guy didn't hustle, didn't run out a ground ball, it went right in the report. They knew up there that they'd reached the big leagues. There was not a league above the big leagues."

Early in the 1986 season, when Boros was in the process of losing his grip on the Padres at the major league level, Bowa was having no easy time making the transition from his playing days to his managing days. Bowa had been so anxious to obtain his first managerial job, he turned down a $250,000 contract to be a utility player for the 1986 New York Mets, who ultimately came from behind to beat the Boston Red Sox in seven tough games to win the World Series.

"I had set myself in a situation in which I could manage in the minor leagues for about three years," Bowa recalled, "at that money. I said, 'OK, I want to do this. I want to give it a shot. But if it doesn't happen in three years, forget it.'"

Not only had Bowa rejected a six-figure salary, but he had lost out on big postseason money and a chance to earn his second championship ring. Instead, Bowa opted for $28,000 and the 100-degree summer days of Vegas, where the lights may shine on the strip but rarely waver to the north side of town where the Stars once played their baseball games at cozy Cashman Field.

Going back to the minor leagues was a tough transition for Bowa, who hadn't been there even as a player since 1969 in the Phillies organization.

Terry Collins, who managed the Angels a decade later and would hire Bowa to coach third base, was manager of the Triple A Albuquerque Dukes in the Dodgers' organization during that 1986 season. As times change, so do affiliations. The Dodgers are now affiliated with the minor league franchise in Las Vegas, and Collins is back with the Dodgers as their minor league field coordinator. In 1986, Collins got to know Bowa as an opposing manager.

"He'd been at it a month when we went to play them in Vegas," Collins said. "Before a game he asked me, 'How can you stand this?'

It was his reaction to being exposed to the minor leagues for the first time in many years and to the patience you must have with all the young players. I told him not to worry about it. It would come. It just takes some time to understand again what the minor leagues is all about. Of course, in the end, the Stars won the league."

The Pacific Coast League used to use a playoff system, which split the season into halves. At midseason, records reverted to zero and the first-half winners met the second-half winners in the play-offs. Bowa was fortunate. His team finished 36-35 during a first half in which he was suspended several times because of a running feud with Pam Postema, one of the few female umpires in baseball history but a woman who never realized her dream of working in the major leagues.

During one of the suspensions, Bowa was involved in a club-house confrontation with Stars outfielder Gary Woods, a former Chicago Cubs teammate, who was thrown out at the plate to end a game. When a reporter from the *Las Vegas Star* wrote up the incident, Bowa wound up having a shouting match with the writer, too.

But with the Padres signing former major league slugger Steve Kemp to a minor league contract and Bowa softening his hard-edged attitude, the team soared into first place during the second half.

"It wasn't easy playing for him at first," said pitcher Ed Wojna, who pitched for Bowa at Vegas in 1986 and for a short time in San Diego in 1987. "He was tough. He pushed us. Some guys resented him. But he got the most out of us. He got us to do our best. We respected him. And he changed as a manager over the course of the year. He still drove us, but he became more tolerant. More relaxed."

Bowa: "A coach of mine in Vegas, Rob 'Peach' Picciolo, came up to me and said, 'Larry, these guys are scared of you. They're scared, they're scared, they're scared.' He had a clubhouse meeting to tell them, 'You don't understand what Larry is trying to get across to you. That he cares about you. That he wants you to get out of Triple A because that's not where you're supposed to play.' ... That meeting must have broken the ice or something. Because it seemed like from that day on they started responding.

"Peach was the guy who came up with the idea: Don't listen to the level of his voice. Listen to what he is saying. Don't listen to his harshness or look into his eyes when he squints. Listen to the words he's saying. That's all."

Picciolo would also make it to the Padres as a coach and is now in his 15th season with the team.

In 1986, someone must have begun listening, because the Stars started playing Bowa ball, a combination of aggressive running tactics, bunts and squeezes, mixed with a power game that capitalized on the light desert air.

"Later on in the summer they were playing us in Albuquerque, and they had a pretty big lead," Collins said. "It might have been 11-1 or 12-1, something like that. His pitcher was up late in the game with a runner on first base, and he had him bunt. I remember all the guys on our bench were complaining, 'What's he doing, rubbing it in?' And I told them that he was preparing his players. When that pitcher goes to the big leagues, he'll be ready to bunt. That's what the minor leagues is all about, boys, developing players. And I learned something from that."

In a short minor league season, Bowa had exhibited sizeable growth as a manager. During the tumultuous first half, when Bowa was alienating his players and being ejected from games at a record pace, Padres general manager Jack McKeon noted that Bowa was probably "a few years away from managing in the big leagues."

But with the playoffs on the horizon as the minor league season concluded on August 31, McKeon had already changed his mind.

"In August I realized Larry was probably ready. He had learned how to deal with players. He had made adjustments in his managing style. His players were responding. He'd come an awfully long way."

McKeon had seen the potential in Bowa a year earlier, setting him up as the manager in waiting just in case the team flopped under Boros. When it did, McKeon turned to Bowa.

"I was asked for my recommendation, and I suggested Larry," McKeon said. "I said, 'Larry was a highly competitive individual as a player, and I think he has shown it will carry over as a manager. I think he's got a chance to be an outstanding major league manager.' He was the only man I recommended for the job."

What happened to Boros in such a short span of time is another contributing element to the Bowa odyssey. It was pure timing and good luck that Bowa's amazing acceleration coincided precisely with the deterioration of the major league club. On July 13, 1986, when the Stars had yet to round into shape, the Padres were only three games out of first place, having ridden the crest of a 45-43 first half.

At an All-Star Game function that summer in Houston, Ballard Smith, taken with the team's seemingly positive position, had proclaimed these Padres superior to the 1984 team that came back from a 2-0 deficit to beat Bowa's Cubs in the last of the five-game league championship series.

It was to be the zenith. By early August, Boros had lost control of a club that took a severe nose dive into the cellar, 10 games out of first place.

And Smith fled San Diego to Cashman Field to view Bowa's young prospects—catcher Benito Santiago, pitcher Jimmy Jones and shortstop Gary Green, all youngsters who would play for Bowa in the major leagues. It is highly implausible to find a major league club president in a minor league clubhouse talking baseball philosophy with a novice manager.

"I'd never heard of anything like that before," Bowa said.

It was at that point Smith made a decision not to bring any of the young Stars up to the major leagues unless it was absolutely necessary. They might win the title. The Padres were beyond redemption and as punishment would be left to flounder for the remainder of what had been nothing short of an ugly season.

The Padres' troubles had really begun in November 1985 after the defending National League champions had concluded a disappointing run at a second consecutive pennant. In September of that season, with only one year remaining on his contract, Williams began telling cronies that he would not return to the club in 1986 as a lame-duck manager. And so he sought a contract extension, but none was forthcoming.

Williams thought McKeon was plotting against him. But in essence, Williams's paranoia and angry binges would take a quantum leap as the pressure of the seemingly endless baseball season increased. Williams, who won pennants in Boston and San Diego and a World Series with Oakland, is one of baseball's most gifted managers of all time. He could tactically manage the socks off his contemporaries, and often did, besting the likes of the Dodgers' Tommy Lasorda and Joe Torre, who was then with the Atlanta Braves. But as he ultimately did in all five of his managerial jobs, he alienated almost everyone in the Padres organization.

It was too bad. Williams was probably the best baseball man the Padres ever had as a manager. The numbers speak for themselves. The Padres won 337 games, a division title and a pennant under Williams. They were a .500 team or better for his four years as manager, something they had only accomplished once in the 13 seasons prior to Williams's arrival in 1982. To put that into perspective, the Padres haven't had a winning season under their current manager, Bruce Bochy, since the New York Yankees swept them out of the 1998 World Series.

Williams's demise is what really began the Padres' fall from grace and Bowa's rapid ascent.

By February 1986, it became increasingly plain to Williams that he had isolated himself within the organization and that he was not prepared to return to the club for spring training to honor the final year of his contract. Days before the opening of camp, Kroc called Williams and asked him if he was sure he was ready to return. She gave him his out. Williams said he didn't have the heart to try it again that year.

Recognizing that a crisis was on her hands, Kroc had to make an around-the-world telephone call to Smith, who just happened to be in Australia for the opening of a new McDonald's restaurant. Her message to Smith, then a member of the McDonald's board of directors, was succinct: "Williams does not want to return as manager. Come home."

On February 24, with the team gathered in its Yuma, Arizona, clubhouse, Joan and Dick faced the media in the same Stadium Club where Bowa would eventually take over the team. They each made brief statements. Answered no questions. Kissed. And left the room. The Padres announced that Williams had resigned and would be paid for the full term of his contract.

That left the Padres scrambling for a manager. McKeon was asked to draw up a list of names, but he had already hired Boros as the minor league coordinator in anticipation that Williams might opt to step aside. Boros, who was at the camp in uniform, was whisked to San Diego, where after one session with the hierarchy, he was promoted to manage the club for the season on the stipulation that he could return to his former position if the club was not satisfied with his ability to manage. That, of course, didn't happen. He was finished with the Padres after that season.

It wouldn't be an easy one for Boros, a scholarly man whose soft approach was a neat contrast to the grumpy Williams in the early going. But he could never earn the respect of many of the same players who blasted Williams.

His most significant handicaps seemed to come off the field. The day after Boros was hired, pitcher LaMarr Hoyt was whisked away for drug rehabilitation. It was learned that he had been arrested for trying to smuggle over-the-counter drugs across the U.S.-Mexico border and had also been cited in San Diego during a routine traffic stop for carrying a small amount of marijuana and a switchblade. Hoyt, a Cy Young Award winner with the Chicago White Sox in 1983 and a 16-game winner and All-Star with the Padres in 1985, would never be a factor.

The Padres then decided to ban beer and liquor from the home clubhouse in San Diego. This incited a mini-revolution led by relief pitcher Goose Gossage, who would eventually be suspended for his nationwide diatribes against Kroc and Smith.

Gossage began the salvo by calling Kroc a hypocrite for banning beer when she "poisons the world with her cheeseburgers."

After one particular clubhouse meeting about player gripes, Smith was so surprised when he was confronted by a group of anxious reporters that he called them a bunch of "flies."

Bowa's problems with Pam Postema seemed infinitesimal in comparison. Despite a series of injuries to Padres pitchers and all of the off-field distractions, both McKeon and Smith had seen enough of Boros. McKeon, a longtime friend who had hired Boros when he managed the Kansas City Royals, was despondent. He and Boros had never built the communication he anticipated.

Smith lamented the fact that Boros could not handle disciplinary matters. Smith said he had implored Boros to handle player problems and had assured him that management would back his decisions. But Boros was neither able nor willing to make those decisions. Smith blamed the Gossage suspension on Boros because he felt the manager should have handled it at the club level. Instead, it turned into another public fight with the Major League Baseball Players Association, who in 1985, had contested the way the Padres handled the late second baseman Alan Wiggins when he was treated for the second time for cocaine abuse. The Padres tried to banish Wiggins, but instead sent him to the minor leagues before trading him to Baltimore. Now the union was threatening to take the Padres to arbitration because of their suspension of Gossage. Gossage and the Padres settled their dispute, but later on, the association would claim that the Padres acted, as a franchise, above baseball rules in the handling of both Hoyt and Wiggins in regard to their serious drug problems. Tragically, Wiggins would be dead at 32, the victim of AIDS due to drug needle use.

Undoubtedly, all of these elements had to coincide for Bowa suddenly to earn his first shot as a big-league manager. He was aggressive and feisty, the spitting image of a younger Williams when he was a utility player for five major league teams, including the Brooklyn Dodgers. And Smith wanted him to reinstill a sense of discipline and order. In eight months, the Padres had gone from the hard-nosed Williams to the scholarly Boros—an early devotee of writer W.P. Kinsella (*Shoeless Joe, The Iowa Baseball Confederacy*)—to the defiant and hard-nosed Bowa, who was already shooting from the hip.

"I told them, 'Don't expect me not to get thrown out of games,'" he said. "'Don't expect me to be a choirboy.' I'd never done that. I was very competitive. I wasn't saying I was going to get kicked out of 50 ballgames, but I wanted us to take the field with a little cockiness and let the other clubs know, hey, we had a good ball club."

By nightfall, though, Bowa began to find out what it is like to be associated with the Padres. That evening, Hoyt was arrested again—this time trying to smuggle 400 Quaalude and Valium pills across the border. Hoyt was then severed from the ball club, which stuck hard by its edict that second-time drug offenders would not be tolerated.

McKeon had already begun to gut the team of its veteran players. He traded catcher Terry Kennedy to Baltimore for pitcher Storm Davis. The trading of Kennedy opened the position to young Benito Santiago, who was valued highly by the organization but had played only a handful of major league games. Davis, who might have been a cog in another trade, became a valuable commodity because of the problems facing Hoyt.

Veterans Graig Nettles, Jerry Royster and Dave LaPoint were not extended new contracts, further lowering the experience level of Bowa's team.

And then in December, the Padres traded their one pure power hitter, Kevin McReynolds, to the Mets for a group of youngsters including Kevin Mitchell, Stanley Jefferson and Shawn Abner. Mitchell, a rookie in 1986, was expected to replace the aging Nettles at third base, and it was hoped that Jefferson would replace McReynolds in center field.

With that, the transition was all but complete. Only four starters remained from the 1984 pennant-winning club—right fielder Tony Gwynn, who was the Padres' only reliable talent; shortstop Garry Templeton, who was hampered by a sore knee; left fielder Carmelo Martinez, who was coming off a disappointing season; and first baseman Steve Garvey. There was plenty of suggestion within the organization that Garvey, at 38, had outlived his usefulness. Because of shoulder problems, Garvey, in fact, played in only 27 games that year under Bowa. His career was over.

The pitching staff was in shambles. Mainstays Eric Show and Dave Dravecky had missed the final five weeks of the 1986 season because of elbow tendinitis. Show would die far too young from a drug overdose. Dravecky would lose his once potent left arm to bone cancer. Gossage, who appeared only twice in game action during the final five weeks of the 1986 season because of his problems with management, was also a real question mark. His age was also becoming a factor. His best days, in fact, were well behind him.

Plus, Kroc, tired of dealing with the incessant public criticism and the ever-expanding drug issue in baseball, had decided to place the Padres up for sale.

This was the club that the brash Lawrence Robert Bowa had agreed to guide with so much panache for a mere $100,000 salary in his first season as a big-league manager.

"Larry would have accepted a half-year contract. That's how much confidence he has in himself," McKeon said.

In retrospect, Bowa concedes now that he was uneducated about the machinations of the baseball world and that he really wasn't ready to deal with the politics of managing.

"I go to meetings now and realize that there are so many dynamics," Bowa said. "You don't know how important it might be to keep a kid in the minor leagues for a while. You talk about how many options he has. When you're talking trades, how much money does the guy make? When you first start, you don't care about any of that stuff. You could care less. Now you realize it's very important.

"The one thing the Phillies have done with me when I first got hired [was] they laid down their game plan and said this is what we're going to do. Within range, this is what our payroll is going to be this year. And they have not lied or deceived in any way. They've followed it to a 'T.' When you know going in what it's all about, you can't complain."

But during his chaotic tenure in San Diego, the team would be tentatively sold and then taken off the market again by Kroc. Upper management would change, making it that much more unfriendly to Bowa.

The next 18 months would be a costly lesson. After the Padres fired Bowa on May 28, 1988, he wouldn't get another chance to manage in the big leagues for 13 years.

"I was really naïve back then," Bowa said. "I let a lot of those things roll off me now. I realize that it's not personal. It's just the way the business of baseball operates."

— 9 —

12-42 Horse...

T rue to form, Bowa was thrown out of his first home game as manager of the Padres. On Opening Night, April 13, 1987, in San Diego, Bowa treated hometown fans to one of his famous snaps when he argued long and hard with second base umpire Bob Engel after Engel allowed a San Francisco Giants double play. The umpire ruled that Tim Flannery had slid out of the baseline to drill shortstop Matt Williams, who bounced his pivot throw by first base.

Certainly, that the call negated a Padres run and turned what would have been a one-run game into a Giants blowout was a determining factor. But when Engel ignored Bowa, who was pointing at skid marks in the infielder dirt that seemed to indicate that Flannery had not slid out of the base line, the real fun began.

With veins a-popping, his neck jerking violently and his cap on the ground, Bowa stunned everyone by ranting and raving for more than two minutes after he had been ejected. Bowa had ardently noted that it certainly would be a feather in Engel's cap to run him out of his first home game since Bowa became a big-league manager.

"I deserved to be kicked out," Bowa said. "I was not saying I didn't deserve it. I needed it. I had some built-up frustrations in me."

His first spring training with the Padres, then held in the Colorado River town of Yuma, Arizona, had been trying. Joan Kroc had tentatively sold the team to George Argyros, who owned the

Seattle Mariners. The possible free agent signing of Tim Raines collapsed under the weight of the owners' attempt to drive down salaries by failing to offer big contracts to prime-time players. Bowa began battling with some of the youngsters, including Stanley Jefferson, a tough kid from New York City who had just come over in a trade with the Mets. That relationship would explode into near fisticuffs in a Pittsburgh clubhouse early in the season. To make matters worse, the Padres finished spring training with eight consecutive losses and opened the season with five more.

Bowa's mother, Mary, became so sick that she and his father, Paul, couldn't make the 90-mile trip from Sacramento to San Francisco when the Padres opened the season against the Giants, who at the time still played in windy Candlestick Park. After the Padres were swept in that opening three-game series, Bowa issued a comment that would be the hallmark for the first few months of the season.

"Good teams create things. Horseshit teams just wait to get beat. And that's just what we are now—horseshit. Oh and three, horseshit. The manager is horseshit. The coaches are horseshit. The players are horseshit. We're all horseshit. Everybody. We're horseshit because we're 0-3. And you can dissect that up any way you want."

After finally winning his first game the following weekend in Cincinnati, the club returned to San Diego for its home opener and set a major league record by opening the game with consecutive homers by Marvell Wynne, Tony Gwynn and John Kruk, whose bats all were whisked away to the Hall of Fame. Bowa put on a show in front of 48,686 at Jack Murphy Stadium with his demonstrative performance, airing out Engel. "It was a big ego thing, I guess, who ran me out first," Bowa said. "Now that was out of the way."

But the Padres lost, 13-6, leading Gwynn to note: "When you looked up at the scoreboard and you had six runs and 12 hits and you weren't even in the ballgame, well, danger signals were sounding off, and it didn't look good."

As a player, Bowa found that he could relieve some of his tension by wreaking havoc on material items. Light bulbs, toilet bowls, fixtures, bats and helmets. When Bowa was playing for the Cubs, Cubs president Dallas Green once billed Bowa for the commode he smashed apart in the home dugout at Wrigley Field after a particularly galling strikeout.

But, said Bowa, "I always made sure none of my teammates were around me when I went crazy. That way, nobody got hurt."

As a manager, Bowa became even more demonstrative, although he knows he can no longer succumb to his usual display of raw emotions on inanimate objects. Instead, he is reduced to biting his fingernails to the bone and building up anger over the course of several days like a pressure cooker.

In his first few months managing in 1986 at Las Vegas, Bowa learned the hard way that he had to begin to control his temper.

"He was so intense on every pitch," said Larry Koentopp, who was the Stars' general manager at the time and had more than his share of soul-searching talks with the novice manager. "Every time the umps made a call, he was out on the field. He was driving himself, and everyone else, crazy."

In the spring before the 1986 season—when Bowa was invited to Yuma to help coach the Padres' big-leaguers—the star players opened a cash pool to pick the game of Bowa's first ejection as Las Vegas manager. He was tossed in the Stars' 21st game by Pam Postema, the first woman to umpire at the Triple A level. Postema was involved in a running feud with Bowa and was responsible for three of his first four ejections, all coming in one week.

Postema's report about the debacle to the Pacific Coast League office was legendary. In the report, she claimed that she did not so much mind being referred to as a particular part of the female anatomy, but she was aghast when Bowa questioned her femininity. The feud led to Bowa's first suspension.

"Jack McKeon called me and told me to lighten up a little," Bowa recalled. "And for the rest of the Stars' season I was good. I didn't get tossed until the league playoffs."

Early in the 1987 season, things on the field didn't improve one bit. By April 25, the Padres were 4-15 and already nine and a half games out of first place in the National League West after losing two in a row to the Dodgers in Los Angeles. Bowa closed the clubhouse and just went nuts. He tossed over the buffet table in the middle of the room, sending autographed baseballs bouncing and milk cartons flying spilling milk into lockers. His tirade was expletive-filled, but in retrospect he tidies it up:

"I told them they didn't know how to win. They were going through the motions," Bowa recalled. "I said if we didn't play harder, with more intensity, we'd get everybody out of there. I told them that if anybody wanted to get out, they should come in and see me. We'd get them out of there today. I thought I was going to have a stroke. I swear I did. My heart was pounding. I think it was the maddest I had ever been. I started out good, though. I started out by saying that I wanted to apologize to the seven or eight guys who were busting their butts out there for me. But the other 16 or 17, this was for them."

After the meeting, Gwynn went into the manager's office and said to Bowa: "I hope I'm one of the seven or eight busting my butt, Larry."

Bowa told Gwynn, ultimately an eight-time batting champion and a future Hall of Famer: "You're one through eight, Tony."

By the beginning of May it had become obvious that Steve Garvey's career as a player was effectively over. He was trying to play through a damaged tendon in his left shoulder, and no longer had any power in his compact stroke. Garvey was a .294 lifetime hitter, but for Bowa during the first weeks of the 1987 season, he was struggling along at .211 with a homer and nine runs batted in. Playing in a National League-record 1,207 consecutive games from 1971 to 1983 had obviously taken its toll.

The team arrived at Chicago's Wrigley Field for a three-game series against the Cubs. And by the end of the Cubs' sweep, Bowa had told Garvey he was taking him out of the lineup in lieu of a platoon of the left-handed-hitting John Kruk and the righty-swinging Carmelo Martinez. Garvey would thereafter be used as a pinch hitter and spot starter.

How the world turns. It was Garvey's Dodgers who bedeviled Bowa's Phillies by bouncing them out of the 1977 and 1978 playoffs. It was Garvey, then a Padre, who hit the big home run to win Game 4 of the 1984 National League Championship Series that Bowa's Cubs lost in five games. Now it was manager Bowa doing the benching of the aging and injured Garvey.

"He took it super. I've got to tell you, the man had a lot of class," Bowa said. "We talked a little about it, but he said he understood what I had to do. You know, we were going with young guys. Garvey took the news with his usual grace. You've got to remember, this was a man who was not only used to playing every day, but he was used to playing just about every inning of every game. He was the iron man."

As usual, Garvey said all of the right things. Garvey was the Padres' big free agent signing before the 1983 season, and with his acquisition, the franchise rose to the next level. He broke Billy Williams's National League consecutive-game playing streak as a Padre early that season, ironically at Dodger Stadium. And not long after that, the streak ended when he came sliding home trying to score a run and dislocated his thumb. The five-year contract he had signed was about to expire at the end of the 1987 season. At 38 years old, a forced career change was in the offing.

"It was something that was a realistic possibility," Garvey said then about his benching. "Anything I can do on or off the field to get us back on track, I'll be glad to do it. I had two goals when I came here: to help the team win and build a winning tradition. The team did win and the winning tradition has been a little sidetracked, but I think I've fulfilled my obligation. And so, chapter two unfolds in this year's book."

The Padres had certainly not reached their low-water mark. Neither, in fact, had Steve Garvey. When the club returned home,

Garvey decided to undergo a battery of tests with the team physicians to find a cause for his shoulder problems. He would learn that a biceps tendon had severed in his left shoulder and needed to be surgically repaired if he wanted to continue his baseball career. On May 23, in San Diego, Garvey took his last major league at-bat—a ninth-inning pinch-hit appearance against Montreal's Neal Heaton. He flew out lazily to center field. A day later, Garvey began to prepare for surgery. He was through not only for the year, but for good. There was not enough power left in the shoulder for him to make a comeback in 1988.

By the time of Garvey's departure, Bowa's problems had reached a boiling point. On May 13 they exploded in the visitor's clubhouse at old Three Rivers Stadium in Pittsburgh. The catalyst was a blown 5-2 lead in the sixth inning and a 9-5 loss to the Pirates. The focal point was Stanley Jefferson, Bowa's favorite antagonist of the early season.

Back in spring training, after the last exhibition game—a loss to the Cubs in Denver's old Mile High Stadium—Bowa finally let loose on Jefferson, whose pain tolerance had been questioned by Bowa all spring.

First, Jefferson had arrived with a badly sprained wrist he sustained during his cross-country trip from the East Coast. Jefferson said he had parked his car at a scenic viewpoint, slipped on the snow, and jammed the wrist while breaking his fall. Jefferson wore a fiberglass cast on that one for a while, although the team reported that X-rays and bone scans had proven negative.

As spring training ended, Jefferson confided that he thought he was playing with a hairline fracture of the wrist but was scared to sit out of the lineup because Bowa might think he was faking it. During the middle of spring training, Jefferson was hit on the head by a pickoff throw as he slid back into second base. The throw split Jefferson's helmet and sent him back to the hospital for more X-rays.

There were various other nagging leg and shoulder injuries, but the coup de gras was Jefferson's ankle injury. With a week left,

Jefferson led off a game at Palm Springs by driving a shot to left field that appeared to be a double. As he rounded first base, his left foot hit the bag wrong, and Jefferson collapsed several feet up the line as if he had been felled by a sniper.

"I never saw anything like that before," Bowa said. "I thought he had broken his leg in six places."

Jefferson, who could be found later stretched out on a training table with ice wrapped around his foot, had merely twisted the ankle. But Jefferson was advised not to play until team doctors gave him clearance. The club, which played an exhibition game in San Diego, then traveled to Denver for the two games, where, evidently, Bowa expected Jefferson to play.

It was cold enough that Jefferson was excused from his fifth straight game. But several hours before the last spring training contest, Bowa asked Jefferson if he could play. The rookie gave an affirmative nod. Everything was fine until Jefferson took a few flies in the outfield and realized that his foot would not loosen up. He then went to trainer Dick Dent and told him that he couldn't go. "Go tell the manager," Dent evidently told Jefferson. Jefferson, still in the process of learning clubhouse protocol, did just that. And predictably, Bowa erupted.

"That was my big mistake," Jefferson said. "I was told by a couple of players I should never go to the manager and tell him I can't play. I'll never make that mistake again."

But for this day, the damage had already been done. Jefferson was yanked out of the exhibition game lineup, and reporters covering the team were also informed that he would not start on Opening Day the next day in San Francisco. "If I was a kid, I'd want to be in the opening day lineup if it was my first year in the big leagues," Bowa said. "I talked to Jack McKeon about it. Jefferson was just a body then. [I thought] if he was hurt, maybe he was better off going to Triple A."

But Jefferson remained with the team. The next morning, Jefferson went to Bowa's hotel room to talk over the situation with the manager. He had been told by a number of people that he had to open up lines of communication with Bowa. Jefferson, a quiet man who did not like to talk about his problems, had become a whipping boy for Bowa's verbal attacks.

The result of the talk might have been encouraging for the short term. "I had a long talk with him," Bowa said. "He knew that everything was OK. Too many guys were telling him what to do. When too many guys pull your chain, you don't know what to do."

Jefferson agreed to go back in the lineup for the second game of the season despite the painful ankle. That decision might have made Bowa happy for the moment, but it would turn out to be his first major mistake. Jefferson wasn't ready physically to play.

"It was a combination of me not knowing him and him not knowing me," Bowa said about the early phases of his strained relationship with Jefferson. "I take the blame for that. He was the kind of guy that if you watched him on the baseball field, just watched his mannerisms, you'd say he was not giving everything he had. But that was just his mannerisms, and it took me a while to find that out. Another thing that I found out was you've got to understand that everybody's tolerance for pain is different. Just because I could play on something didn't mean another guy could. I'd be the first to admit I made a lot of mistakes handling different personalities. But I tried like hell with Jefferson and couldn't figure him out."

Jefferson reinjured the ankle during the first week of the season and went on the disabled list for nearly a month. He came off the disabled list on May 7 and would be disabled again on May 31 because of a sore shoulder. But Jefferson's sin in Pittsburgh was not showing up for early practice.

Bowa thought Jefferson had been told to attend by Deacon Jones, one of his coaches. Jefferson said he wasn't told. Jones, though, claimed he had notified the rookie outfielder. "In my mind, I told him," said Jones.

Countered Jefferson: "It was a miscommunication between me and a coach. That's all it was."

Larry Bowa, vintage 1972, his third big-league season. "You couldn't help to be impressed by his passion for the game and the incredible way he had to maximize his skills," said Dave Montgomery, the team's president now and in Phillies season ticket sales back then. "I'll never see another shortstop that had Bowa's throwing accuracy. It was amazing." ©*The Phillies*

A natural right-hander, Bowa had to learn how to switch hit as a young professional player. Here is No. 10 taking a cut from the left side of the plate. "I mean, you ever do something with one hand for 20 years and now they say do it with the other hand?" Bowa recalled. "It was the worst feeling I ever had in my life." ©*The Phillies*

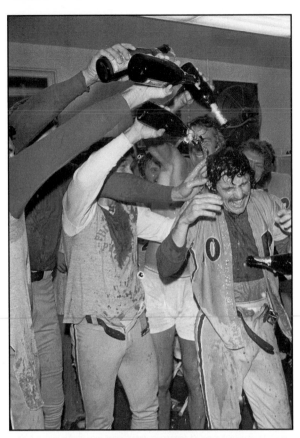

Teammates douse Bowa with champagne in the locker room in Chicago after the Phillies beat the Chicago Cubs 15-9 and clinched the National League East division, on September 28, 1977. The 1970s were a golden era of Phillies baseball. The club opened a new ballpark, Veterans Stadium, and built itself into a competitive franchise. *AP/WWP*

Philadelphia Phillies Bowa, left, and World Series Most Valuable Player Mike Schmidt wave to the crowd as the team victory parade moves through confetti from City Hall down Broad Street before more than half a million cheering fans on October 23, 1980, in Philadelphia. Bowa and Schmidt anchored the left side of the infield and were key components in the Phillies' first World Series championship. *AP/WWP*

Bowa took over as manager for the Padres after the 1986 season on general manager Jack McKeon's recommendation. "I said, 'Larry was a highly competitive individual as a player, and I think he has shown it will carry over as a manager. I think he's got a chance to be an outstanding major league manager,'" McKeon recalled telling upper management. "He was the only man I recommended for the job." *AP/WWP*

Bowa inherited a difficult situation over the course of the 1987 season with a roster full of inexperienced, unfocused players. As the season progressed, injuries and off-field antics would continue to make Bowa's tenure more trying as he adjusted to leading the team. "I was at the point where I would listen to anybody," Bowa said. "We'd try every avenue. We'd given most guys a chance to play. God knows every pitcher had had an opportunity. Even though some of those guys had been hurt, the guys around them had been hurting us more. The middle of the lineup was basically kids... Like I said, you tried to be optimistic, but before you even took the field, you looked at the lineup card of the team you were playing against, you went position by position, and just talent-wise, raw talent, we were outmatched." *AP/WWP*

Early in Bowa's second season, he would be replaced by the man who recommended him, Jack McKeon. McKeon said: "I figured, 'Well the club's going bad. [Feeney's] firing Bowa. I'll be the next one to go. What have I got to lose?'" McKeon made his reputation as a manager taking young teams and turning them around. Under McKeon, the Padres played with more polish. *Otto Greule Jr./Getty Images*

After disappointment at the helm of the Padres, Bowa returned home to Philadelphia to coach third base. As a coach, Bowa was able to distance himself from the highs and lows clubs go through: "As a coach you want to win. When you don't win, it's disappointing, but it's a different feeling as opposed to when you're a manager. When you're a manager and you lose, it goes right down from your head to your toes. It rips your insides out." *AP/WWP*

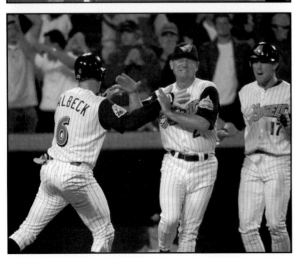

Bowa was the third base coach for the Angels under manager Terry Collins from 1997 to 1999. Here he's celebrating a victory in Anaheim with Darin Erstad (right) and Matt Walbeck (left). "Larry worked endlessly with Erstad after we converted him from an outfielder to a first baseman," Collins said. *AP/WWP*

Bowa's return to the Phillies as manager after the 2000 season. That's Phillies general manager Ed Wade on the right helping Bowa hold up his jersey. "He's a Philly guy, the most popular Phillie probably in our history," Wade said. "He's the guy who the fans look at as the real symbol of what Phillies baseball was and should be." ©*The Phillies*

Because of his passion for the game and for winning, Bowa has always been willing to debate calls and face off with umpires throughout his career. Over the course of his career on the diamond, Bowa has been able to temper his outbursts and channel his anger to driving his team to victory. ©*The Phillies*

Bowa's daughter, Tori (left) and wife, Sheena (right), the day he was hired to manage the Phillies. Bowa said Sheena has always given him good advice during the course of his baseball career. Like the day in 1988 he was fired by the Padres. "Sheena told me if they wanted to fire me, I should just let it happen," Bowa said. "That I didn't need the aggravation. She was right. She's always right." ©*The Phillies*

Scott Rolen, center, and Bowa argue with umpire Mark Carlson over Carlson calling Rolen out at home plate. Rolen and Bowa had a rocky relationship, but Rolen was Bowa's kind of player. "He didn't need to be motivated. The uniform motivated him. He plays the game hard whether it's a spring training game or an American Legion game. He goes all out." *AP/WWP*

Bowa at the press conference after he was named the National League's Manager of the Year for 2001, his first season as Phillies' manager. The 86-76 season and second-place finish vindicated general manager Eddie Wade, whose decision it was a year earlier to bring back Bowa. "He's the right guy for us," Wade said. "We're making the moves...to put the team together that best handles Larry's personality or exemplifies what he's all about." *©The Phillies*

Bowa signs autographs for fans before a game at the Vet, a regular occurrence. "Larry put us back in touch with fans that had checked out on following the Phillies," Dave Montgomery said. "Just his hiring, just because of the image of the overachieving guy with a tremendous work ethic, who eats and sleeps baseball, a person who was part of the Phillies' high moments, Larry was able to bring us back." *©The Phillies*

Bowa on the mound contemplating a pitching change. That's catcher Mike Lieberthal with his back to home plate. Lieberthal said Bowa was very upbeat when spring training opened in 2003. "I don't know if it's fair to say he's in better spirits, but he's more at ease because of the veteran players he has," Lieberthal said after the team's first meeting. "He showed how excited he was." ©*The Phillies*

Here Bowa congratulates pitcher Randy Wolf after Wolf threw a five-hitter and a win in 2003. In his first season as manager, Bowa gave Wolf a choice of going back to the bullpen to develop his game or being reassigned to the minor leagues. Wolf chose the bullpen and was back in the pitching rotation after the All-Star break. *AP/WWP*

This time he was able to celebrate a win with Phillies left fielder Pat Burrell, who struggled in 2003 after a mammoth 2002 season. "He's not on the outs with me," said Bowa, who tried a number of methods to coax Burrell out of his season-long 2003 slump. "If he was on the outs with me and I didn't like him, I wouldn't have played him. I believe in this kid." *AP/WWP*

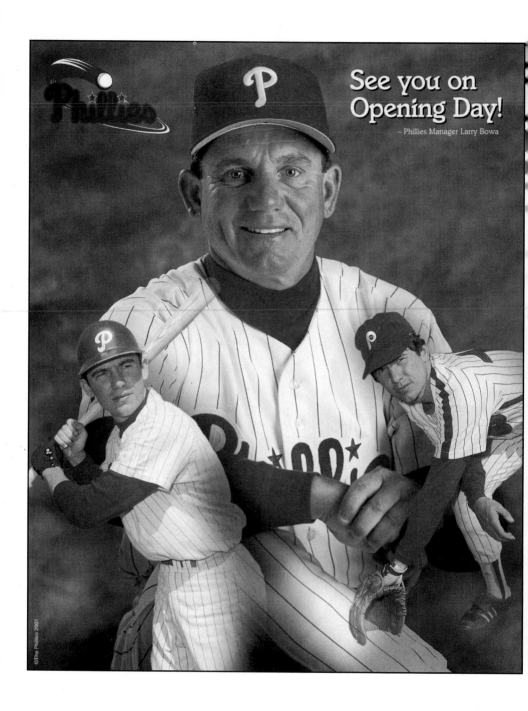

The Phillies promote Bowa in a poster. ©*The Phillies*

That miscommunication turned into a fracas. The game was replete with missed popups, a blown suicide squeeze by Joey Cora—another rookie for whom Bowa had little tolerance—and a balk by loser Craig Lefferts that brought home the go-ahead run. Jefferson seemed to have no direct effect on the outcome.

During a 20-minute postgame tongue-lashing of the team, Bowa fined Jefferson $100 for not coming out early. Bowa was working up a good froth when reporters were stopped outside the clubhouse door only minutes after the game. He went over the litany of errors before turning his attention on Jefferson. "Is that a smile I see on your face?" Bowa shouted, addressing Jefferson.

Jefferson said he was not smiling.

"You're smiling," Bowa continued. "What do you think this is, a joke? I told you and Cora to be out here early."

"Nobody told me to be out here early," Jefferson said, his voice now rising.

"You were told to be out here," Bowa countered.

"I wasn't."

"You were."

"Nobody told me to be out here," Jefferson screamed in a loud shrill. "I'll pay the damned fine. I bust my butt out here for you."

With that, there was a momentary pause and a crush of bodies. From within the depths of the locker room, somebody yelled, "Break it up!" A split second later, Jefferson was being pushed from the clubhouse by his teammates. Bowa, quickly cooling down after another major blowup, shut himself behind the door of his office.

Jefferson, 17 years younger than Bowa, was literally carried out of the locker room by five players—Marvell Wynne, Tony Gwynn, Carmelo Martinez, Joey Cora and Kevin Mitchell. Jefferson was twisting, ranting and raving while being ushered down a dark hallway to the dugout. Jones, Garry Templeton and Rich Gossage followed suit.

"Stanley was grabbing Bowa by the throat," Gwynn recalled long after with a chuckle. "I thought he was going to kill him."

Trying to avoid a mutiny, the next day Bowa called another meeting and apologized to Jefferson and the team. He rescinded the $100 fine and told them to just go out and play.

Bowa was calm, but the incident had a ripple affect.

"I said, hey, that was my fault. You shouldn't have been fined," Bowa said. "We said every day we had the field early, we wanted Jefferson and Joey Cora out there to work on little things—bunts, Stanley stretching his arm out, practicing leads. They didn't even have to hit. But Jefferson didn't know. Because he was temperamental, Jefferson took it wrong. That is the difference between guys who played 20 years ago and now. Now, if you even think about criticizing anybody, they go into a shell for a week.

"You're not supposed to do that. And then, if you let it go without saying anything, it's as if you don't care. So it's a catch-22. You don't say anything to anybody. Don't bring up their mistakes. Just let them play. Then he thinks, 'If he doesn't say anything to me, he doesn't care.' But if you bring up something, he'll think, 'Oh, he's too critical. I can't play like that.'"

Still, the Padres went out and lost again to the Pirates—their 15th loss in 17 games. By week's end in Philadelphia, the Padres would be 8-30 and 15 games out. The clubhouse had turned into a cesspool with no help coming from the veterans of earlier seasons and the rookies feeling browbeaten and totally lost. Bowa was looking for any thread to hang on.

"The same guys who blamed it on [previous Padres managers] Dick Williams and Steve Boros were blaming their problems on me," Bowa said. "I was to the point now where I'd listen to anybody. We'd tried every avenue. We'd given most guys a chance to play. God knows every pitcher had had an opportunity. We'd used all of them. Even though some of those guys had been hurt, the guys around them had been hurting us more. The middle of the lineup was basically kids. It was an inexperienced lineup. That's basically what it was. Like I said, you tried to be optimistic, but before you even took the field, you looked at the lineup card of the team you were playing against, you went position by position, and just talent-wise, raw talent, we were outmatched. When we made these mistakes, we would get buried."

Then on May 29, the Padres' front office personnel shifted again, really leaving Bowa to float on thin air. Kroc's deal to sell the team to Argyros had been annulled. Ballard Smith, the team president who had studied Bowa late in the 1986 season at Las Vegas, was out. Resigned. McKeon, still the general manager, was virtually pushed aside. Chub Feeney, the former National League president who had his own history with Bowa, the player, replaced Smith.

Feeney was well aware of the Bowa psyche. As league president, he read the reports about Bowa's well-documented snaps during his playing days. "He suspended me once for pushing umpire Jim Quick. And I deserved it. I didn't push him. I bumped him. The fines... Oh hell, he did that so many times I couldn't count. He was president of the league for practically my entire career. I know he got more than $5,000, easy. When I first started getting kicked out, it was $100. Then it started going up—$300, $500, $700. In 16 years I'd have to say I was kicked out 40 or 50 times. I'm serious."

Actually, Bowa wasn't ejected nearly that many times as a player, even if he was in his own mind's eye. From 1974 to 1981 with the Phillies, Bowa was only ejected from seven games. No records were available charting the first four years of Bowa's career, but by his own admission, "I was a lot more toned down during my first five years."

During his four years in Chicago from 1982 to 1985, Bowa was ejected five times. In his brief one-month stay with the Mets before his retirement at the end of the 1985 season, Bowa was thumbed just once—in his third game after being signed by the Mets.

The tantrums and explosions wouldn't sit well with the stately Feeney. The former general manager of the New York Giants took over in 1947 and presided over their move to San Francisco a decade later. He was equally aghast at the antics of Leo Durocher, the crazy onetime infielder and manager of the Cubs, Dodgers and Giants, who allegedly as a player slugged an over-the-hill Babe Ruth and pushed him into his locker.

Feeney was hoping for a more reserved approach from his manager than a Durocher ... or a Bowa, for that matter.

As far as Argyros was concerned, he didn't have enough votes from fellow owners in the National League to secure the franchise. And as the months dragged on it became apparent to Kroc that Argyros would slim down the front office staff and might even try to move the team, whose stadium lease was set to expire at the end of the season.

When Joan called the office staff together to tell them about her decision, there was an outpouring of positive emotion that surprised even her. She received a similar response from the usually stoic ballplayers, whom she visited in the clubhouse prior to a night game in San Diego against the Mets. During the press conference, she made mention of a recent disclosure that right fielder Tony Gwynn, a .380 hitter and the rock of the team, had filed for bankruptcy because of various problems involving his former agent. The agent apparently co-signed sizeable loans in Gwynn's name, took the money and left Gwynn to handle the bills.

When asked what had made her change her mind about keeping the team, Kroc said, "The agony of defeat. I don't like what's happening. Ray Kroc wouldn't like what's happening. I haven't had much fun the last year. I can tell you that. But I want to tell you that when we have young men like Tony Gwynn who have had adversity that none of us realized and has been out there pounding his butt day in and day out—I love him. And I think we've got the nucleus of a good team. I think we're heading in the right direction.

"You know, it takes more than one tuba player to make a symphony. It takes more than one ballplayer to win a pennant or have a winning attitude. I'm asking these young men to get together in spirit. Adversity can tear a community apart or it can bring it together. I love this community. There is no way in the world this team will ever be moved."

In the clubhouse, Joan gave the players a similarly motivational speech. "She told us that all our hard work was appreciated," Gwynn said. "She turned to Goose and said, 'Come on, Goose, let me see a smile.' Goose kind of looked around at us and then broke into a smile. We all smiled. Then she came over to me and asked for a hug. It really meant a lot to me. I mean, how many times does the owner come to the clubhouse and ask for a hug?"

On a baseball level, the sudden decision promised a fresh start for a team that had already been counter-punched into oblivion by all its incessant on- and off-field miseries. Perhaps the resolution of the ownership struggle would mark a turning point for the team.

"Maybe I'm wrong, but I don't see how who's buying the team should affect the way we're playing," Bowa said then. "I mean, when you put on the baseball uniform, you don't worry about how much money you're making, you don't worry about who your boss is, you don't worry about what you're doing after the game. Basically, you go out there and try to do whatever you can to beat the other team. If you've got that other stuff on your mind, you're not really concentrating."

He has a different take on that now.

"The worst thing you want to see as a manager, player or coach is when you're in an organization and in the middle of the year or the end of the year the team's up for sale," Bowa said. "Because you know what? It destabilizes everything. It doesn't matter how good you are, they're going to bring in their own people. That's a hard thing to settle in your mind because you take it personal. But it's really not personal. If I'm the new owner I'd want to bring in people I'm comfortable with. That's just the way it is."

But the club didn't stabilize immediately after Kroc's decision to keep the team. On June 4 in Montreal, Bowa called another team meeting, this time before the game. There was no ranting and raving. He benched a few players and just presented the cold, hard facts.

"I jotted down some notes," Bowa said. "I felt like a high school coach going in there or something. But we had reached the end of the line. The night before we lost another one-run ballgame [4-3 to the Expos]. What was our record—12-41? What a disgrace. I was beginning to feel like nobody was listening to me anymore. That nobody even cared."

As if this particular day hadn't been long enough already, Bowa had one more incident to deal with. This incident didn't involve mental errors on a baseball field. It involved Kevin Mitchell and the United States Customs Service.

After Bowa's most solemn team meeting of the season, the Padres dropped an 8-5 decision to the Expos. Facing the specter of a game the next night in Atlanta, the team bus made its quick escape to Dorval Airport where the usual charter flight would whisk the club overnight back to the United States. Unlike most American cities, Dorval had a strict midnight curfew on all departures, making it a tight fit to get out that night anyway. The prospect of pushing 24 ballplayers through customs in their re-entry from Canada to the United States was no thriller either. Normally, these return voyages aren't a problem. But on this late night, Mitchell took care of that. With 20 minutes remaining before curfew, Mitchell was stopped at the gate by customs agents checking a plastic carrying bag containing $2,000 worth of newly purchased suits. In an attempt to skirt the duty tax, Mitchell told the agents he had purchased those suits on a trip to Canada a year earlier and had brought them back simply for alterations. Customs agents asked Mitchell to produce the receipt, and that's when the fun began. Mitchell started shouting at the agents, claiming that he was being harassed.

One agent told Mitchell: "You better watch it, or you'll stay here."

"Fine. All I need is a pillow."

"Where you're going, you won't need a pillow."

Bowa and Doc Mattei, the Padres' scruffy traveling secretary, were then summoned off the plane. Curfew was now just 15 minutes away. One option considered was flying the plane to Mirabel Airport, some 30 miles away, where there was no such curfew. Bowa and Mitchell would cab it there if the dispute could be mediated.

It was just what Bowa needed. "I was sitting on the airplane," Bowa recalled. "A guy came on the plane and yelled, 'Mr. Bowa? Mr. Bowa? Where's Mr. Bowa?' The guy said, 'You've got to come with me.' We had about 15 minutes to a midnight curfew. If we didn't get out of there, we wouldn't be able to leave. So we went out there, and there was Mitchell standing there with all his bags open and all his clothes. He was holding a receipt. And the receipt was dated something like, June 3, 1987. He told the customs agent that he got the suits altered, and they gave him that receipt.

"The customs agent said, 'Well, we're not stupid.'

"So I asked, 'What are our alternatives?' One alternative was he would go to jail for resisting this. The other alternative was that he would pay the duty on it, something like 150 bucks. So I said, 'I don't think there's any alternative.'

"Mitch said, 'I'm not paying any money.' I thought he was kidding. We were down to about eight minutes, seven minutes."

At that point, Mattei took out his billfold and offered to pay the $150 duty so that the Padres wouldn't lose $20,000 for the chartered flight.

"Now the guy asked Mitch for his social security number," Bowa said. "Mitch said, 'I don't have it.' That made the agent even angrier. I mean, Mitch had already given him a lot of crap. He said, 'Then you're still going to jail.' That's when I said to myself that we were not getting out of there."

It should be noted that Mitchell was one tough character. He has various scars on his face and caps on his teeth from childhood altercations. Mitchell grew up in rough southeast San Diego where he was a gang member. Mitch knew the streets and had plenty of crazy stories to back up his exploits—some of which had long since proven to be unfounded.

Case in point: When Mitchell joined the New York Mets, he told publicity people that he had played football for and had graduated from Clairemont High School in San Diego. They dutifully noted such in the club's 1986 media guide. A bit of investigation proved that not only had Mitchell not played football for Clairemont, but he had never graduated. In fact, he was listed on the rolls of several San Diego high schools but had never graduated. Also during his one-year tenure in New York, Mitchell was fond of telling people that he had not played baseball until he was 18 years old. Mitchell, who was estranged from his mother and still lived with his grandmother in one of San Diego's toughest neighborhoods, could not pass that bit of malarky by his maternal grandmother, who claimed to have driven Mitch to Little League games. During the classic Game 6 between the Boston Red Sox and Mets in the 1986 World Series, New York manager Davey Johnson gazed down the bench in the climactic bottom of the 10th inning looking for Mitchell to pinch hit. The Mets were trailing in the game and were one out away from losing the series. Johnson found Mitch on the clubhouse phone already stripped to his underwear, trying to make a plane reservation back to San Diego. Mitchell pulled on his uniform quickly and hit a single. The Mets came back to win the game, 6-5, on the Mookie Wilson grounder that skidded through the legs of first baseman Bill Buckner.

In his short stay with the Padres, Mitchell had already been fined and chastised by Bowa for a number of missed curfews and practices. He reported to camp late with painful back problems, sustained, he said, when he was knocked off his bicycle by an automobile in a hit-and-run accident. He often took the three-hour drive back and forth to San Diego after practice and could be found the next day snoozing in front of his locker. When he remained in Yuma, he'd take his assault rifle out into the desert and shoot up some snakes and cacti just for recreational purposes.

Since the season began, he had hurt his leg running down a fly ball. At the time of the Dorval incident, he was nursing a toe broken when hit by a pitch during an exhibition game in Las Vegas. Mitchell had clearly been Bowa's most puzzling problem during a first two months rife with problems. Mitchell had immense talent, but Bowa viewed him as overweight and not mentally prepared to play the game. Bowa seemed to have no reading on the man who was supposed to have solved long-term Padres problems at third base.

"The only read I had on Mitch was that it didn't seem like his priorities were in order," Bowa said. "I think he had a rough childhood. You know, I'd sit down and talk to him. I thought he was a pretty good kid. The big mistake we made was you make a trade and then right away you say the guy is your third baseman. It shouldn't be that way. You should say he's going to have the opportunity to win a job. Not unless you get an established player. You can't give away jobs to players who aren't established."

The Padres did make it out of Dorval with Bowa and Mitchell on board the flight.

"I told him, 'Why don't you start cooperating with them a little bit and get it out of the way?' So he started cooperating a little bit," Bowa said. "He asked the guy, 'Why are you always picking on guys like me?' I don't think he used any swear words. At least, when I was there, he didn't. If he did, I think the guy would have thrown him in. They were upset. But the guy finally took the money, let him go, and we sprinted toward the airplane. When we got on the plane, Mitch gave Doc the $150 back. Before we left, the customs agent told Mitch, 'You'll be hearing from us.' So I couldn't imagine what was going to happen the next time we went up."

As it turned out, Mitchell's next trip to Canada would be his last with the Padres. This bit of trouble was over. Nobody knew it yet, but so were many of the problems that had plagued the Padres during the first months of that season. As they winged south from Canada, though, there was one thing that nobody could change: In Bowa's own parlance, the team was horseshit, 12-42 horse....

10

No Retreat, No Surrender

As George Harrison once so aptly wrote, "All Things Must Pass," and so too passed the initial grief of Bowa's only full season as manager of the Padres. With the team at 15-46 on June 11, 1987, the Padres suddenly ripped off six wins in a row and seven in eight games. It is the most reliable of axioms that plagues all teams during any given baseball season, says no less an authority than Tommy Lasorda, the Hall of Fame former manager of the Dodgers.

"The good teams will hit at least one long losing streak," Lasorda sagely said. "And even the worst of teams will find a way of having at least one long winning streak. For the good teams, ultimate success depends on how you weather it."

The Padres under Bowa weren't a good team. So ultimate success wasn't a concern. Survival was. A dearth of solid pitching mixed with an inexperienced core of raw talent among his everyday players was the cause of the season's early fluctuations. Before the team could begin to right itself, it had to be purged of the players who were the contributing factors. After Steve Garvey's demise, the next to go was Joey Cora, who was sent to the minor leagues to try to rid himself of the numerous mental errors that he was committing. Right behind him was Kevin Mitchell, who never seemed to be able to focus with his friends and family hounding him as he tried to play in his hometown.

Both players would go on to make significant contributions to other teams as they grew and matured—Mitchell to playoff runs in 1987 and 1989 with the San Francisco Giants, the latter season producing a National League Most Valuable Player trophy for him and a World Series trip for his team. Mitchell, overweight and plagued by personnel problems, retired at 36 and never again enjoyed the success he had with the Giants. The happy-go-lucky Mitchell went on to manage in the independent leagues. Cora, as a rangy second baseman, helped anchor infields in Seattle and in Chicago for the White Sox. Cora had to retire at the relatively young age of 33 because of a chronically bad knee. He returned to Chicago in late 2003 as a coach under new White Sox manager Ozzie Guillen, who was the shortstop next to Cora in Chicago for most of four seasons—1991 to 1994.

But at the time, neither player had the maturity to contribute to Bowa's Padres in 1987, and Bowa didn't have the patience to bring them along slowly. Even recently, Cora rolled his eyes when Bowa's name was mentioned.

"Wow, Bowa, what a piece of work," said Cora, whose younger brother, Alex, is a smooth-fielding, light-hitting second baseman for the Dodgers.

Cora was trying to make the jump two levels from Double A to the majors that season and obviously wasn't ready. Even he figured that a demotion to Triple A Las Vegas might be the best thing for all parties and anticipated the move for weeks.

"The disappointing thing was that if you asked all of the coaches, they would have told you we thought he was one of our most intelligent players," Bowa said. "Maybe it was the pressure of trying to make it in the big leagues. I don't know. All I know is that every double-play ball was an adventure. Every steal, every hit and run. [Catcher] Benito Santiago had a half-dozen throwing errors just because [Cora] had been late getting to the bag on his throws from behind the plate.

"One game in Philadelphia was the most incredible thing I had ever seen. He must have run into everybody. He looked like a linebacker."

The game in question—a 6-5 Padres win in Philadelphia on May 17, 1987, that broke a 10-game road losing streak—would have been a horror story for anyone. Cora collided with left fielder James Steels and shortstop Garry Templeton on one pop fly, bowled over first baseman John Kruk on another one, and sped by right fielder Tony Gwynn when he lost the ball in the sun for an error. Toss in a throwing error and a missed tag on a potential double play. What a day.

On June 8, Bowa made it official, optioning Cora to Vegas for the remainder of the minor league season. He didn't return to the big-league team until after the Pacific Coast League playoffs on September 7.

The Padres were in Houston, and Bowa called Cora into his office in the visiting clubhouse at the Astrodome.

"He sat down. And he hadn't looked at me yet," Bowa recalled. "I said, 'We're going to make a move, and I don't want you to think this is punishment or failure. Physically, you can make all of the plays. You have a nice hitting stroke. You put the ball in play. But you're pressing in the field, and it's hurting us. Do you have anything to ask me?'"

"Nope," Cora said.

"Do you think I'm being fair with you?" Bowa asked.

"Yep," Cora said.

"You've got to feel something. Are you upset? Are you hurt?" Bowa prodded.

Cora just wouldn't answer.

Bowa closed the conversation by saying: "You can do one of two things: You can go down to Vegas for two or three weeks and you can play your butt off and be back up here, or you can go down there and we might not ever hear from you again. It's up to you."

At the time, Bowa bemoaned having to make the decision less than two years after he was cleared out himself as a player with the Cubs to make way for Shawon Dunston. Now the proverbial shoe was on the other foot.

"I guess I felt for him because I saw a lot of me in him. I was very moody as a player. I had a lousy temperament," Bowa said.

Cora also played the entire 1988 season in Vegas and returned to the Padres in 1989, long after Bowa had been fired. His career with the Padres lasted 140 games before he was traded to the White Sox for two no-name pitchers just before the start of the 1991 regular season.

Today, Bowa feels that he might have been a little hard on Cora, who was only 22 at the time.

"I liked Joey. He never really gave me any problems," Bowa said. "I always thought he could play, which he did after he filled out a little bit. Maybe I should have handled it differently. I'm sure I would handle it differently now."

Mitchell's career with the Padres would last only 20 more games. The deal that brought him over from the Mets along with Jefferson and an outfielder named Shawn Abner for Kevin McReynolds was misbegotten from the start. As general manager, Jack McKeon loved engineering those off-season blockbusters that gave him his trademark nickname "Trader Jack." But this wasn't one of his better acquisitions. McKeon and his scouts gawked at Mitchell's strength and talent and hoped he would replace Graig Nettles at third base. He had batted .277 with 12 homers and 43 runs batted in as a part-time player for the World Series-champion Mets in 1986. That was the good news. The bad news was that Mitch liked to run with the Mets' bad boys—Darryl Strawberry and Dwight Gooden. Those two immensely talented players were on their way to the Hall of Fame until drugs and alcohol virtually extinguished their careers.

Mitch partied with them, and the rumors about their antics on road trips, particularly in Mitchell's San Diego, ran rampant. The last thing Joan Kroc needed after deciding to keep the team was another problem child, certainly not so soon after the careers of Alan Wiggins and Lamar Hoyt literally went up in smoke. On top of that, Mitchell was batting only .245 with seven homers and 26 RBIs in 62 games for the Padres.

Mitchell could never adjust to Bowa.

"Really, I could never understand his baseball," Mitchell said. "I think he scared a lot of people with all his screaming and yelling. When I grew up, I wasn't the kind of person who was too easily intimidated. Larry didn't intimidate me. But we really didn't talk. Just a few words back and forth. As far as I'm concerned, we really didn't get along."

It was no surprise then that on July 4, 1987, Chub Feeney, in his first real act as club president and de facto general manager, dispatched Mitchell to San Francisco along with pitchers Dave Dravecky and Craig Lefferts for Chris Brown, another third baseman, and three other pitchers, including Mark Davis, a future Cy Young Award winner.

The deal came down after another lackluster performance in Montreal only a month after Mitchell's fiasco with the customs service leaving Dorval Airport. It stunned Bowa, who was left completely out of the loop. At least, though, getting Mitchell out of Canada wouldn't be his problem. Mitchell would have to find his own way on to Chicago, where the Giants were playing the next day.

"It stunned me because I didn't know we were that close to making any deal," Bowa recalled. "There was Chub on the phone after a tough loss telling me that we just made a trade. He said, 'Do you want to tell the people involved that we'd like them to be in Chicago tomorrow and wish them luck?' I told him I'd take care of it. At the end of the conversation [Chub] asked me what I thought of it. I told him I liked Chris Brown, but I really hadn't thought about the rest of it."

Brown, and his hypochondriac ways, would turn out to be the bane of Bowa's existence in his last months with the team. But on this day, Bowa had to call in Mitchell, Lefferts and Dravecky and give them what amounted to joyous news: They were leaving a club mired in last place, 17 1/2 games out, to go to the third-place Giants, who would go on to win the National League pennant.

The nuts and bolts of the trade went like this: A few weeks earlier in San Diego the Giants had asked for Dravecky, a mainstay of the team since the early 1980s. The Padres wanted Brown. When Giants president Al Rosen finally put Brown's name on the table, Feeney started talking seriously about trading Dravecky. Once the Giants agreed to part with Brown, they realized that they would need another third baseman to fill in for the short term, so the Padres gladly gave them Mitchell. Feeney and Rosen ultimately worked out the deal.

"I'd heard that when Ballard Smith was president, Jack worked out most of the deals," Bowa said. "Now he had handed the ball over to Chub. Jack said he didn't care as long as everything was being done for the good of the team."

McKeon cared, all right. He was blowing smoke out of one of his famous cigars. He played it coyly at the time.

"Chub wanted to be involved in everything," McKeon said. "There was nothing wrong with that. I had no problem working with him. As long as he kept me in cigars and I kept him in cigars, we were fine."

Less than a year later, the relationship between Feeney, Bowa and McKeon would fracture, leaving Bowa as the odd man out in a typical game of inside baseball politics. Bowa was hardly equipped for that fight, and McKeon was and still is one of the game's best at maneuvering himself into a position of power.

The newly re-equipped Padres, with the .242-hitting Chris Brown at third base, flew off to Chicago themselves the next day after another loss to the Expos, their sixth in six tries that season in Olympic Stadium.

It was at Wrigley Field that the driving forces of Padres right-hander Eric Show and Cubs slugger Andre Dawson would meet in a head-on collision and Bowa would emerge as the peacekeeper in an explosive situation.

Even though the series in Chicago was between two teams that finished the season in last place, the Cubbies had no problems beating up on the Padres in 1987. They won five of the six games that season over the Padres at Wrigley, including the three that week by a combined score of 26-13. By the third inning of the game on July 7, Dawson had homered three times off Padres pitching in two days. The third came in the first inning off Show. A long-forgotten infielder named Paul Noce opened the fateful third inning with another long ball—the 20th Cubs homer off Padres pitching in half a season.

Then Eric Show's pitch exploded in Andre Dawson's face. The pitch, a high inside fastball, dropped Dawson face first to the ground.

Did Show snap and launch a high hard one at Dawson on purpose? The video replay seemed to back Show's contention that once again he was a sad victim of circumstance. Dawson's long arms and head were dangling across the middle of home plate. But Dawson thought otherwise. Ditto for his teammates.

Cubs pitcher Rick Sutcliffe charged the mound and plowed into Show with his long arms extended shoulder length. That emptied both benches and sent 26,615 Wrigley Field crazies into a frenzy. Several players slowed Sutcliffe's initial thrust as Dawson continued to lie prone at the plate, his face dripping blood.

As Dawson climbed slowly to his knees, he decided to charge the mound himself, doing a neat impersonation of the late Bears running back Walter Payton until he was gang-tackled by a combined group of Chicago and San Diego players short of a 60-foot, six-inch gain. Unknown to Dawson, Show was well behind the mound talking to pitching coach Galen Cisco when Dawson made his futile charge. It was Cisco who parried a second onslaught by Sutcliffe after Dawson was herded at the mound. Several Padres came to Show's defense. Newcomer Chris Brown was standing next to Tony Gwynn when umpire Charlie Williams motioned Show toward the Padres' dugout, which was on the first base side of the field at Wrigley. Before Show could get there, Dawson, running with the abandon of a wounded bull, made one last dash at the offending pitcher. Show scampered into the dugout, and Dawson, the front of his white pinstriped Cubs uniform streaked with red, was stopped from behind by Brown and Gwynn.

When the fracas was over, Dawson and Sutcliffe were ejected from the game. Dawson was taken to the hospital where he was given a CAT scan and 24 stitches in his cheek and upper lip.

"I think it was blown out of proportion, I really do," Bowa said. "I didn't blame Dawson for getting so mad. He got a gash in his face. But first of all, these people didn't know Eric. He wouldn't intentionally hurt anybody. Then Joe Torre went on some TV show and said Eric was a headhunter. Where did he come off saying something like that? He was basing it on some 1984 incident when he was managing the Atlanta Braves and his club, and the Padres were involved in an all-out beanball war. And from what I understand, Eric wasn't even in the game that day. The whole thing was ridiculous."

On August 12, 1984, all hell broke loose among the Padres and Braves, in Atlanta. Only 11 Padres on Bowa's team—nine players and two coaches—were there that day when Dick Williams turned the game into a circus. Williams let a host of Padre pitchers throw at Pascual Perez because Perez had the audacity to open the game by plunking Alan Wiggins in the back. By the time Craig Lefferts hit Perez during the eighth inning, the day was so hot and muggy that tempers were frayed to the boiling point. A pretty fair fight followed that encounter. And when Donnie Moore nailed Graig Nettles to open the ninth, it really became ugly. That was when the fans entered the fray.

Show was not ejected or warned. But in a move that boded well for even wiser moves to come, Bowa took Show out of the game. Only an inning later, Bowa told Show to leave the ballpark. Armed guards escorted him to the club's downtown hotel. Before Show left, he issued a statement. "I apologize to the Cubs, the fans of Chicago and especially Andre Dawson," said the note scribbled in Show's own handwriting. "It was unfortunate, and I'm sure I'll regret it for the rest of my life. I don't know any other words to express my feelings at this time."

Dawson wouldn't accept Show's apology until he received a personal letter some days later, and the fans howled for the remainder of the series. Show did not emerge again in public, switching hotel rooms in his own form of covert activity. He took no phone calls. He showed his face only when the team bus left for O'Hare Airport several days later, having spent the time deep in reflection. He even received a death threat through the mail that was investigated by the FBI.

Show was not around to witness the Cubs' retaliation that day during the top half of the fourth inning. He also missed Bowa's finest hour in his short tenure as Padres manager.

Everyone in the ballpark knew the Cubs would retaliate. It was just a matter of when. Bowa didn't say anything to his team before it came to bat in the fourth. He apparently had already made his decision. It didn't help tensions any that the first batter to face then Cubs hurler Greg Maddux was Chris Brown, who, in a San Francisco Giants uniform on May 4, had had his jaw splintered when St. Louis Cardinals pitcher Danny Cox lost control of a pitch. Brown walked cautiously to the plate. Maddux threw a curve. Brown bailed out with a meek swing.

"He had me," Brown said.

Brown struck out without incident. So did Tim Flannery, who was playing in place of the banished Cora on a badly twisted ankle that would hamper him all season. It lulled everyone into believing that the Cubs might not strike.

Forget it.

Maddux slammed Benito Santiago, the next batter, just above the left buttock. To his credit, the rookie catcher, bat dangling in hand, jawed briefly with Maddux, who immediately was tossed from the game. Catcher Jim Sundberg blocked Benny's path to the mound. Outfielder Carmelo Martinez lumbered out of the dugout and gestured angrily toward Maddux.

"Benny was so mad," said Bowa, "he couldn't even see straight. I don't even think he knew what the score was."

Both teams took one step out of the dugout. Round one had been fought after Dawson was decked. Round two figured to be a lot worse.

It was a moment of truth for Bowa, who calmly strode up to Santiago with his hands characteristically tucked in his back pockets. He calmed the catcher down. He walked him to first base. As he returned to the dugout, he raised both hands in the air, palms out, to gesture his players back inside.

The danger was over, at least for the moment.

"Hey, I could have let Benny go. He was pretty upset," said Bowa, who also remained calm when Scott Sanderson uncorked a wild one behind Brown in the eighth inning. "Brown was worked up. I don't think you're going to solve anything like that. Let's put it this way: If you're going to play this game, you can't be intimidated. But you can't be ridiculous either."

It was the absolute zenith of Bowa's time in his No. 10 Padres uniform and would give any serious student of baseball a glimmer of the man entrusted by president Dave Montgomery and general manager Ed Wade to guide the Phillies more than a decade later.

It was the last incredible incident of an incredible first half, which the Padres just happened to conclude with five losses in their last six games. At the break, they were looking down the nasty gullet of a 30-58 record. And the season wasn't nearly over.

Bowa wouldn't long support Show, who finished the 1986 season with a sore right elbow and was on his way to an 8-16 record in 1987. If the game in Chicago showed a calm side of Bowa that no one expected, his "I hate to lose" attitude was never quelled as the season headed toward its 97-loss conclusion. As July turned into August, Bowa was back to an old refrain after a 10-run loss the Reds at Cincinnati. Only the numbers had altered somewhat from that early-season blowout meeting in Los Angeles.

"Twenty guys will go through walls for me and, frankly, four others don't care," Bowa said at the time.

Bowa later qualified the statement, "Maybe the words 'don't care' were wrong. I thought there were four guys whose attitudes were on a different level than the rest of the team. They were at the stage of their careers where their attitudes weren't going to change. When you brought up a lot of kids who saw that, it was not helpful to your program. It had a tremendous effect on them. I don't have to mention any names."

One of those guys was Show, who was going through the motions and just seemed to be losing interest in his baseball career. Bowa wouldn't rant and rave at the veteran Show, who made 34 starts for him that season and was at least reliable enough to take his turn every fifth day.

"Larry says things to me differently from what he says to other people," Show said at the time. "I think that what he does sometimes is, he's frustrated like we all are and he'll think about isolated incidents that he can single out as a reason for why generally we're going bad. Larry is a good baseball man and knows the game. I hold no anger toward him. I just wish he would confront me one time and tell me what's on his mind.

"I think you ought to figure out what you're deep down dissatisfied with and try to help the problem, rather than scream about something to try to give your argument some validity. And if you notice, he also has individuals he likes to single out, who usually are safe for him to do that with."

Show had long been the Padres' iconoclast. An accomplished jazz guitarist with right-wing religious leanings, Show helped shatter the harmony of the clubhouse in 1984 when he, Dravecky and another pitcher, Mark Thurmond, manned the John Birch Society booth during the annual county fair at the Del Mar Fairgrounds in North County San Diego. The trio revealed shortly thereafter that they were card-carrying members of a group that, rightly or wrongly, had been noted for its anti-Semitic and racist tendencies. But

Show, a born-again Christian, argued that he joined as an anti-communist.

Ever more the iconoclast, Show was the pitcher at Cincinnati's old Riverfront Stadium on September 11, 1985, who allowed one of the most significant hits in baseball history: a first-inning single to left field by then-44-year-old Pete Rose. It was the 4,192nd of his career, allowing him to pass Ty Cobb for the most in baseball history. As the flare of fireworks lit up the nighttime pre-autumn sky and the celebration swirled around him, Show didn't retreat to the Padres' dugout. He sat down on the mound.

Show would eventually become the top starter in team history with 100 wins, which gives any baseball fan a quick clip of the Padres' shortcomings over their first 35 seasons. He would also succumb to his own demons, dying at a treatment clinic in 1994 of a drug overdose. He was only 38 years old and three years beyond pitching in his last major league baseball game.

Chris Brown was another one on Bowa's list of malcontents, along with Goose Gossage and Storm Davis, a starting pitcher who was injured on and off all season and never reached his potential with the team. Davis was traded before the season was out. Gossage, who had lost the fastball that made him one of the most potent of baseball's all-time closers, would be traded prior to the 1988 season.

"I haven't known my role all year," complained Gossage, whose 11 saves in 40 appearances were his low-water mark to that point in his career as a reliever. "I would like to be used more, and for whatever reason, I haven't been. I don't like to be kept in the dark, but that's what it's been like. I really haven't talked to Larry all year."

As far as Brown was concerned, he was in the process of missing 15 consecutive starts because of an injured left wrist. Brown claimed he had originally sustained the injury before leaving San Francisco when Giants batting coach Jose Morales inadvertently hit him in the wrist with a pitch during batting practice just a day before the trade. The Giants would not substantiate that claim.

Brown evidently reinjured the same wrist just after the All-Star Game when, in a game against the Chicago Cubs in San Diego, he dove for a grounder off the bat of Keith Moreland. Teammates had been surprised before by Brown's injuries.

"The craziest injury I ever heard of," said pitcher Mark Grant, who was Brown's teammate both in San Francisco and San Diego, "was one spring when a guy missed a week because he said he slept on his eye. I don't think I have to tell you who that was, do I?"

The situation hadn't gone unnoticed by Bowa, who was trying all kinds of psychological means to reach the 25-year-old third baseman. Brown obviously had the physical talent to be a force in the National League if he ever recognized his ability. Bowa tried calling him in for meetings. He tried ignoring him. He tried penciling him into the lineup, and he tried leaving him out of the lineup until Brown asked back in. It was a perplexing problem.

"There was no doubt he was taking a beating from his teammates," Bowa said. "I mean guys got on him, calling him a jake. It was rough. But he dealt with it. He was a very complicated and sensitive person to get to know. When you talked to him one on one, he seemed like he was sincere and he wanted to do well. Physically, I really thought the guy could play. But if you're not mentally involved in the game, if there's something bothering you mentally, it's going to show up out there."

For his part, Brown admitted playing at about 60 percent of his physical capability because of the wrist injury and backlash from the Danny Cox pitch that shattered his jaw. Brown also admitted anticipating a quick end to the season. That turned out to be a self-fulfilling prophecy when former teammate Mike Krukow fractured Brown's right hand with another pitch late in the season. For Chris Brown, 1987 was quite a year.

"I got traded," he said back then. "I got hit in the jaw. I had shoulder surgery. Then there's my wrist. It has just been one of those years. My 1987 hasn't been the greatest. I hope '88 is a better year. It can't help but be a better year, barring injuries."

But 1987 wasn't over.

On August 21 at New York's Shea Stadium, Bowa was back to his old ways on the field. He was thrown out of a game for the first time in three months, but it happened with the National League president, the late Bart Giamatti, and the entire Padres brass—owner Joan Kroc, president Chub Feeney, former president Ballard Smith, and general manager Jack McKeon—in the stands to witness the explosion.

By season's end, Bowa would be banished five times. But on this occasion, Bowa completely lost it. He tossed his brown cap to the dirt. Eyes wide with passion, blue veins protruding dangerously from his forehead and neck, Bowa charged home plate umpire Steve Rippley, apparently grazing Rippley with his chest and hips in the onslaught.

Giamatti fined Bowa $500, and Feeney called Bowa into his office to admonish him days later when the team returned to San Diego.

"He told me, 'You don't help your team,'" Bowa said, recalling the meeting. "'It's not very professional.' He made sense. He thought what I did was right, sticking up for the team and all that, but after the umpire said no way, I should have dropped it. And I said I would have. But then the umpire said, 'I'm running the show here.' And when he said that as I was walking away, that just upset me. Chub didn't like managers to get thrown out of the game. I thought I did pretty well in that category."

August was good to the Padres, who won seven in a row at one point and nine out of 12. From opening at 12-42, the Padres finished the season with a 53-55 record in their last 108 games. Benito Santiago sparkled down the stretch, finishing his first season on a 34-game hitting streak, the longest at the time for a catcher, a rookie or a Latino player. He is the only Padre ever to be honored as the National League's Rookie of the Year.

By mid-September, Feeney had decided that the team had improved enough under Bowa to rehire him again for the 1988 season. Feeney was from the old school. He worked under a one-year contract, and he expected his manager to do the same. It's a practice largely unheard of in today's baseball world of skyrocketing salaries for both players and managers. Feeney figured that if the late Walter Alston managed the Dodgers in Brooklyn and Los Angeles for 23 years from 1954 to 1976 under a series of one-year contracts, why couldn't Bowa do the same?

Feeney anticipated the best from Bowa heading into the new season.

"Here is a highly motivated, highly intelligent man with a fine personality," Feeney said about Bowa months later. "He made himself into a good baseball player. He's highly competitive. As league president, I had only gotten to know him in an adversarial relationship, fining him a couple of times. I've really gotten to know him as a person since coming here to San Diego. I consider him to be a manager of the future. I think he obviously knows baseball. He's wrapped up in baseball. He's a fine tactician. He's not afraid to make moves. He's not afraid to do things on the field. He does what he thinks is right. He makes the game exciting by using the skills of his team. By stealing bases, using hit and runs.

"His limitation right now, stopping him from becoming a great manager, is the fact that he has a tendency to blow his top and to not maintain his cool. That's reflected in his attitudes toward both umpires and players. I have no objections about talking to umpires when you think they're wrong. But it's the way you do it. The attitude you have. And Larry has a tendency to lose his head at that moment. I also think he has a tendency to talk about his players publicly, and that's not going to help him as a manager. I think he will get over both of those things. I think he's working on it, which is the most important thing. On the few occasions I've talked to him, I think he already understood before we even sat down that what he did was not in the best interests of the Padres or himself.

"The best thing he did was to keep the ballplayers in a state of mind so they played as hard as they could every day. When I got here, we were obviously out of any pennant race, so everybody could have rolled over and played dead. I think they needed that motivation. I think each individual player has to motivate himself, but the manager was responsible for putting us into the position where for most of the second half of the season we played the best baseball in the division, except for the Giants. So he had to have success in keeping these guys motivated, which is a tough thing to do."

In six months, Bowa had obviously matured as a manager. His day-to-day dealing with players had become less frenetic. Although he still tended to take his shots in print when he was angry, many of the comments were of a more general nature. Perhaps the difference in styles of two distinct club presidents could account for much of the change. Under Ballard Smith, a hands-off president, a free-wheeling, opinionated man like Bowa was able to fly. Even in his most energetic days with the club, Smith rarely interfered with on-field personnel unless it involved a matter of front office policy. There was little accountability to the top of the organization with Smith in control.

That all changed with the coming of Feeney. Say what you will about Feeney's expertise when he was general manager of the Giants—and many critics have—but with 40 consecutive years of experience during major league baseball's most formative stages, he was an expert on the inner workings of the game. Feeney took the job in San Diego so that for the first time in his career, he could fully saturate a club. During Smith's final years, as Smith became more distracted with other business interests, the club began to lose focus. Like the last stages in the life of a cloud, the Padres were about to drift into clear, blue nothingness. Joan Kroc decided she should halt the process.

Under Feeney, a sense of order seemed to have been reinstituted. There was no doubt now who was to make the final decisions when it came to the baseball end of this highly complex business: Feeney. That shift of authority met with resistance from some people who were carried through the transition. But even with that, for a time, his regime ushered in one of the more serene baseball eras in Padres history.

So too did Bowa feel a shift in how he had to approach his job and his attitude toward upper management. No fool and certainly a survivor, Bowa seemed to become far more conciliatory under the Feeney regime. When negative connotations toward players appeared in a Bowa newspaper quotation, Feeney picked up the telephone. Even when names appeared in print without attribution to Bowa, the manager heard about it.

"I told him, 'I have no control over what those guys write,'" Bowa said about one such conversation with Feeney.

Feeney was indeed a hands-on president. And Bowa was certainly one element Feeney had his figurative hands directly on.

"When he does something wrong, I'm going to tell him," Feeney said back then. "As far as I'm concerned, he gets a baseball team from Jack McKeon and myself—with his input—to put on the field. What he does with that team is his. We're not going to second-guess him, help him strategize or tell him what players to use. But if I think he does something wrong when it involves his actions in regard to players and umpires, I'm certainly going to tell him about it."

After what seemed like an endless season, no one in the organization seemed to disagree about Bowa's expertise as a manager. It was the method that at times even Bowa himself questioned.

McKeon, who had hired Bowa only a year or so earlier, also put his stamp of approval on Feeney's decision to bring Bowa back.

"In time, Larry will be a damn good big-league manager. It's like anything else, the more experience you get, the better you become," McKeon said back then. "He's on track to becoming an outstanding big-league manager."

But would it be in a Padres uniform? That question was answered less than two months into the 1988 season.

11

IN THE END,
IT WAS BACK TO JACK

The Padres who gathered in Yuma for spring training in 1988 were not much different from the ones who closed the 1987 season. Another old baseball axiom is that teams live and die with their pitching. The Padres had perished the previous season largely because of their pitching. The staff earned run average was 4.27, and veteran starters Storm Davis, Eric Show, Andy Hawkins, Ed Whitson and Dave Dravecky combined to win only 26 games. Dravecky and Davis were traded before the season was over, leaving Bowa to rely on the young arms of Jimmy Jones and Mark Grant to take their places. Jones, a first-round draft pick in 1982, was 24 years old, and general manager Jack McKeon had projected a bright future for him. Grant came over with third baseman Chris Brown and reliever Mark Davis in the midseason deal that sent Dravecky to the Giants. The projections were misconceived. Jones would be traded to the New York Yankees after the 1988 season, and Grant would win 22 games in his career, faring far better as a Padres broadcaster than he did as a pitcher.

"I told Larry that first year, 'Hey, if you stay 15 to 20 games under .500 you've done a hell of a job,'" said McKeon, who at age 72 would manage the Florida Marlins to their 2003 World Series championship. "'I'll get you the players, but it's going to take some time. You've got eight or 10 decent ones here. Polish them up.' But he's such a dedicated and intense guy he couldn't stand it. That, I guess, comes with experience."

McKeon, though, no longer had the ability to get the players. He continued to work the phones, but Chub Feeney, from his perch as club president and with Joan Kroc's blessing, called all of the shots. McKeon had built the 1984 National League champions and subsequently tore that team apart. Some of the elements of those earlier deals still remained—Garry Templeton, who came in a 1982 trade of shortstops with the St. Louis Cardinals for Ozzie Smith, and outfielder Carmelo Martinez, who was obtained in a 1983 three-way deal with the Chicago Cubs and Montreal Expos.

But the more recent deals had Feeney's fingerprints all over them. The Chris Brown deal with the Giants; Storm Davis to Oakland for pitcher Dave Leiper and first baseman Rob Nelson; reliever Goose Gossage to the Cubs for first baseman Keith Moreland. Not one of the players obtained by Feeney had any long-term impact on the organization, although Mark Davis won the Cy Young Award in 1989 before splitting as a free agent.

"I wasn't in favor of the Chris Brown deal, and Chub wanted me to go along with it," McKeon said. "The Giants kept wanting us to throw in more players—Dravecky, Craig Lefferts. I told him, 'You can't do that.' He said, 'Come on, I'm right here with [Giants general manager] Al Rosen. Let's make it.' I said, 'You're the boss, go ahead and do what you want to do.' Yeah, that was his deal. I was in Wichita on a scouting trip when that happened. Chub was on his own. He did all those deals. I figured he was the boss. Let him do it."

Four years after winning the pennant, the Padres opened 1988 with only three position players remaining from the 1984 team—Templeton, Martinez and Tony Gwynn, who despite sore knees and all of the team's problem, still batted .370 to lead the National League in 1987. From the pitching staff, only Show, Hawkins, Whitson and Greg Booker—a reliever and McKeon's son-in-law—remained. And Whitson had returned from the Yankees in a trade after a miserable season and a half as a free agent signee in New York. Add utility infielder Tim Flannery, and the veteran portion of the team was complete.

These were the cards dealt to Bowa in his second season, and he knew the prospects didn't look good although he had re-signed for $150,000, a $50,000 raise over 1987.

"Probably the most helpless feeling as a manager is when you know in your heart that you're a good baseball person, but if the players don't perform to the level the front office wants them to, then you're the guy out," Bowa said. "You feel like you failed. But when you sit back eventually and digest it, you say to yourself, 'Hey, there are just some things I had no control over.'"

Bowa said he noticed a difference in McKeon's approach under Feeney as opposed to Ballard Smith, the previous club president.

"When I first got there and Jack wanted to make a deal, he didn't have to check with anybody," Bowa said. "But the next year he'd always tell me he had to check with Chub. I didn't really think much of it at the time. I just figured we had a guy coming in who was president of the National League, a pretty high-profile guy. But when I first got there, it stopped at Jack's desk. Jack was the guy."

Bowa, of course, had no control over the roster, and Bowa had no control over McKeon's relationship with Feeney. Kroc had given Feeney a free hand to replace McKeon in the organization, but his frugality got the best of him. McKeon had two years remaining on his contract, and Feeney wasn't about to pay him to stay home or work for another team. Bowa was on a one-year deal. Replacing him on the field with McKeon was ultimately the most expedient thing to do. If McKeon failed, Feeney could dispose of him, too.

In reflection, the 1988 season began with this elaborate dance of spiders and could have had no other conclusion. When McKeon was in control, it was he who had chosen Bowa among all other candidates to replace Steve Boros as manager. It was McKeon who took Bowa, just freshly retired as a player, and gave him a chance to manage in the Padres' farm system at Las Vegas. McKeon and Bowa had no prior personal relationship. What made the novice Bowa so attractive?

"I saw the same things in Larry that I saw in myself," McKeon said. "I'm probably a little bit more patient, though, than Larry. And maybe that was because of my long minor league career [17 years overall] as a manager. I had acquired that patience, that understanding that I can't win if I don't have enough talent. But I saw the same things. I saw the fire, that competitiveness. He was highly intelligent. No shit, he's a good baseball man. That was the thing that sold me. And talking strategy, he thought just like I did."

After the 1985 season, Bowa said he put out the word through his agent that he wanted to quit playing and start managing. He had a $250,000 offer to return to the Mets as a utility player in 1986.

"But I didn't want to be a backup," Bowa said. "I had been a regular my entire life. Utility player is a tough job. I figured I was done. So I told my agent that if he saw anything that popped up in the organizations he was familiar with to get me an interview. I was thinking Single A ball or rookie ball. Then Jack called and said they might be interested in me managing their Triple A club. That was unbelievable. I had no relationship with McKeon before that. He was in Vegas all the time that year, and we became friendly there. The one thing he liked about me is that we worked hard on fundamentals. He appreciated the fact that I spent so much time teaching the kids how to play the game."

By 1988, though, McKeon had begun to build a shabby short list of managers ultimately jettisoned by the club. McKeon had been with the Padres in his front office capacity for nearly eight years and had engineered around 45 trades. But he had already authored four managerial changes. Boros had been McKeon's choice to replace Dick Williams, and it hadn't been a good one. Firing Bowa so quickly after that debacle would've put another quick ding in McKeon's reputation.

"I didn't fire the guy; man, I didn't even think of it," McKeon said. "That would've been a bad rap on me for poor judgment."

But right from the outset, the rumors of Bowa's demise began running rampant. The Padres opened up the season the same way they did in 1987—with five losses in a row. Feeney had to immediately deny the validity of those rumors. Feeney called Bowa in to tell him not to worry about winning or losing—just develop the young players. But Feeney didn't give Bowa his best shot at it. A young Roberto Alomar, after a spectacular spring training at second base, was sent back to the minor leagues for more seasoning. Again, Feeney's frugality got the best of him.

"If we had started the season with Robbie, maybe it would've been a different story," McKeon said. "But Chub just wanted to keep him away from arbitration for another year."

By April 20, Alomar was with the club, and by April 26, the Padres had fought back to 8-9, the closest the team would come to reaching .500 during Bowa's tenure. They then lost eight of their next nine, and Bowa's job was left dangling by a thread. Feeney had to dispel another rumor that he had given Bowa 40 games to alter the course of the season. At that point, he also advised Bowa to change his managing philosophy. Sure, work with the young players, but it was imperative to win some games.

"At the beginning it was just get our young kids going," Bowa said. "We would get them some experience, and they were going to become pretty good ballplayers. We would win some games, but don't worry about it. But after that it was, 'We've got to do both.' You couldn't do both. If you played the young kids, you were going to get your butts beat. If you played the veterans, the young kids were going to sit and were not going to get the experience. There had to be a happy medium."

But around the 40-game mark, Feeney had evidently made his decision. On May 23, the team left San Diego for a nine-game eastern swing through Montreal, New York and Philadelphia. But not before Feeney called Bowa in one last time to quell the manager's fraying nerves.

"He literally said all the stuff in the papers about me being fired was hogwash," Bowa recalled. "Was he lying to me? What else am I supposed to assume? It was hogwash; then all of a sudden it became reality."

The Padres lost three straight in Olympic Stadium, where they failed to ever win under Bowa, going 0-9. On May 26, Feeney called in McKeon, who was just about to embark on another scouting sojourn. McKeon was off again to the Midwest to look at a pitcher named Andy Benes, who would be taken by the Padres with the first pick in the June 1988 draft of amateur players.

McKeon had set up a lunch at a Holiday Inn near the airport in San Diego so afterward he could make a quick escape for his flight. His sidekick, Bill Beck, then the team's director of media relations, and agent John Boggs were scheduled join him at that lunch.

"That was my plan," McKeon recalled. "I came to work that morning at nine o'clock, and Chub told me he wanted to see me. I went to his office, and he said, 'We're going to make a change in managers.' I asked him whom he had in mind. I'm thinking he had some ex-Giant—Tom Haller or Jim Davenport. He said, 'You!' I asked him how much time I had to think about it. He said he'd give me until two o'clock. So I canceled the flight, but I still met those guys for lunch. We talked about it. I called my wife and the kids. It was like a 2-2 vote. The girls said, 'Forget it dad, you don't need it.' The boys said, 'Go for it.'

"I figured, 'Well the club's going bad. He's firing Bowa. I'll be the next one to go. What have I got to lose?'"

At that stage of McKeon's illustrious career, he hadn't managed in the major leagues since 1978. In all, out of 22 seasons as a manager, he had spent about five seasons managing the Oakland A's and Kansas City Royals, amassing a 286-310 record. At the time, McKeon's prior big-league managing job was a decade earlier with the A's, a franchise in its waning days under the irascible owner Charlie Finley, who ran a carnival sideshow. There were four people in the front office, including McKeon. And he was thrown into the dugout one June day in 1977 when the incumbent manager, Bobby Winkles, got so fed up with Finley's meddling that he just drove away from the stadium in Oakland and never came back.

Finley, who lived in Chicago, would think nothing of calling the dugout to tell McKeon what move to make during a game. McKeon would act like the phone wasn't working. By the time he took over, the A's teams that had won the World Series three years running from 1972 to 1974 had been stripped bare by free agency and Charlie's inherent cheapness. Finley once traded a manager for a catcher—Chuck Tanner to Pittsburgh for Manny Sanguillen. McKeon won only 71 games in two seasons and was ushered out.

McKeon was still a popular figure in San Diego, so from a practical standpoint the move back to the field made sense to Feeney, who in one fell swoop would rid himself of Bowa's maniacal antics and McKeon's footsteps in the front office. McKeon had been neutered as a general manager, so from a personal standpoint it was his only option if he hoped to salvage his career with the Padres.

All this was going on behind Bowa's back while the team was 3,000 miles away. There is, of course, no good way of firing a manager or coach. The events are at best a public flogging, and at worst a pretty ugly vetting of the team's problems. But through leaks to reporters and the carping of the players, a climate can certainly be created for any pending dismissal. Such is what happened that week in Montreal as the team barreled toward a 15-30 record and a season-worst 15 games under .500. The drums of impending doom grew louder and louder as events were playing out simultaneously in two time zones. And McKeon was sworn to secrecy, so he couldn't even give Bowa a heads up.

"The only thing about it that still bothers me is how it happened," Bowa said. "When I called Jack from Montreal because I heard little rumblings and I wanted to talk to him, his wife told me he wasn't in. Maybe he wasn't in, but he never returned the call. That should have gotten my attention. I had never been through this as a manager. I guess it's like getting traded as a player. You sort of expect a warning from the guy who hired you, but maybe you're supposed to see it coming. I don't know."

So Bowa was completely in the dark. The next day, May 27, the passion play continued into its next act. The Padres were in New York playing the Mets at Shea Stadium. Feeney and McKeon took separate flights to get there. McKeon went to the team hotel and stayed out of sight. Feeney, who was sequestered in a private box during the game—a Padres victory—wouldn't address the issue or answer questions. But this was no secret. The three newspapers that regularly covered the team at the time—the *San Diego Union, San Diego Tribune* and *Los Angeles Times*—had been carrying stories speculating about the inevitable all week. No one, though, figured that McKeon would be the guy to replace Bowa. That was the ultimate twist of fate.

The firing came on the following morning, and Bowa found out about it from a reporter long before Feeney called at 8:30 a.m. and asked him to come up to the president's room. Bowa was livid and refused the request, telling Feeney he already knew he had been fired. But Bowa didn't let Feeney off the hook that easily. The Padres had been 81-132 under Bowa, but he still came out blasting.

"I said, 'Before I hang up, what's the reasoning behind this?'" Bowa recalled. "He said, 'We're better than 16-30.' I said, 'Oh, without Tony Gwynn for 21 days? Without John Kruk for nine games? Without the so-called franchise turnaround Chris Brown for 20?' He started muttering some stuff, and I said, 'I don't want to talk to you. I've talked to you enough.' Why would I want to go up, to listen to more lies?"

Bowa's wife, Sheena, and his daughter, Tori, then four years old, had joined him in New York, coming up from their home in Philadelphia. Bowa's plan was to drive down to Philly with his wife after the Sunday game in New York to open a three-game series at the Vet. The drive came a day early.

"Sheena told me if they wanted to fire me I should just let it happen," Bowa said. "That I didn't need the aggravation. She was right. She's always right. A hundred people must have told me I did a good job. I did everything I could do with that team."

But the obvious question was why Feeney had opted to re-sign Bowa if he intended to panic after only 40 games?

There were obvious reasons for the Padres' early problems that season. Gwynn, Bowa's best player, had been on the disabled list for three weeks and was recovering from strained ligaments in his right thumb suffered during a base-running mishap. Brown, Bowa's biggest problem child, had missed 21 games with various ailments and hadn't been in the lineup since May 10 when he left a game after the first inning with a cyst on the back of his hand and tendinitis of the right wrist. John Kruk had missed nine games and struggled all season with a bruised knee and tendinitis in the left shoulder.

In 1987, Kruk, then 26, was Bowa's biggest project, and he responded with a .313 batting average and a team-leading 20 homers and 90 runs batted it. Bowa was sharp enough to place Kruk under Gwynn's wing, and the stellar work habits of the punk manager and the batting champ rubbed off on the brash kid from Charleston, West Virginia.

Kruk was as green a rookie as one can imagine. While riding the team bus from Chicago's Wrigley Field downtown along Lake Shore Drive, he once turned to Tim Flannery and pointed to Lake Michigan. In his most innocent southern drawl, Kruk asked: "What ocean is that, the Mediterranean?" Now he's an acclaimed Phillies broadcaster and personality in his own right.

"I enjoyed playing for Larry," Kruk said. "He taught me more about baseball than anyone else, any other coach or manager I've ever had, as far as doing the little parts of the game, situations. He made me think when I was playing."

Bowa has always had his backers and detractors. Players either love him or hate him. There are no gray areas. In the dugout, Bowa wears his emotions on his sleeve, rolls his eyes and bleats and moans as events unfold during a game. But Bowa definitely left San Diego with a sour taste in his mouth.

"I thought I got screwed," Bowa said. "But when you think about it, I didn't get screwed. I was probably in the wrong place at the wrong time. Things didn't happen right. It was a situation in flux. But looking back on it, I was rushed into the major leagues. I could have used another year in the minor leagues, maybe two. I don't think I needed any more time as far as strategy goes. It was dealing with all the other things. The players. The press. Baby-sitting guys. I had no idea. I was a self-motivated guy when I played."

The irony of it all is that McKeon pulled the 1988 season and his own job out of a hat like a mystic magician, establishing another facet of his reputation—the ability to give young, faltering teams a chance to win. The Padres made only one trade after Bowa was gone, and it was a big help. In June they sent Candy Sierra, a pitcher of little consequence, to Cincinnati for left-handed starter Dennis Rasmussen, who went 14-4 in San Diego that season. Otherwise, the walking wounded returned to the lineup. Gwynn won another batting title, this time doing it while hitting only .313. Chris Brown's career petered out. He hit .235 with only two homers and 19 RBIs in 80 games. Still, the Padres went 67-48 under the calming, grandfatherly like hand of McKeon, who earned himself another contract as manager while losing the title of vice president of baseball operations in the bargain.

Joan Kroc forced Feeney's hand near the end of the season and demanded that he extend McKeon's contract, which only had one year remaining. Feeney, of course, was loath to give managers long-term agreements.

"The season gave me a new lease on life, especially my managing life," McKeon said. "I never thought I was going to manage again. And Joan gave me a new three-year contract."

McKeon recalled a meeting he had with Feeney, Kroc and Beth Benes, the team's general counsel, about his future with the team near the end of the 1988 season. Kroc told McKeon that she wanted him to manage. McKeon had the year to go on his contract for $300,000. Feeney made the offer: three years for $310,000, $315,000 and $325,000.

"Joan asked me how that sounded. I said no way. I wasn't going to do it for less than $400,000 a year," McKeon recalled. "She said, 'I don't have any problem with that.' I told them I'd let them know tomorrow. So the next day, I go into Chub's office to tell him I was going to take the contract. He said, 'I wouldn't have paid you that much.' Can you imagine that? Not happy to have you back or let's keep this going, but I wouldn't have paid you that much!"

By the end of that week, Feeney was gone anyway. On Fan Appreciation Night at Jack Murphy Stadium, he made a gesture from his box at a group of fans in the deck below carrying a sign calling for his ousting. McKeon would eventually regain the dual titles and keep them as long as Kroc owned the club.

Bowa says now that he has a better understanding of how the inside game of baseball politics works.

"Jack and I get along good," Bowa said. "I have no animosity toward Jack. He was good with me. He never gave me any indication that anything was really wrong. Hindsight being 20-20, forget Chub Feeney taking over, I should have never accepted that job for the second year, no matter who was the GM, no matter who was the president."

Bowa returned to Philadelphia that August as the Phillies' third base coach under old friend Lee Elia, who himself was fired as manager before the end of the season. Bowa wasn't interviewed to fill that job.

—12—

BACK TO PHILLY

Save for Mike Schmidt, who was nearing the end of his career, the Phillies that Bowa returned to as third base coach on August 11, 1988, were almost unrecognizable compared to the team Bowa had left as a player only six years earlier. Since losing the 1983 World Series to the Baltimore Orioles, the Phillies had imploded, falling to the depths of last place in the National League East. They were in the midst of a 10-year absence from the playoffs and had been run by four different managers since Dallas Green pulled up stakes in 1981.

Veterans Stadium, less than two decades old at that point, looked worn around the edges. The artificial surface was noted by most players to be the hardest and worst in the league, with seams that seemed carved from a baseball.

With the departures of mainstays such as Bowa, Steve Carlton, Tug McGraw and Greg Luzinski, Schmidt had become the standard-bearer, but he was the captain of a sinking, creaking ship. The Phillies were one of the few teams to risk the free agent market before the 1987 season, but the signing of Detroit catcher Lance Parrish had paid few dividends. And these Phillies, built around center fielder Von Hayes and second baseman Juan Samuel, had been a disaster. On June 21, Phillies president Bill Giles brought in Lee Thomas from the St. Louis Cardinals to take over as general manager with the aim of trying to straighten out the mess.

"We weren't real good. That was probably the low point," Bowa recalled. "When I say hitting rock bottom, I'm talking about the minor league system. It was really depleted. We neglected it. We tried to patch something here and patch something there, but there was no light at the end of the tunnel."

Schmidt had hit his 500th lifetime homer on April 18, 1987, in Pittsburgh's old Three Rivers Stadium off Pirates right-hander Don Robinson—a two-out, two-run, game-winning shot—and then used the occasion of the press conference hyping a videotape of that historic home run to question Phillies upper management about the direction of the organization.

"My overriding goal is to do whatever it takes to get this Phillies organization back on top," Schmidt said at the press conference. "We're not polished anymore. The minor league system is depleted. The fields are the worst in the league. The dugouts are filthy. The clubhouse is dirty. The pride factor is not what it used to be. We used to have the best field; now it's the worst. We used to have the cleanest dugouts; now they're the dirtiest. We used to have the best minor league system..."

And on and on and on...

When Schmidt arrived at the Vet not long after his critique of the facility, he found lush, green ferns hanging from his locker and candles surrounding his folding chair. Workmen were scrubbing down the runway from the clubhouse to the dugout where only minutes earlier Schmidt had whiffed the telltale signs of "cat piss." The next night, as Schmidt sat in the dugout, the cleanup on the field continued. Someone seemed to have listened.

"Eyewash," Schmidt said at the time. "You know what I mean? Now they're trying to make me look bad. To stick it to me because I opened my big mouth."

The tirade made Bowa laugh, but he understood better than anyone the root of the problem.

After all, Schmidt had become accustomed to winning. With Bowa playing to his left, the two had been to the playoffs and won the World Series in 1980. After Bowa left, Schmidt went on to the World Series again in 1983. Since then the Phillies hadn't finished higher than second place. By the time Bowa reentered the scene, Schmidt's numbers had begun to plummet, leaving him no platform to stand on.

In one season alone, the difference was stark. In 1987, Schmidt hit .297 with 35 homers and 113 runs batted in, pretty standard for the first 15 years of his career. But in 1988, he sank to .251, 12 homers and 62 RBIs, his worst year ever. Forty years old at the end of that season, Schmidt began to ponder retiring.

"I remember him asking me what it felt like to get to the end of your career," Bowa said. "I said, 'There were some plays I thought I could make that I wasn't making.' The Mets wanted me to come back as a utility player, and I didn't want to play utility. I just told him about my scenario, which was completely different than his. I still thought he could have played a little bit longer, maybe two more years. But he was pretty proud. I didn't think he'd have embarrassed himself, but he went out his way."

When Schmidt opened the 1989 season hitting .203 with only six homers and 28 RBIs, he called it quits. The Phillies were in the middle of an 11-game losing streak and on the West Coast when Schmidt called a press conference on May 29 before a night game in San Diego to announce his decision. He had gone hitless in three at-bats with two walks the day before at San Francisco.

Schmidt broke down in tears in front of the media, and the decimation of Ruly Carpenter's Phillies was now complete.

Bowa, though, needed a respite after his chaotic 20 months as manager of the San Diego Padres. And so, for the first time during the summer months since he signed his first professional contract back in 1966, Bowa took a 75-day break during the baseball season.

Like Bowa's departures as a player from Philadelphia and Chicago, he had left San Diego with much acrimony.

"It took me a long time to get over the animosity because I thought I was deceived by the whole organization," Bowa said about the Padres. "Where did the three-year plan we were working on go in a year? We weren't ready to win yet. We had kids, and the veterans weren't good enough to win. They were on their way out. I just think that instead of everyone being on the same page, everyone was on different pages. But here's the bottom line: The regime was different in San Diego from when I came in. No matter what I did, I wasn't one of their guys. It doesn't matter if you're a dope or if you're a genius. If they don't want you, that's just the way the game evolves."

So Bowa spent the months of June and July home with his family in Philadelphia before his old friend Lee Elia, then the manager of the Phillies, called.

"It wasn't bad. I got to spend some time home during the summer just sort of sitting back and reflecting on things I could have done better," Bowa said. "Obviously, you're beating yourself up over getting fired. There's a first for everything. When you get released as a player it's a first; when you get traded, obviously, that's a first; when you get hired as a manager and then get fired, that's another first. Those are transitional phases you go through.

"You think about things you could have done differently. Then you realize it might not have mattered if you did things differently. It was just the situation you were in. It wouldn't have mattered. You beat yourself up for a little while and then you move on."

Bowa's and Elia's paths had often crossed before. Elia was a coach on the Phillies when Bowa was a player. Elia was the manager of the Cubs when Giles traded Bowa to Chicago. Now, Elia was managing the Phillies, and he wanted Bowa back to replace the veteran baseball man Dave Bristol in the third base coaching box. There was no point to waiting until the end of the season to make the change, Elia said.

"There had been some strong consideration for Larry to coach for the Phillies," Elia said at the time. "Why wait until next year? Let's see if it's good for both parties. Let's see if it's just what the doctor ordered."

Bowa, of course, was fortunate to be back. He left as a player in 1981, flailing away at Giles, the new owner, because of a contract dispute. There had been harsh words between both men and a public vetting of the dispute in the newspapers. Giles, though, a promotion man at heart and always a carnival showman, hoped he might appease the hostile fan base by putting Bowa back in a Phillies uniform and making him a most visible component coaching third base. Attendance at the Vet had remained remarkably steady during the 1980s despite the play of the team. The Phillies drew two million or more three times, and attendance never fell below 1.8 million during that decade.

Bringing Bowa back would provide a glimmer of the recent good old days. And after all, Giles knew the Bowa psyche better than anyone and hadn't harbored a grudge about the dispute.

"I never really held it against him," Giles said. "I knew he had a temper. He believed one thing and I believed another at the time. So I wasn't ever bitter about it."

The team was in Los Angeles on August 16 when Bowa returned to the field, and as fate would have it, the Phillies ended that trip in San Diego with Bowa's first visit back since his dismissal. The Padres, much like the second half of the 1987 season, had begun to play with some polish under Jack McKeon, who kept chanting the "don't worry, be happy" mantra of let's have fun. The Padres did just that. (Mark Grant, the team jokester, was even caught on camera during a game in Philadelphia reaching under the bench to hot-foot a teammate. The video, complete with flaming lighter, was broadcast on the Vet's scoreboard to an appreciative crowd.) The Padres had also picked up left-hander Dennis Rasmussen from Cincinnati, and he helped transfigure a beleaguered pitching staff. But Bowa still obviously didn't have the events of earlier that season out of his system.

"I didn't have Dennis Rasmussen. I didn't have a left-hander in the starting rotation," he said in Los Angeles before his return to Jack Murphy Stadium. "Take away his numbers [9-1 as a Padre] and what is the team's record? I didn't have Tony Gwynn for three weeks. Now he's vying for the batting title. What bothers me most about being fired is that nobody picked us to win the division. A lot of teams, at one time or another this season, were 14 games under .500, teams that were supposed to be contenders. That still bothers me.

"When I was hired, I was told the team needed discipline," Bowa added. "When I was fired, I was told that there was too much discipline."

Still the Padres had a 40-33 record under McKeon at the time of Bowa's initial San Diego visit, and some of the Padre players, who had rebelled under Bowa's leadership, were eagerly taking some shots at the former manager in his absence. Bowa chaffed under the criticism.

"You have got Mark Grant, who made a statement that it's more fun coming to the park now," Bowa said back then. "I gave the guy an opportunity to pitch every fifth day. Now he's 2-8. It must be a lot of fun coming to the park. And Andy Hawkins seems to take a slam every time he gets a chance. He still thinks I was the big reason for trading his buddy Goose Gossage [to the Chicago Cubs]. I wish I had that much power. Everybody in the organization seemed to think Gossage was finished: Everybody except Hawkins. Goose has blown something like 13 of his last 21 save opportunities. If it weren't for him, [manager] Don Zimmer would have had a pretty good season."

None of this, though, was Bowa's problem any longer.

His problem was now learning the nuances of acting as third base coach, relaying signs from the manager to the players, waving runners around third base, and working with the infielders. Bowa had coached third base while he managed the Las Vegas Stars, primarily because minor league staffs are not as deep as those provided to teams in the major leagues. But even then, he was the manager relaying his own signals. It would take a different mindset and be a position he'd perfect for the next 12 years, although Bowa had no way of knowing that at the time.

"When you're a coach you're involved in one area," Bowa recalled. "I was in charge of the infielders and base running. That's basically what you stick to. I was very lucky to have worked for managers who let me do my thing. As a manager, you oversee things. You let your coaches coach. Looking back on San Diego, that's one thing I learned. I tried to do everything myself. That's impossible, and you shouldn't even try. That's why you have to get people around you who you know and trust and you believe in."

But the more things changed, the more things remained the same. While the Padres would finish in third place that season with an 83-78 record, Bowa and the Phillies would continue losing. From the moment Bowa took his new position at third base, the Phillies reeled off a streak of 11 losses in 12 games, the only victory coming against the Padres on August 22, Bowa's first game back in San Diego. From August 13 to September 10 the Phillies won only five games. But the losses didn't bother Bowa nearly as much as when he had the responsibility of managing.

"As a coach, you want to win," Bowa said. "When you don't win, it's disappointing, but it's a different feeling as opposed to when you're a manager. When you're a manager and you lose, it goes right down from your head to your toes. It rips your insides out. It's hard to describe. That's why it was a great experience watching another manager deal with personnel moves and stressful situations. As a coach I don't think you beat yourself as much when you go into a long losing streak. You feel like you were shouldering all the weight when you were the manager.

"Sure you feel like hell as a third base coach when you have a guy thrown out at the plate. That sticks in your mind, especially if it's the tying run in the bottom of the ninth and he gets thrown out. You take something like that home. But there are so many variables that go into when you send a runner: Who's the next guy up? Is he swinging the bat good? Is there going to be a pinch hitter? How's your pitching? Is it strong? How many guys do you have left in the bullpen? So many things go into that one move. People don't understand it. But if you don't have guys thrown out, you're not a very good coach."

All of the losing, though, would have a deleterious effect on the man running the team. Lee Thomas, the Cardinals' director of player personnel since 1981, had been hired in June to evaluate personnel and make any changes he deemed necessary to restore the ball club's health. Elia had been used as a tourniquet midway through the 1987 season. John Felske, in his third season, had managed the Phillies to second place in 1986. But Felske was fired on June 18, 1987, and replaced by Elia with the club in the middle of a six-game losing streak.

The move worked for a time. The Phillies drew as close as six and a half games out of first place under Elia during the last week of August and then finished the season in fourth. Elia had managed a 51-50 record. But during the second half of the 1988 season, things began to collapse. Injuries to Schmidt, Parrish and young catcher Darren Daulton were contributing factors. At the All-Star break, the Phillies were 13 games under .500 before things really started to go south. The Phillies were 29-57 the rest of the season, finishing in last place with a Padresque 96 losses.

For a time, Bowa said Elia seemed to be rolling with the rip tide.

"Lee was fairly under control," Bowa said. "I guess he learned through experience to channel his anxiety somewhere else. He didn't show any emotion."

Perhaps this was true on the field, but an off-the-field incident proved to be his undoing. Bowa recalled a late-season bus trip back from New York to Philadelphia when Elia aired out the driver with Thomas in attendance. The Phillies had just lost a three-game series to the Mets at Shea Stadium, giving them an 8-17 record for September.

"It was ugly, and the people involved were embarrassed," Bowa said. "Elia just snapped at him. He was pissed at all the losing and pissed that we had just lost the game."

The incident was the catalyst for change, and Elia was fired the next day, September 23, replaced for the last nine games of the season by bench coach John Vukovich. Vuk was a coach with the Cubs under Elia and had his own ambitions to manage. But he was bypassed in Chicago when general manager Dallas Green had a falling-out with upper management and abruptly left the Cubs. Vuk returned to Philadelphia, where he warmed the bench as a utility player from 1976 to 1981.

As a member of the Phillies' coaching staff in 1988, he was reunited with Bowa. The two men had a long timeline together. Both grew up in Sacramento and played American Legion ball there. They were both signed by the Phillies on the recommendation of scout Eddie Bockman and came through the minor league system, finally emerging together for the Phillies during the 1970s. When Bowa was traded to the Cubs in 1982, Green hired Vukovich as a coach.

Years later Vuk recalled watching Bowa during an American Legion game. "He was running his mouth," Vukovich told Paul Hagen of the *Philadelphia Daily News*. "We were 16 years old, and he was chirping. He hasn't stopped since."

Neither Bowa nor Vukovich was considered as a candidate to manage the Phillies in 1989. Thomas gave the job to an old Cardinals associate, Nick Leyva, who had managed for six seasons in the St. Louis minor league system and had been a Cardinals coach from 1984 to 1988. Leyva had no big-league managing experience and was only 35 years old.

"I didn't even interview," Bowa said. "Lee had his man already picked out. Nick had been with him in St. Louis for a while, and they had a pretty good relationship."

Bowa remained on the coaching staff, but Leyva would have an undistinguished two and half years as manager of the Phillies. When Jim Fregosi replaced him, the Phillies would embark again on the path to winning.

13

LONG ROAD TO THE 1993 WORLD SERIES

The guys who have been through it at both ends say there's no comparison. Winning the World Series as a player is far superior to doing it as either a coach or a manager. Mike Scioscia, the manager of the Anaheim Angels and native of Upper Darby, Pennsylvania, just outside of Philadelphia, has experienced it as a hard-nosed catcher, winning twice with the Dodgers. He also managed the Angels to a come-from-behind victory over the San Francisco Giants in a seven-game 2002 World Series that was short on pitching, but long on thrills.

The top moment of his career: "It just has to be taking part in winning the World Series as a player with the Dodgers in 1981 and 1988," he said. "The second one was the best one. It was a team that wasn't expected to win against Oakland. We did anyway in five games. It was like David against Goliath. We got the confidence and just took it from there. It was very rewarding."

Ditto Larry Bowa, who played on the Phillies team that won the 1980 World Series over Kansas City and was the third base coach on the Phillies team that lost the 1993 World Series to Toronto.

"To me there's no greater thing than winning it as a player," Bowa said. "It's a result of the dedication, the hard work, the long hours that you put in. When it's over you say to yourself, man, this is worth it. As a manager, would I like to experience it? No question. But no matter what, it's never going to measure up to being in it as a player. I don't care what it is. It's just not going to do it."

It is, of course, up to the front office powers to assemble the necessary pieces, and in 1988, it was no small task that Phillies general manager Lee Thomas had in front of him. He had to rebuild the team from its roots up without much help from the farm system. He also had to find the right combination of manager and coaches. Both would take a while.

"We had a group in the late '80s that wasn't quite there as Schmitty's career was winding down," said Dave Montgomery, who was an executive vice president under Giles then. "Juan Samuel was a gifted player but never reached the level we quite hoped. Von Hayes was a much better player than people would remember; however, he was not the next Richie Ashburn, which we projected him to be."

Thomas started shipping players out. Almost immediately after the devastating 1988 season, catcher Lance Parrish was traded to the California Angels. And then in 16 days the following June, the face of the team almost completely changed. Chris James was traded to the Padres for Randy Ready and Bowa's protégé, John Kruk. Juan Samuel, the team's once vaunted franchise player, was swapped to the New York Mets for center fielder Len Dykstra and pitcher Roger McDowell. Veteran reliever Steve Bedrosian went to the Giants for Terry Mulholland, Dennis Cook and Charlie Hayes.

The changes didn't have an immediate positive effect on wins and losses, but they had a pugnacious feel to them. Guys such as Kruk and Dykstra would run through walls for managers and coaches, and Dykstra had starred for the 1986 Mets, a team that came from behind to beat Boston in that World Series. Third baseman Dave Hollins, a rookie with promise, was plucked off the Padres' roster in the 1989 Rule 5 draft when Jack McKeon, back in his dual role as manager and general manager, failed to protect him on the 40-man roster. It proved to be an inexpensive acquisition for $50,000, considering the fact that Hollins came right up to the Phillies in 1990 and remained until he was traded to Boston midway through the 1995 season. Thomas even tried to resurrect two-time National League Most Valuable Player Dale Murphy, who was obtained in a trade with Atlanta along with pitcher Tommy Greene. Murphy would barely make it through two seasons with the Phillies. Greene, though, would have a longer-lasting impact.

"It was a great group of guys," Bowa said about this edition of the Phillies.

There would be plenty of growing pains and a number of other trades and free agent acquisitions to come before the Phillies won another pennant. Under Leyva in 1989, they finished sixth again with 95 losses, and in 1990, ended in a fourth-place tie with only 85 losses. It should be noted that in 1989, the Cubs went back to the playoffs under general manager Jim Frey and manager Don Zimmer and lost to the Giants.

On April 7, 1991, a day before the Phillies' season started, Thomas unwittingly set the spiral in motion that would result in one of the great moments in World Series history and one of the most heartbreaking for the Phillies when he sent two players to the Cubs for Mitch Williams. The left-handed reliever was nicknamed "Wild Thing" after the character in the movie *Major League* because of his propensity for throwing the ball hard and wild around the plate.

As the roster shifted, Nick Leyva would prove ineffective. He was too young and inexperienced to succeed under the scrutiny of the tough Philly fans. By April 23, with the Phillies opening the 1991 season 4-9, Leyva was out. Thomas replaced him with Fregosi, a former major league infielder who had six years of experience managing the White Sox and Angels, taking the California franchise to the playoffs for the first time in 1979, where they lost to the Baltimore Orioles.

The hiring of Fregosi came from within the organization and happened swiftly. There was little time to lose. Thomas had brought Fregosi in as a special assistant early in the 1989 season to help with the reorganization of the minor league system and to scout the major leagues. For the second time since his return to the Phillies, Bowa didn't even get a sniff at the top field job.

"It was a bam-bam move," Bowa said. "I wasn't even considered."

Bowa was marginally considered, but the long shadow of owner Bill Giles and the way Bowa departed the Phillies as a player still hung over Bowa's career.

"We considered him almost every time we had a managing change, and we had a quite a few of them," Giles said. "But I knew I wasn't going to name him manager when I was in charge of those decisions. I hired Lee Thomas, and I gave him that responsibility. I told him, 'I don't care if you hire him or not. It's up to you to make those decisions.' I wasn't going to push him either way."

Under Fregosi, the team neared the .500 mark in early May, and then off-field tragedy struck. In the wee hours of the morning of May 6, 1991, just hours after a day game at the Vet, the team attended a bachelor party for John Kruk at the first baseman's house. Afterward, Dykstra ran his Mercedes into a tree, seriously injuring himself and catcher Darren Daulton. Dykstra was charged with driving under the influence and suffered three broken ribs, a broken collarbone and a broken cheekbone. Daulton injured his left eye. Both players were lucky. Daulton was on and off the disabled list until June 18, suffering stiffness and the after effects of the accident. He batted .196 that season. Dykstra missed 61 games and didn't return until July 15. On August 26, he ran into the outfield wall in Cincinnati, broke the same collarbone and was finished for the season. Dykstra still hit .297 and led the team with 24 stolen bases.

The Phillies battled through it all to finish in third place with a 78-84 record, but only one game better than what Leyva had accomplished a year earlier. They hadn't had a winning season since 1986 and had averaged close to 96 defeats a season since then.

"It wasn't the happiest of times," Bowa said. "The accident sent us all back to earth. It's life, but you wonder how something like that can happen? Baseball for an instant wasn't really that important. It was a tough, tough season."

The concurrent period hadn't been particularly pleasant for the Padres, either. It had started out with potential. Jack McKeon had stocked the team again with stars, bringing in sluggers such as Jack Clark from the Yankees and Joe Carter from the Cleveland Indians. Youngsters such as Benito Santiago and Roberto Alomar just kept improving. Bowa's problem players—Stanley Jefferson, Chris Brown, Andy Hawkins and Jimmy Jones—were all banished.

"I wish I had had a shot at it with Joe Carter and Jack Clark," Bowa lamented. "Not with some of the players I was strapped with over there. I could have done something with that team."

In 1989, the Padres finished just three games behind the division-winning Giants, but that would be McKeon's apex as manager. The team had enough All-Stars in 1990 to make a run at it. But the chemistry wasn't there.

"We had the players," Carter said recently. "There just seemed to be something missing. Something negative always seemed to be happening. I could never put my finger on it."

Perhaps the ball club cracked under the pressure of the pending ownership change, which didn't become official until midseason. New ownership, headed by majority partner Tom Werner, took over and was sorting through the wreckage just as baseball was entering another cycle of escalating player salaries and protracted labor problems that exploded in 1994 with the most devastating strike in baseball history. McKeon had finally played out the string. With the team sagging at the All-Star break, he voluntarily gave up his job as manager to Greg Riddoch and was ousted as general manager before the disappointing 75-87 fourth-place finish in the NL West, 16 games behind the eventual World Series winners, the Cincinnati Reds.

Joe McIlvane came over from the Mets to replace McKeon as general manager, and in his first major move he traded Carter to the Toronto Blue Jays along with Roberto Alomar for Fred McGriff and Tony Fernandez.

Carter was devastated. He was attending a players association meeting in Florida and was playing a round of golf when he heard the news inadvertently from a caddie.

"I had just built a house in San Diego and had moved my family there from Kansas City," said Carter. "The caddie asked me if I had heard about the big trade—Joe Carter was traded to the Blue Jays. Then he realized who I was. I thought, 'You've got to be kidding. This is a mistake.'"

It was no mistake. Carter ran into union director Don Fehr, who confirmed the news as they headed toward the clubhouse. "Obviously the trade to the Blue Jays turned out to be a blessing in disguise," Carter said.

The trade would ultimately prove to be ruinous for the Phillies. Carter would get the best of Mitch Williams in the 1993 World Series. At this juncture in Bowa's career, it seemed that though the Padres once giveth, they continued to taketh away.

Bowa and Fregosi, meanwhile, had their little imbroglios. Both were and still are strong-willed men with combative personalities.

"I have a whole bunch of stories, most of them you can't print when they're concerning Larry," said Fregosi, who's now a consultant and scout in the Braves organization. "Without being specific, let's put it this way, I had more meetings with him than I did with the players."

Again it was about Bowa wearing his emotions so openly, a reaction that would continue to stalk him from job to job and city to city throughout his post-playing career.

"I get into a bad habit. If a guy swings and misses or swings at a bad pitch, I'd drop my head," Bowa said. "Jimmy would call me in and tell me that the players were getting pissed because I was doing that. It was just a habit I got into. I used to do that a lot. Really, I didn't mean anything by it."

Under Fregosi, though, Bowa really began to see the error of his ways when he managed the Padres.

"I think the one thing I learned is that if a player is really aggravating the shit out of you or not doing what they're supposed to do, let the coach handle it. Let him be the asshole first," Bowa said. "In San Diego, if I saw something, I would step in and do it. I thought, 'Hey, you're the manager; it's your responsibility.' But I discovered that when you hire coaches, like the Phillies hired me, you hire them because you believe in them. They're good baseball people. You've got to let them do their job. I liked being trusted to do my job."

In the front office, Thomas continued to wheel and deal, acquiring the component parts of the 1993 team. After the 1991 season, Giles and Thomas admitted what Phillies fans had discovered long ago. Not only was Von Hayes not the answer, he wasn't even the question. Acquired before the 1983 season from the Cleveland Indians for five players, Hayes had 351 at-bats for the Phillies team that lost to the Orioles in the 1983 World Series, but in his subsequent eight years in Philadelphia, he never hit more than 26 homers or 98 RBIs in a single season. In 1991, he spent most of the year on the disabled list, had no homers, batted in 21 runs and hit .225. At the end of the season, he was traded to the Angels for infielder Ruben Amaro, Jr. and pitcher Kyle Abbott.

And just before the 1992 season opened, Thomas traded pitcher Jason Grimsley to Houston for right-hander Curt Schilling, the anchor the Phillies needed for their starting rotation. With a few notable exceptions—Milt Thompson, Danny Jackson, Pete Incaviglia and Jim Eisenreich—the team that would win the pennant in 1993 was already assembled. But it was a big flop in 1992, falling back into last place with a 70-92 record. In the nine seasons since they last appeared in the playoffs, their record was 679-777 and the Phillies were a .466 team.

"In 1992 we basically had the same players we did in 1993," Giles said. "But in 1992 we had a lot of guys get hurt. In 1993 people stayed healthy."

It would have been easy for Giles and Thomas to change managers again. After all, teams with much better records and equal expectations were doing it elsewhere. But they kept Fregosi to guide a team heading into 1993 with no expectations.

"We were picked for dead last," Fregosi said. "But it was the only year we had this club together that they stayed healthy. The guys on that team loved to play, and they loved the game. They stayed at the ballpark late and came early. They were really baseball junkies."

That team, with only three homegrown players in the lineup—catcher Darren Daulton, second baseman Mickey Morandini and rookie Kevin Stocker at shortstop—jelled from the first day of the season. The Phillies fell to second place after the fourth game, hopped back into first place the next day, and never dropped out of the lead again. April 9 constituted the only day the Phillies weren't in first place in the NL East. Call it a fortuitous journey. The Phillies finished 97-65, three games in front of the Montreal Expos. Meanwhile, in the West, the Atlanta Braves went to the wire to defeat the San Francisco Giants by one game on the final day of the season. The Braves, who won 104 games, would have won the East handily that year. The Giants, with 103 wins, didn't make the play-offs. The Braves shifted to the East in 1994 when the leagues each split into three divisions and wild-card berths were added. They haven't lost an NL East title in a non-strike season ever since.

The five Phillies starters, led by Schilling and Tommy Greene with 16 wins each, all had at least 10 victories. And Mitch Williams had the best year by far of his career and saved 43 games.

"It was a team that was definitely old school," Bowa said. "The players policed themselves. The big difference between guys playing now and then is that in those days, teammates would jump on each other. If you didn't run out a ball, the coach didn't have to say any-thing to those guys. Veteran players would. There were older guys, like Dykstra and Kruk, getting toward the end of their careers, and they were giving it one last run. They were a hell of a lot of fun to be around. They really were. We caught lightning in a bottle early. We got out of the gate fast and then just maintained."

Giles echoed Bowa's sentiment: "It was an unusual year. It was a lot more fun for me than 1980 because I had a lot more to do with the personnel on field. The cast of characters that we had were people I really got along well with. It was a heck of a lot of fun. It's too bad the strike hit in 1994, because we might have done it again."

No one gave the Phillies, though, much of a chance to defeat the powerful Braves in the National League Championship Series. After a decade of futility, cable mogul Ted Turner had finally found the right management combination in general manager John Schuerholz and manager Bobby Cox. Much like the Phillies, the Braves had won a division title under Joe Torre in 1982 but then floundered for the next eight seasons as the team built around Bob Horner and Dale Murphy began to age. Four times from 1986 to 1990, the Braves finished in last place. But that's where any comparison to the Phillies ends. With a strong, young starting pitching staff in Tom Glavine, John Smoltz and Steve Avery, they went from worst to first in 1991 and have continued a winning tradition with a record 12 consecutive division titles.

The Braves team that met the Phillies in the 1993 playoffs had been to the World Series the past two seasons, losing to the Minnesota Twins in 1991 in an enthralling seven games and to the Blue Jays in six games in 1992 on the vagabond Dave Winfield's two-run double during the 11th inning of Game 6. But the Phillies shocked the baseball world by beating the Braves in six games. The big blow of the series came in Game 5 and belonged to Dykstra, whose 10th-inning homer off Braves reliever Mark Wohlers in Atlanta gave the Phillies the game 4-3 and ultimately the series. Dykstra was to carry this kind of production into the World Series, as he had done with the Mets in 1986, blasting six big homers for the Phillies in both the playoffs and the World Series.

"We got on really quite an emotional roll," Giles said. "Beating the Braves in the playoffs was a big surprise to many people. The Braves had better talent, but we beat them."

And that emotional roll continued into the World Series against the Blue Jays, who were built to kill by general manager Pat Gillick. In 1992, they had borrowed Hall of Famer Dave Winfield as a one-season free agent and won the World Series. In 1993 it was Paul Molitor, who would win the World Series MVP and stay for three seasons. Joe Carter had blossomed as a five-time American League All-Star and had torn up the circuit in the three years since being traded by the Padres. The team was averaging four million fans a year in the new state-of-the-art SkyDome with its retractable roof and triptych video screen. The Blue Jays had won 95 games in 1993, taking the AL East easily by seven games over the New York Yankees. Add Rickey Henderson, Al Leiter, Todd Stottlemyre and Dave Stewart, and, well, the odds again were not with the Phillies.

In Game 1 on October 16, in the Skydome, Schilling didn't have it, giving up seven runs in six and one third innings. The Phillies blew leads of 2-0, 3-2 and 4-3 before the Blue Jays scored five times to win the game 8-5. In Game 2, the glowering Stewart, who had won three pennants and the 1989 World Series as the ace of the Oakland A's, didn't have it. Jim Eisenreich hit a three-run homer, and Dykstra hit his first of four homers in the series. Mitch Williams earned the save. The Phillies won the game 6-4, taking the series back to Philadelphia for three games with an even split.

Take note that up to that point in the postseason, Williams had had a hand in all five Phillies wins with two victories and three saves. But in the end, no one would remember that contribution.

"People in Philadelphia wanted to know why we went so much with Mitch," Bowa said. "Mitch got us there. It was a no-brainer. Mitch was our closer. If Mitch wasn't on our team, we never get to the playoffs."

In Game 3 at the Vet, the Blue Jays pummeled the Phillies, 10-3. Because the designated hitter is not utilized in National League parks during the World Series, Toronto manager Cito Gaston had to decide whom to play at first base. He opted for Molitor over John Olerud, and Molitor went three for four with a homer and three runs batted in.

But Game 4 would be one for the archives. The Phillies had a 14-9 lead heading into the eighth inning in a game that set World Series records at the time for length (four hours, 14 minutes), total runs (29) and most runs by a losing team (14). There were also 31 hits and 14 walks. In this game, Gaston played Molitor at third base and Olerud at first. The middle of the lineup had Carter, Olerud and Molitor hitting behind Roberto Alomar. The Blue Jays would explode for six runs in the eighth to win, three of them off Mitch Williams, who came in but couldn't stop the bleeding after Carter singled, Olerud walked and Molitor doubled. The Blue Jays won 15-14; Williams took the loss.

With the Blues Jays leading 3-1 in the series, the stage was all set for the Phillies to go easily and quietly. But Schilling wouldn't hear of it. He threw a five-hit complete-game 2-0 shutout in Game 5, walking three and striking out six.

Sages craft eloquent odes about the heartache sustained each year by Red Sox and Cubs fans, but the Phillies' faithful suffer no less angst. The Phillies never seem to travel the path of least resistance. The ghosts of 1964 had been revived, and it appeared that all hope would be shattered at the last possible instance.

The series shifted back to Toronto for Game 6 on October 23, and the Blue Jays jumped off to a 3-0 lead in the first inning off Terry Mulholland and were ahead 5-1 going into the seventh. But the Phillies scored five runs in the seventh off the usually impregnable Stewart. Stocker walked, Morandini singled and Dykstra hit a three-run homer. The Phillies carried a 6-5 lead into the bottom of the ninth inning with Mitch Williams back on the mound.

"I thought for sure in Game 6 when we went ahead late in the game, we were going to win the whole thing," Giles said. "But we didn't. Mitch threw that pitch."

Henderson opened with a walk and sat tight on first base when Devon White flew out to left field. Molitor, who hit .500 in the series (12 for 24 with two homers and eight RBIs) singled to center, Henderson stopping at second.

That brought up Carter, who just relished these big-game situations.

"I came to the ballpark every day, and I always wanted to be the player with the game on this line," Carter said. "I was like [the NBA's] Michael Jordan in that way. He always wanted to take the last shot. Win or lose, just give me the ball. That was the same thing for me."

Carter worked the count to two and two and was sitting on a Mitch breaking pitch because one had just fooled him earlier in the count. Mitch, trying to keep the runners from moving, took a short slide step toward home plate rather than his usual kick forward.

"People say Mitch threw a bad pitch, but he didn't," Carter said. "He came back with a fastball, and I was way out in front of it. If I had been sitting on a fastball, I would've fouled it over the dugout. I just reacted. You see the ball and hit it."

Fregosi, who has watched the replay a thousand times, doesn't agree.

"I've looked at the tape a number of times. I don't think it was a good pitch to Joe," Fregosi said. "It might have been a good pitch to somebody else, but not to him."

Bowa watched the events unfold from the dugout.

"Mitch did a slide step that he hadn't done all year, and I still don't know why he did that," Bowa said. "When you do a slide step, it takes something off your velocity. Mitch threw a lot harder than that. Obviously, though, when it goes out of the park, it's a horseshit pitch."

And that's what it did. Carter's shot soared out over the left field fence for a three-run homer and an 8-6 Toronto victory, ending the World Series for only the second time in history on a walk-off homer.

The Blue Jays and their fans erupted with sheer ecstasy.

"When I hit it at first, I wasn't sure it was out," said Carter. "And I never did see it go. All I saw was the flash cameras popping and suddenly the place was bedlam. The only thing I can remember thinking at the time was to make sure I just touched every base. I was ecstatic—like a kid in a candy store. To this day I watch the video in wonderment. Like, yeah, that really did happen."

The Phillies left Canada in despair.

"After Joe Carter hit that home run, I was in shock for about 12 hours," Giles said. "I couldn't believe it. I watched the replay over and over again the next day. Mitch Williams put a two-and-two pitch in the wrong spot. It was kind of devastating."

Mitch Williams would never throw another pitch for the Phillies. He was so vilified by the fans in Philadelphia that for his own good, Thomas and Giles traded him to Houston less than two months later. Williams unfairly took it on the chin for the Phillies' loss, Bowa thought.

"Everyone remembers the last thing that happened," Bowa said. "No one remembers us popping up with the bases loaded. They don't remember us blowing that game in Philly with a huge lead. They talk about Mitch giving up a home run. To me it's unfair, but that's the way the public perceived it. It was tough around Philly for a while. He had to fly home on a different plane. He got death threats. The thing about Mitch, he was up front. He took it like a man. Again, without Mitch we don't even get to the playoffs and World Series."

Mitch would throw only 27 1/3 innings over the next three seasons for Houston and California. He'd have six more saves. By 1997, at 33 years old, his career was over. In 1998, Carter finished his career with Baltimore and San Francisco. The two didn't face each other again in a game.

After the two retired, Carter was invited to Mitch's bowling alley outside of Philly for a made-for-TV production. Carter, a skilled bowler, smoked Mitch again.

Neither the Blue Jays nor the Phillies have been back to the World Series.

14

EXILED FROM PHILLY, AGAIN

L arry Bowa's chapter as a third base coach in Philadelphia would ultimately come to an end after a little more than eight years. It would take the firing of Jim Fregosi, but Bowa and the Phillies would have to endure a few more indignities before it happened.

It was a shame. Bowa had thrived under Fregosi.

"When I was with Jimmy, he let me do what I wanted to do," Bowa said. "If I wanted to jump on a guy, he didn't give a damn. If I saw a guy slacking off on a ground ball, I'd go up to him and say, 'Let's go, man. Get it in gear.' He wanted me to do that. If it was in my area, if one of my infielders was late, I'd say, 'What the hell is going on here? Let's go. I don't want this to happen again.' If it did happen again, then I'd go back to Jimmy and tell him that the guy wasn't listening to me. You better bring him in."

The national baseball scene would play no small part in the changes confronting the Phillies both on and off the field.

As fate would have it, for the second time in their long history, an in-season strike would derail the Phillies again after a pennant-winning season. It had happened in 1981 a year after the Phillies had won their only World Series title, and it happened again in 1994. Only this time, when the players went out after the August 11 games, there would be no more baseball that season. This time, there were no playoffs and no World Series, but the Phillies weren't even in the hunt. They flirted with .500 for most of the season and fell under that mark for good on July 5. On the day the season prematurely ended, they were in fourth place, 20 1/2 games behind the Montreal Expos, with a 51-64 record.

It was the darkest season in this era of baseball history, and the pitched battle between owners and the players over revenue sharing and the sport's economic system took some strange twists. This time, the owners tried to post new working conditions, meaning their last and best offer rejected by the players would become the new Basic Agreement. The owners also brought in replacement players to spring training. The tactics backfired. The union hierarchy proved that enough back-channel negotiations had taken place. A federal judge ruled that the owners could not post conditions and the strike was over. By that time, many fans had lost patience and interest. They couldn't have been angrier.

Any threat to open the 1995 season with replacement players faded. The regulars returned 23 days late on April 26, albeit to hostility from the populace across North America never seen before in the annals of the sport.

The hostility was reflected in attendance around the league, especially in Canada. In Montreal, the Expos never recovered. And in Toronto, attendance has never equaled the four million fans who had flocked to the Skydome each season before the strike. In 1993, the Phillies drew more than three million fans to the Vet for the first time in franchise history—3,137,674 to be precise. But by Fregosi's last season of 1996, the fans were so fed up by the labor problems and the Phillies' return to their losing ways that home attendance had dwindled to 1.8 million and would continue to slide.

That rough-and-tumble Phillies group that succumbed in the World Series on Joe Carter's home run scattered to the wind. Len Dykstra played through the 1996 season and then retired. John Kruk suffered from testicular cancer and left the team as a free agent, signing with the White Sox in May 1995. Kruk had 159 at-bats in Chicago that season and, on the occasion of smacking his 1,170th career hit, walked off the field and never looked back. At 34, he finished with a .300 lifetime batting average. Pete Incaviglia was traded to Baltimore near the end of the 1996 season. Milt Thompson was traded to Houston just before the strike. Jim Eisenreich lasted through 1996, when he signed as a free agent with the Florida Marlins. Darren Daulton was traded to the Marlins, Mickey Morandini was shipped to the Cubs, and Kevin Stocker was swapped to Tampa Bay, all at various points in 1997.

It was a hell of a sendoff for the one-year wonders, but Giles and Thomas kept the revolving door spinning.

At the same time, Philly's sports arena and stadium scene, which had been static for 25 years since the opening of the Vet, began changing. The name of the game was now generating revenue, and lots of it. The current buildings were considered outmoded, without the requisite number of suites to sell the corporate community and club season seats to sell to well-heeled fans.

A spate of new baseball stadiums across North America had left the have-nots panting. The first wave of new ballparks in Toronto, Chicago, Baltimore, Cleveland and Denver led, for the most part, to financial, artistic and on-field success. It was a phenomenon that every major league club wanted to match. The question was how to pay for the construction. The best deal was utilizing public dollars to build the facility with much of the revenue streams—ticket sales, concessions and parking—turned over to the teams, giving them the ability to keep signing players to increasingly outlandish contracts. Over time, as the economy began to soften and taxpayers lost the stomach to finance such endeavors, private facility ownership or at least an investment from the particular club owner became a necessary part of the package.

In Pennsylvania the state legislature was kind enough to set aside funds to build new football and baseball stadiums in both Pittsburgh and Philadelphia. The Vet and Pittsburgh's Three Rivers Stadium were almost identical: enclosed circular concrete multipurpose stadiums that opened at virtually the same time in the early 1970s and had already become outdated. To make their new $350 million stadium a reality, the Phillies would have to substantiate the state funds with city and private money. They would also have to partner with the city administration and determine where it was best to build the new ballpark—downtown in Center City or in South Philly on land adjacent to the Vet.

Bill Giles, the club president, would be a significant factor in piecing all that together.

After the strike-delayed 1995 season finally opened, the Phillies jumped off to a 19-6 start and maintained first place in the National League East until the Braves tied them on July 4. From there, it was a long, steady decline. Fourteen players were sent to the disabled list 19 times, and the Braves, as they are wont to do, ran away with the division. The 69-75 Phillies finished in a second-place tie with the Mets and 21 games out.

The Phillies hosted the All-Star Game for the second time at the Vet in 1996. Season tickets were linked to the guarantee of All-Star tickets, keeping attendance artificially high. But the season was an unmitigated disaster. The Phillies were a season-best four games over .500 at 16-12 on May 4 but collapsed to 17 1/2 games out and in fifth place by the break.

Ricky Bottalico, the Phillies' ace reliever at that juncture, was their only representative in the All-Star Game they hosted. He pitched one inning of scoreless ball for the National League and wowed the 62,670 in attendance by registering pitches thrown faster than 100 miles per hour on the auxiliary scoreboard. How the mighty had fallen. The season ended with the Phillies at 67-95 and in fifth place, 29 games behind the Braves.

For Fregosi, it was all over except the bloodletting, and Bowa wasn't far behind him. In Fregosi's six years as manager, the Phillies had enjoyed one winning season and surprised everyone by going to the World Series. In the other five seasons they were 64 games under .500.

Thomas at least did afford Bowa an interview for the vacant position this time, but the job went to Terry Francona, a former major league player and son of Tito Francona, another former major league player. Francona, with only four years of lower minor league managing experience, had one claim to fame: He managed Michael Jordan at Class AA Birmingham in 1993 during the basketball star's shot at attempting a baseball career.

And when Jordan called Thomas personally to recommend Francona, the job was sealed, much to Bowa's chagrin.

"I thought I had good interviews. Lee told me that I had been the best third base coach he had ever seen," Bowa recalled. "But with Francona, Michael Jordan called Lee Thomas during the process. Jordan just gave him the highest accolades you can give a guy. I'm sitting there figuring, man, what chance do I have when the guy I'm going against just got recommended by the greatest basketball player to ever put on shoes? Terry's a good baseball guy, but to this day I'm sure it had some influence on the decision."

There was another factor as well. After the Fregosi years, the Phillies weren't ready for another rough-and-tumble manager. In baseball usually a tough manager, one who has burned out the players, is followed by a feline, who coddles and strokes. In San Diego, the intellectual Steve Boros followed the tough Dick Williams. The nerve-wracking Bowa was next after Boros. The calming influence of McKeon was an elixir after Bowa. In Philly, Leyva was the young, silent manager followed by Fregosi, the cantankerous father figure. Bowa was out of sequence.

"We were a young ball club in 1997, and we asked Terry to be a nurturing manager," said Montgomery, who was by now co-general partner with Giles and in the process of taking over the club. "If you look at our managerial selections, Larry wasn't the right fit. You wouldn't even necessarily have considered Bo because of the makeup of his personality. I really think that wasn't the right time for Larry to take over."

Passed over again, Bowa wasn't ready for the next jab. Thomas didn't even want Bowa back to coach third base under the 37-year-old Francona. Instead, Bowa was offered a chance to manage again in the minor leagues for either the Phillies' Triple A club in Scranton, Pennsylvania, or at nearby Double A Reading. John Vukovich, who has survived every Phillies purge since he rejoined the organization in 1988, was moved over to coach third base.

"I interviewed twice," Bowa said about that particular shot at managing the Phillies. "Then they finally called me in and said they were going to go in another direction. I figured I was still going to be the third base coach. When I mentioned that to Lee, he said, 'We talked about that. We don't think it would be good for Terry for you to be coaching third. You're popular here. But we might have something in the minor leagues.

"I couldn't believe it. I went home. I didn't mind so much not getting the managing job, but now I was losing my third base job? Looking back on it, it had nothing to do with Francona. Lee just thought it would be easier for him to do the job without me breathing down his neck. He didn't need to take all that heat. I didn't understand it back then, but in hindsight I can see it."

Bowa told Thomas he needed a day to make the decision. But when he called back the next morning to take the Triple A job, Bowa was given another wrenching blow to the gut.

"He said they already gave that away," Bowa said. "It was less than 24 hours. They said I could have the Reading job if I wanted it. I didn't mind going back to the minor leagues to manage. Maybe that was just what I needed. But I didn't want to go all the way down to Double A. So I hit the phones."

One of his first calls was to Terry Collins, who had just been fired as manager of the Houston Astros. Collins had survived a lengthy, complex interview process among a number of candidates and was taking over the Angels. Collins, whom Bowa met in 1986 when both men were managing in the Pacific Coast League, was in the middle of putting together his staff. The two had developed a friendship back then and kept it going when Collins was managing the Astros and Bowa was a coach for the Phillies.

"I told him I'd certainly think about it," said Collins, now the minor league field coordinator in the Dodgers' organization. "About two days later I called Jim Leyland [then manager of the Florida Marlins] about something else, and Jim asked me if I had hired all my coaches. When I told him no, he said, 'You ought to hire Larry Bowa. He's a great baseball man, and I think he's as good a third base coach as there is in the National League.'"

It was around January 1 before Bowa heard back from Collins, and he went out to California for an interview that also included Angels general manager Bill Bavasi. Bowa was offered the job.

"In the end I figured I could use a guy with his stature and his background," Collins said.

Collins replaced the fatherly Marcel Lachemann, who asked out with 50 games to go in the Angels' 91-loss 1996 season, the first under ownership of the Disney company after buying it from Gene Autry. In Anaheim, the Angels were going through many of the growing pains Bowa had experienced in 1981 when the Phillies were transferred from the hands of Ruly Carpenter to Bill Giles and his group of corporate owners.

After purchasing the Angels, Disney had gutted much of the team's business and marketing operations, combining them with similar departments run by their NHL team, the Anaheim Mighty Ducks. Tony Tavares, the Ducks' tough president, was also put in charge of the Angels. It was a move that had become commonplace in other cities, like Dallas and Atlanta, where the same corporation owned multiple sports teams in the same area.

Tavares and Bavasi had perceived a lack of toughness in Lachemann's managerial style as the 1996 season wasted away. This failure came fast on the heels of the 1995 debacle when the Angels blew a big September lead in the division race to Seattle and lost the American League West in a one-game playoff to the Mariners.

"Lach was very much a players' guy," said Tavares, who is now president of the Expos. "There was an atmosphere around the Angels where failure was tolerated. Billy felt that way as well, that we had just fell into an acceptance of losses. People talking about curses. We felt we needed to toughen things up."

Tavares liked Collins, who had managed the Astros to three better-than-.500 seasons before his hard-nosed approach wore thin on the players. Tavares wanted more drive and discipline. Collins was hired to deliver it. What better person than Bowa to back him up?

"Billy went out and got Terry and put together a more demanding staff than had existed in the past," Tavares recalled. "Certainly Larry was a big part of that. As you know, he doesn't take many prisoners."

And so for the second time in his career, Bowa left the Phillies organization. Anaheim is just 90 miles north up Interstate 5 from San Diego, but it may as well be in a different world. It isn't a city as much as it is a suburban sprawl with two centers—dueling Disney amusement parks and a sports complex with a baseball stadium on the west side of Route 57 and an indoor arena on the east side.

Renamed the Anaheim Angels, their opening day lineup in 1997 already had some of the key elements of the team what would go on to win the 2002 World Series—Darin Erstad, Tim Salmon and Garrett Anderson. Dave Hollins, who played on the 1993 Phillies team that won the National League pennant, was the third baseman. Troy Glaus, who would later be named MVP of the 2002 World Series, was on the bench.

Bowa worked tirelessly with the young infielders to try to turn them into exciting players.

"Larry worked endlessly with Erstad after we converted him from an outfielder into a first baseman," Collins said. "He spent a lot of time with Glaus. He took Troy over to the instructional league and spent two weeks with him alone and just worked him out. We knew that eventually Glaus was going to be our third baseman. I can just remember Larry hitting a thousand ground balls to this guy a day."

Elsewhere in baseball that season, Jack McKeon resurfaced as a manager, taking over a downtrodden Cincinnati Reds team with 63 games to go in the season and leading them to a 33-30 record. He would manage the Reds through 2000, finishing with consecutive second-place finishes and a loss to the Mets in the 1999 one-game playoff for the National League's wild-card berth. Like his 1988 experience in relief of Bowa with the Padres, McKeon had earned the same accolade: He was the elixir for getting the most out of young players, thus jump-starting the team in the process.

The Phillies, meanwhile, would continue to struggle and lose 94 games again under Francona. And on December 9, 1997, Lee Thomas was fired, replaced by Ed Wade, who is still the general manager. Wade would become a major force in the organization and would attempt to bring Bowa back to Philly.

In Anaheim, the Angels responded to the aggressive approach of Collins, Bowa and the rest of the staff. The first two seasons produced second-place finishes and 84 and 85 wins, respectively. In 1998, Collins was suspended for eight games after a succession of bench-clearing incidents on June 2 in Kansas City. The Angels finished only three games behind Texas, who won the AL West.

Thus far, Collins and Bowa had gotten the most out of some players and alienated several others. As Tavares said, they were taking no prisoners.

"Just like everyone else in life, Larry has his faults," Tavares said. "And I put a big question mark next to this fault because I would probably be the same way. He expects people to play the game the way that he did—hard-nosed, play every game, every pitch to win. Bottom line: That can get to today's players. The old guys were warriors. You left it all out on the field. If you came in and lost, you knew everything was left out there.

"There were times when I thought Larry Bowa and Jim Edmonds were going to come to blows. What Larry saw in Jim Edmonds was a guy who has immense amounts of talent, but periodically would take at-bats off and appear that he wasn't trying as hard as he could. Larry really believed that Jimmy could be one of the best players in the game if he didn't have those mental lapses. So Larry was all over him. And that was a good thing. You had to understand the motivation. Larry wasn't doing it to help Larry; Larry was doing it to help Jimmy."

But in 1999, the words began falling on deaf ears. During that off season, the Angels signed the overweight and recalcitrant former Red Sox first baseman Mo Vaughn to a huge free agent contract that paid him $61 million over five seasons. Vaughn was supposed to give the Angels' offense the pop they needed to put them over the top. It didn't happen. Vaughn hurt his left foot on opening night after falling into the dugout while trying to catch a foul pop and was placed on the 15-day disabled list.

Vaughn, hobbled all season, still hit .281 with 33 homers and 108 runs batted in, but the clubhouse came apart around him.

By the end of May, the Angels were 25-27, and although in last place in the AL West, they were still only six and a half games out. Several players petitioned Tavares for Collins's ousting, but instead the manager received a vote of confidence and a contract extension.

"Then he lost the club," Tavares said. "While Larry can be animated and challenging, Terry would get upset at plays being made in the field and couldn't control his emotion on the bench. He'd groan when something happened in the field. Some players thought it was a personal attack. I don't believe it ever was. I always thought he had the best of intentions—to win at all costs."

It's all perception, of course. The same charge that has been made against Bowa throughout his managing and coaching career was now directed dead on at Collins: that the players thought he was too emotional, that the roll of the eyes, the inopportune curse, the turning of the back was detrimental to the team.

"If you gave them some constructive criticism, they'd say, 'To hell with him, why is he mad at me?'" Bowa said.

The managing greats, John McGraw, Miller Huggins, Gil Hodges and Casey Stengel, must be turning over in their graves.

Tavares, who now has the sometimes demanding Hall of Famer Frank Robinson as his manager in Montreal, knows that none of them would have been capable of coddling the modern player.

"Larry and Frank get away with more of it because of the careers they had at the major league level," Tavares said. "Terry struggled because he didn't have a great major league career. So you're starting at a deficit when you're trying to manage today's major-leaguers, especially if you're being a hard-ass."

Collins didn't have a major league career. In 12 minor league seasons he never broke through the Triple A level.

The clubhouse became a feeding frenzy. By September 1 with the Angels on a road trip through Boston and Cleveland, they had fallen 30 games under .500 and were on a nine-game losing streak.

"We were in Cleveland, and Mo Vaughn and Troy Percival got into it in the clubhouse, pointing fingers," Bowa said. "They had to be separated. It was like a zoo."

"The fight between Mo and Percy, that was just frustrations boiling over," Tavares said.

But the argument between the team's top hitter and best relief pitcher finally was a good enough reason to make a change. A few days later, Collins was fired, by general manager Bill Bavasi, saying tearfully at the time: "I tried everything I could think of to get them going. I decided that if I'm the reason they haven't, then I'm out of here."

Years later, Collins said he knew it was time to go.

"Some things happened, and I needed some big-time support and I didn't get it," Collins said. "My authority had been questioned, and I was criticized by the players. In fact, Larry stood up and told me I had to go right back at them. I said, 'No, that's not the way I'm going to do it.' It was just time for me to go. I figured I'd done my thing. We had finished second for two straight seasons, and when we got Mo, everyone said we were going to win it, but there were so many injuries—we didn't have enough."

Tavares said he thought Collins was given plenty of support.

"I'm surprised. I think Billy always supported Terry in a big way," Tavares said. "I have a lot of respect for Terry. I think he did a really good job for us. But when you cut to the chase, when a manager loses his players, and that's indeed what happened, the judgment was made at that point that it was time to move on."

With Collins gone, it left Bowa without a bridge going into the 2000 season. In Philadelphia, Francona was heading into his fourth year as manager, but during his three seasons, the Phillies hadn't approached .500. It was one of those classic Phillie downward spirals. The Phillies hadn't had a winning season since the 1993 World Series. He would have one last season to turn the Phillies around.

In Anaheim, bigger changes were to come. Tavares told Bavasi that he wanted to internally gut baseball operations, which had essentially gone unchanged during the era when Autry ran the team. Bill Bavasi is the son of Buzzie Bavasi, who ended his legendary career as vice president and general manager of the Angels.

"Our scouting staff was antiquated, arcane in many ways," Tavares said about the Angels. "We just felt there needed to be significant changes. Billy, to his credit, grew up with these guys. A lot of these people were friends of Buzzie. Billy knew them when he was a kid breaking into the industry. I remember vividly him telling me that he knew it needed to be done. 'I'm just not going to be the guy to do it. I've got too much loyalty to these people. At the end of the day, I'm going to resign.'

"There are not many guys who would do what Billy Bavasi did, to give up a job on a principle. I have nothing but respect for Bill."

With the general manager and the manager gone, there was no guarantee that Bowa would have a job in Anaheim for the 2000 season. Indeed, Tavares hired as general manager Bill Stoneman, the former Expos pitcher who had given up the first hit at Veterans Stadium in 1971—a single by Larry Bowa. Stoneman hired former Dodgers coach and player Mike Scioscia. Under those two men, the staff turned over dramatically.

"Tavares said he'd like to have [the coaches] back, but 'I'm going give the manager his options,'" Bowa said. "You should go out and talk to other people. If we can take you back, we'll take you back.'"

And Bowa looked elsewhere, to the Pacific Northwest, where Seattle manager Lou Piniella had an opening.

The Mariners, long the doormat of the American League, had climbed to respectability under Piniella, who won World Series titles in 1977 and 1978 playing for the New York Yankees and in 1990 managing the Cincinnati Reds. He had six years of big-league experience managing the Yankees and Reds before he took over the moribund Mariners in 1993.

Under Piniella, the Mariners went to the playoffs in 1995 and 1997, playing in the Kingdome, a cement fortress south of downtown Seattle. But in midseason 1999, they moved into a new retractable roof ballpark, Safeco Field, and were under control of Japanese ownership; they had become another fine example of a once poor small-market team turned into a rich big-market franchise.

Even so, the Mariners had recently shed some high-priced talent. Late in the 1998 season, they traded their top pitcher, Randy Johnson, to Houston rather than lose him that off season to free agency. After the 1999 season, they parted ways with superstar center fielder Ken Griffey Jr., trading him to Cincinnati.

Even so, for once Bowa might possibly have been moving into a decent situation. The team had finished 1999 four games under .500 (79-83) and in third place, 16 games behind American League West-winning Texas; they still had shortstop Alex Rodriguez, one of the top talents in the game, at least for one more season, before he could file for free agency. General manager Pat Gillick had built the 1992 and 1993 Toronto Blue Jays into World Series champions and a team around Cal Ripken Jr. in Baltimore when the Orioles went to the American League Championship Series in 1996 and 1997.

"I had already spoken to Lou near the end of the year," Bowa said. "It was all over the papers that Terry had been fired, and there was a good probability none of the coaches would be coming back. So I told Lou, 'If I ever got an opportunity, I'd like to coach for you.' I remember him asking me what I was doing the next year. I told him I didn't know. So he said to give him a call after the season was over."

A meeting was set up between Bowa, Piniella and Gillick when it became evident that the Angels were going through wholesale changes.

"We talked to him at length and then recognized very quickly that he was an outstanding baseball guy with a good baseball mind," said Piniella. "He had some spunk about him and loved to win. He recognizably did a real nice job as third base coach for the Angels. So we signed him. It turned out to be a real nice move for us."

The comparisons between Piniella and Bowa are myriad. Both had enough innate desire and moxie to go well beyond limited talent and build fine playing careers. Both have combustible personalities and tempers. As managers, they can get thrown out of the game with the best of them—tossing bases while spitting venom at unwavering umpires.

Piniella, in fact, said his biggest problem with Bowa was putting a curb on his, uh, enthusiasm.

"Larry is hyper," Piniella said. "A lot of times we had to tell him, 'Hey, Pee Wee, just sit down on the bench and watch the ballgame. Everything's OK.' He enjoyed chirping at the umpires. But we didn't need the umpires against us. I could take care of that myself."

If Bowa learned anything from Piniella that changed his attitude as a manager, it was to delegate authority to his coaches. Bowa admits now that wanting to control every facet of the game was probably one of his fatal flaws when he managed the Padres. But after having the freedom to do his own job under Fregosi, Collins and now Piniella, Bowa realized irrevocably that he would act that way if he ever again earned a chance to manage.

"In San Diego I tried to do everything," Bowa said. "I wanted to be the hitting coach, pitching coach, infield coach, outfield coach, the base running coach. You can't do that. Physically, you just can't do it. And you shouldn't do it."

The season in Seattle went well. The Mariners and Oakland A's were involved in a scorcher of a pennant race in the AL West that came down to the final weekend of the season. The A's swept a three-game series at home against Texas, and the Mariners won two of their final three at Anaheim. The A's finished first, and the Mariners won the American League's wild-card berth.

Bowa was going back into the playoffs for the first time since 1993, but 3,000 miles away events were unfolding that would have a profound effect on his life. The Phillies had finished fifth again, this time with a 68-94 record, worse than the final year of Fregosi. And this time Francona was fired. His four-year record in Philadelphia was 285-363, a .440 percentage.

"We started down that slope of losing in 1999, and there was no stopping it," Wade said. "So every time Terry stuck his head outside of the dugout, he got hammered by our fans. That was the atmosphere. We had committed in 1996 and 1997 to getting the farm system straightened out. We need to proceed slowly. So there were a lot of elements in place where succeeding was going to be difficult for Terry."

It was the season when Curt Schilling forced his trade from the Phillies to the Arizona Diamondbacks and reliever Mike Jackson, after signing as a free agent, actually hurt his arm warming up and never pitched an inning for the Phillies.

"The season was a disaster," Montgomery said. "It left us no choice but to make a managerial change. I distinctly remember Ed and I talking about whether Larry should be a candidate. We agreed completely on that."

Ed Wade, who began his career as an intern in the Phillies' public relations department in 1977, was waiting. And the door to Bowa's return was slowly opening.

15

YOU CAN
GO HOME AGAIN

The 2000 American League Championship Series between the Mariners and Yankees was about to begin when the rumors started floating that Bowa was going to be hired to manage the Phillies. Sitting in the visitor's dugout at Yankee Stadium before Game 1 of a series the Mariners lost in six games, Bowa traded quips with a group of Philadelphia scribes who had made the trip to New York specifically to see him. Bowa discounted the rumors, particularly while his team was still alive in the playoffs, but as he said, "Where there's smoke, there's usually some fire."

"When the Philadelphia job came open, I talked to the media in his behalf," said Lou Piniella, the Mariners' manager, who chatted up Bowa's candidacy all through the series. "I told them that he was ready to manage."

But the Phillies had left Bowa at the altar a few times before. During his tenure in Philadelphia as third base coach, there had been three managerial changes, all coming under the auspices of deposed general manager Lee Thomas. He was given short shrift when Thomas hired Nick Leyva and Jim Fregosi, and he was ousted as third base coach when Thomas chose Terry Francona. Even though Ed Wade was now the general manager, Bowa had his doubts about the veracity of the rumors. He wasn't willing to be disappointed again.

The Phillies, though, had gone through the process of getting permission from the Mariners to talk to Bowa about the job. After all, it had been more than 12 years since Bowa last managed in San Diego. Twelve years of working under veteran managers, 12 years of learning from their virtues and mistakes and 12 years of mulling over his own.

"I'd been getting a lot of calls from friends in Philly saying that the heat was being put on them for me to be interviewed," said Bowa, recalling the sequence of events that occurred during the final weeks of that October. "But I figured if it did happen, it would be just a courtesy. So I called Eddie; we finally hooked up. I said, 'You and I go back a long way. I know when I played there and coached there I was popular. I know there's probably some heat on you to interview me. But let's do it this way: Let's say we interviewed. I don't want to come in for a courtesy interview. It's a waste of your time. It's a waste of my time. I'll tell people you interviewed me. You can say we had an interview over the phone. That's it. And then we'll just drop it. Move on.'"

But Wade surprised Bowa. He told him that this time the Phillies were really serious.

"We had about a 10-minute conversation where I told him this was not a cosmetic interview," Wade said. "He had made some comments out there that he wasn't going to go through an interview just so we could check him off as somebody we had talked to, that we'd never bring him back. I told him that we were interested and that we were sincere about this thing. We were going to march down the path and that if he was the right guy, he was going to get the job."

Bowa didn't miss a beat.

"I told him that if it was serious, I'd be glad to interview," he recalled. "Obviously, that would be the dream job for me."

There were several significant changes in the organization that led to a change of heart about Bowa. On June 20, 1997, Dave Montgomery replaced Bill Giles as the Phillies' president, general partner and chief executive officer. Giles, because of his past history with Bowa, had been a major impediment to Bowa being hired as manager. In December, Thomas was fired and replaced on an interim basis by Wade, who formally was given the job as general manager in March.

Giles, who became the team's chairman, would still have a significant voice in the destiny of the franchise, but he was finished with the day-to-day decisions of operating the ball club. The changes weren't merely cosmetic. They went to the core of who had financial and operational control of the team.

"The way our club works [is] it's not based on how much you own, it's based on control," Giles said. "Dave had complete control over the rest of the partners, who are limited in structure and the way we operate. Dave can pretty much do anything he wants as long as he keeps the budget in line." Giles had ceded that control.

Montgomery had been with the ball club as long as the Phillies had played in Veterans Stadium. He joined the organization six weeks before the then-new stadium opened in 1971 and hawked season tickets. Montgomery, a salesman at heart, has the cherubic rosy cheeks of a native Philadelphian. As a kid, he lived and died (mostly died) with the Phillies as they bobbled the ball around Connie Mack Stadium, scratching symbols and notations on each play in his scorebook. His ascent within the organization was meteoric. In a decade he went from ticket sales to marketing director to director of sales and by 1981 to executive vice president when the current ownership group, led by Giles, bought the club from Ruly Carpenter. Montgomery added the title of chief operating officer to his tenure in 1992, became co-general partner with Giles, taking an equity share of the team, in November 1994, and succeeded Giles three years later.

"In 1993 our partnership group reached a decision that they wanted to set up a line of succession," Montgomery said. "At that time I made a 10-year commitment. I could leave, but if I chose to stay that long, I could earn a modest piece of sweat equity in the club. Along came 1997, and I think Bill decided that the journey to the new ballpark wasn't getting any shorter. He felt, and we all agreed, that if we ever wanted to shorten that journey, we needed him to focus a good bit of his time on the project. He realized that maybe it was time to give up the day-to-day management of the team."

Wade's background was in public relations when he joined the Phillies as an intern in 1977. He moved to Houston the following off season, and by 1979 he was named the Astros' director of public relations. He jumped from there to the Pittsburgh Pirates for five years in the same capacity. After rejoining his old Astros boss Tal Smith in a private enterprise, Wade came back in 1995 to the Phillies, first as an assistant general manager and then as the big cheese himself.

It is interesting to note that the Phillies' Big Three did not cut their teeth in typical baseball operations like scouting or coaching. None of them is a former player or manager. Giles started in promotions, Montgomery in ticket sales and Wade in public relations. Their collective experience, beginning with Giles in 1969, covered more than three decades and eventually three distinct Philadelphia ballparks.

The three also had this in common: They all knew the feisty Bowa well, having been around at one time or another while Bowa played for or coached the team.

Asked why he thought there had been such a long gap before Bowa had been considered again as a manager, Wade said candidly:

"Volatility. I think Larry's volatility was an issue. People were afraid of Larry. They were afraid of taking a chance on him. During the conversations Larry and I had before the interview process, he said he thought that he had changed, that he had learned a lot under Terry Collins when he was with the Angels. That he had learned even more under Lou Piniella. How to handle situations, how to not be as openly volatile, how to rely on coaches and use them sometimes as sort of whipping boys. Take his frustrations out on the coaches at times and not on the players; that kind of thing.

"He found that Lou did a good job of venting to the coaches rather then venting to the players. I felt that somebody with his baseball knowledge, with his baseball credentials, deserved a second chance. Lots of people get second chances. In the managerial world second chances abound."

It was a brave new Phillies world that Bowa was about to step back into, similar to his entry as a player in 1970 and much different than his most recent departure as third base coach after the 1996 season when the team was on a long downward spiral.

These Phillies now had a new ballpark on the drawing board to be ready by 2004 and a plan to rebuild the team to go along with it.

"It's not like we did anything really innovative," Wade said. "We just dusted off the plan [general manager] Paul Owens used in the 1970s."

It was back to the future. The Phillies were again all about ringing out the old and bringing in the new.

And it started with a return to a natural turf, baseball-only stadium.

The NFL's Eagles would be the first to leave the Vet, moving in 2003 to a monolith of a football-only facility constructed adjacent to the new arena that had opened in 1996. The Phillies' new ballpark, Citizens Bank Park, rose in the parking lot behind the Vet with its red brick façade and stark straight lines. The new park, like most baseball-only facilities built across America in the last decade, hearkens back to the coziness of places such as Connie Mack without the beams, pillars and parking problems and with all of the high-tech amenities fans have become accustomed to in the 21st century.

"The Vet, despite all the criticism of it the last 10 years, was still a solid structure," Giles said. "Physically, the Vet could have lasted another 30 years, probably."

But now the old building was down to its last three. And the Phillies decided it might be a perfect mix to have Bowa back on the field in a significant role for the countdown. Out-of-towners, both the fans and the media, watched from the outside and wondered how Bowa had survived through all of the trials and tribulations. The fact is that the Phillies have had four players in their history who are the obvious icons. Hall of Famer Richie Ashburn, the Whiz Kid who made good, and the trio who played together on the 1980 World Series team: Hall of Famers Mike Schmidt and Steve "Lefty" Carlton, and Larry Bowa.

And Bowa is far and wide the favorite both inside and outside the organization.

"There's no question what Bowa's popularity in the city is," Wade said. "He's perceived as the Everyman in Philadelphia. He was the guy who got cut from his high school team. Everybody knew his story. Everyone saw the passion he played with on the field. Schmitty was viewed as a guy who didn't have that passion. Lefty was a great starting pitcher who was loved by the fans, but he was out there every fifth day. Bowa was there every day. He was there every day after games to talk to the media and face the music. He was there in December and January at banquets because he lived in the city.

"He's a Philly guy, the most popular Phillie, probably in our history. When you listen to the ovations and you get to Bowa, they're at least as loud or louder than anyone else's. He's the guy who the fans look at as the real symbol of what Phillies baseball was and should be."

"His passion for the game is something that our fans have always appreciated," Montgomery said. "To me, he re-energized the Phillies in the community."

With Bowa convinced that he had a shot at the job, the real hiring process started. Bowa was grilled through two rounds of nerve-wracking interviews. In the first round, Bowa went into a room with Wade, assistant general managers Mike Arbuckle and Ruben Amaro Jr., and Dallas Green, who had returned to the organization as a senior adviser to the general manager.

"They just pummeled me with questions," Bowa said. "I got through the first round, and then the second round, and then they called me up. They said, 'We're trying to wind this thing up. We want you to go meet with Dave Montgomery over at his house. So I figure if I'm going over to Dave's house, I'm down to the final two."

It turned out to be a choice between a pair of former Phillies players from the team's two most successful recent eras—Bowa, the shortstop on the 1980 World Series championship team, and Darren Daulton, the catcher for the 1993 National League pennant winners.

And for Bowa, in the end, it all hinged on his relationship with Bill Giles. Some moments in life continually haunt you, and this one had the nature of a recurring nightmare, coming back to bite Bowa in the butt again and again since it happened after the 1981 season. It was the contract dispute to end all contract disputes. The worst part of it, though, was Bowa calling the new Phillies president "a liar" in print, forcing his trade to the Cubs.

Some things one can never change, but an apology was in order, and after all these years, Bowa had yet to apologize.

"I should have apologized a lot earlier," Bowa said. "Bill is a good guy. He just had to do what he had to do. I was a player with a lot of success there, and I just got upset. But I realize now that it doesn't justify what happened—not at all."

Bowa needed to do damage control with Giles, Wade and Montgomery told him, if he wanted to get the job. Montgomery made that clear to Bowa during the meeting at the chief executive's home in Wyndmore, Pennsylvania.

"We talked about Bill, about my leaving [as a player] on bad terms," Bowa recalled. "Dave asked what my feelings were and I said, 'It's over. It's water under the bridge.' They still hadn't told me I had gotten the job, but Dave said if I did get it, 'We want a good transition here.' I told him I had no problem with that. 'Even if I don't get the job, I'll go over and apologize to Bill. It's something I should have done a long time ago.'"

Wade said he told Bowa point-blank that he needed to speak to Giles.

"I actually required him to have a conversation with Bill," Wade recalled. "I told Larry, 'You need to bury whatever hatchets that exist there. We're not checking off all the things that need to be checked off in the process unless you talk with Bill.'"

Montgomery concurred, "One of the things we talked about is we wanted Larry and Bill to feel comfortable. Because there had been an exchange of words in the papers back in 1981 that was inappropriate, we didn't want to put Bill in a situation that our field manager was somebody he couldn't associate with or feel comfortable with and vice versa. To both of their credits, they decided that the past was the past."

At this point in club history, Giles had little impact on the baseball product, but he was still a force in getting the city to help fund brand-new 42,000-seat Citizens Bank Park. Giles was named honorary National League president in 1999, following in the footsteps of his father, Warren, who was NL president for 18 years from 1951 to 1969.

Giles, who spent the 2003 off season recovering from hip replacement surgery, represents the Phillies at owners' meetings. Still the promoter at heart, Giles was the baseball owner credited with coming up with the recent All-Star Game format that gives the winning league in July's Midsummer Classic home field advantage in that October's World Series. It was Giles's plan, and commissioner Bud Selig gave him credit for following it through to a unanimous vote of the other owners in January 2003.

Although Giles doesn't feel he had the power to nix Bowa as manager, he knew Montgomery and Wade wanted them all on the same page. And if Bowa hadn't apologized, Giles believes he might have been passed over again for the job.

"There's some truth to that," Giles said. "They do ask me for my opinions, and I do make suggestions about major moves. But I don't usually tell them what to do."

Bowa did a lot of house-hopping that October, and next he found himself at Giles's home in Villanova. He did a complete mea culpa.

"I told him, 'There's things I said in anger that shouldn't have been said,'" Bowa said. "I apologized for calling him a liar, and I apologized for leaving as a player the way I did. And I told him, 'I've always been a Philadelphia Phillie at heart, even when I played with the Cubs or I went to coach for Seattle or in Anaheim. I constantly watched Phillies games on cable. Philadelphia has been my home. This is where my daughter was raised.' I basically tried to smooth everything out and get it all on the surface."

Giles had long forgiven Bowa for the outburst, although he still had reservations about putting Bowa into such an esteemed position of authority in his organization. When Giles spoke to Wade and Montgomery, he didn't exactly give Bowa a ringing endorsement.

"It's your decision," Giles told them. "I'll give you what I think his pluses and minuses are. It got down to either Daulton or Bowa at the time. I was closer to Daulton than I was to Bowa. But I didn't want to influence it. So I told them, 'If you want to hire Bowa, it's OK with me.'"

Bowa had the backing of the triumvirate, Giles, Montgomery and Wade. He was the popular candidate for the job in win-starved Philadelphia where none of the four major sports teams had won their league championship since the 1983 76ers, with the resplendent Julius Erving swooping down the court, swept the Los Angeles Lakers for the NBA title.

"It took some soul searching," Wade said. "I knew there were some rough spots, generally. There were some rough spots in the past in the organization. And I knew what his volatility was. As much as I heard when he said that he was a changed guy, I knew firsthand that this was still a guy with a very intense approach to things.

"So I had to take some time. We had to discuss it internally. I had to soul search and then stiffen my backbone and go and say, 'This is the guy I think we should hire. This is the guy I want to hire to be our manager.'"

Montgomery had no reservations. "When Ed came back from his last meeting with Bo, he called me and said, 'I think I found the person who should be our next manager.' I was thrilled."

On November 1, 2001, the Phillies announced that Bowa had been offered and accepted his dream job—as manager of the team he grew up with as a player in his adopted hometown.

"Larry put us back in touch with fans that had checked out on following the Phillies," Montgomery added. "Just his hiring, just because of the image of the overachieving guy with a tremendous work ethic, who eats and sleeps baseball, a person who was part of the Phillies' high moments, Larry was able to bring us back. We usually have a holiday fair with our season ticket holders, and I remember at that fair listening to the Q&A. I realized the way Larry responded was just the way a Phillies fan wants to hear their field leader respond."

16

THE END
OF THE ROLEN ERA

It was an inherited problem, but one Bowa had to deal with almost as soon as he took over as manager of the Phillies. Third baseman Scott Rolen wasn't a happy camper. Picked by the Phillies in the second round of the June 1993 draft of amateur players and a unanimous choice as National League Rookie of the Year in 1997, Rolen had developed into a top-flight third baseman and a budding All-Star. He was one of the guys who was supposed to lead the Phillies out of the wilderness.

But Rolen wasn't convinced that the Phillies were committed to winning. At the Vet, the Phillies acted like a poor small-market team, trading their star players such as Curt Schilling and constantly trying to tread water. By the time Bowa returned in 2001, the Phillies had suffered through 13 losing seasons in the previous 14 years, the one oddity being 1993's National League pennant winners.

Bowa knew the defeatist culture needed to change, and Wade assured him that a plan was in place to rebuild the minor leagues and infuse talent into the big-league club, all aiming toward the opening of the new ballpark. Bowa figured the best place to start was with Rolen, who told him right from the outset, "You know, I'm probably not going to be here very long."

It wasn't what Bowa wanted to hear from reputedly his best player. At the time, Rolen was in the final year of a four-year, $10 million contract and couldn't entertain free agency until the end of the 2002 season. And that was two full seasons away. At heart, Bowa thought it was quite a strange position for a 26-year-old ballplayer who had yet to even make the All-Star team. But times had changed. He knew that some of the new young ball-playing millionaires had very thin skin and were easily humiliated by public criticism. They didn't have the Teflon hides players owned as recently as 25 years ago. The new, more mature Bowa had to take a different approach.

"He had some issues with the front office, and, in the end, he obviously had some issues with me," Bowa said. "But my thought process after he told me that was, 'Well, maybe I can change your mind.' You never want to lose a talent like that. He's a Midwest kid who is basically self-motivated. He doesn't need people to push him. And that's where I think he gets confused. As a manager, you know there are some guys who need to be pushed. He didn't think anybody ever had to be pushed, and he felt it was a distraction when I had to motivate other players."

The baggage aside, Rolen was Bowa's type of player. "He didn't need to be motivated. The uniform motivated him. He plays the game hard whether it's a spring training game or American Legion game. He goes all out," Bowa said. "I think he's the best third baseman defensively I'd ever seen in my life. I've never seen anybody better than him. Obviously Schmitty [Mike Schmidt] did it all. But this kid... He's as good as there is."

Rolen's problems with the Phillies were typical of this era's player, who expects everything to be bought, paid for, neatly gift-wrapped and adorned with a tidy nice bow. Players now sweat the little things, such as the location of hotel rooms, travel arrangements and who pays for the airline tickets when their parents fly in.

"I sensed, and some people have told me, that Scott had taken a lot of little issues over time and had built them up," Wade said, "until it became this feeling that we weren't where we wanted to be."

Rolen didn't even like to return telephone calls, even shunning messages at times from Bowa.

"I think the telephone might be the most annoying invention I've ever seen in my life," Rolen told Alan Schwarz for an article that appeared in *Philadelphia Magazine*. "I don't like to talk on the telephone to anybody at any time. I have a cell phone but it's never on. It's for me to call out." Could his agents, Sam and Seth Levinson, reach him? Rolen shook his head. "They wouldn't get any further than a voicemail. And I hate voicemail because it's an obligation."

Wade recognized Rolen as a budding problem, but he trusted that Bowa could handle it. After all, that's why Bowa was signed to a two-year contract with another option year, for just under $1 million a season. Managing the Phillies is never an easy task. Not in any era.

"Scottie may have had issues before Bo got here, and other people were telling us he had issues," Wade said. "But I also take people at face value. And the conversations I was having directly with Scott to me indicated that he wanted to come back with us and be with us going forward. Some people want to portray it as Bowa being the trigger event of Scottie not wanting to be here. I know that they had differences. Candidly, I don't think Scott's view of the world and Larry's view of the world are the same. So maybe it was a relationship that was doomed from the beginning.

"But in retrospect, I would agree with Larry. That Scott probably already had enough issues built up, whether it was Larry as the manager or Terry Francona as the manager."

Wade siding with Bowa would set a pattern established right from the beginning of their new boss-manager relationship. The two would act as a unit, always keeping each other informed about the events in their own domains. In his new job, Bowa had all of the elements that weren't there in San Diego: stable ownership, a plan to build a winning team and a tight relationship with the general manager, a man who would remain the general manager. It was the kind of stability and support that Bowa needed to be successful in his job.

"I'm supportive of Bowa and the coaches because I think that's the appropriate way to be," Wade said.

Even if Wade is not on the road with the team, he said he makes it his business to speak with Bowa at least once every day. And Bowa, for his part, is partial to full disclosure about anything that happens in the clubhouse.

"That's the way it should be," Bowa said. "I tell Eddie everything. Things always come out anyway. What would it look like if something came out and I hadn't told him? It would look like I was hiding something. That's not good, and that's not the kind of relationship I want with my general manager."

They would have plenty to talk about shortly when it came to Rolen.

To everyone's pleasant surprise the Phillies opened the 2001 season playing good, solid baseball under Bowa. They won their first three games in row, failing to replicate the 0-5 starts of Bowa's 1987 and 1988 Padres, and were 7-3 in their first 10 games. The Phillies took undisputed possession of first place on April 10 and stayed there through the months of April and May and well into June.

The unexpected winning streak seemed to be sitting well with Bowa. The players, who had heard all the stories and rumors about their new manager's temper, were still in a feeling-out process.

"If I could come back, I'd play for him again—I'd play for him in a heartbeat," said John Kruk, who played for Bowa when he managed the Padres and was a coach for the Phillies. "That's what I tell people when they tell me they ain't coming to Philly. They say, 'I don't know if I can play for him.' I say, 'Then you don't want to win.' Because that's all he wants, to win."

On May 31, the Phillies had a season-high eight-game lead, but by June 8 when they went into Boston for an interleague series with the Red Sox, the margin over the Braves had dwindled to four games. The Phillies lost two of the three at Fenway Park. Privately, Bowa was beside himself about the offensive production in the series of his Nos. 3, 4 and 5 hitters—Bobby Abreu, Scott Rolen and Travis Lee—who were two for 15 with no RBIs in the pair of one-run losses. Rolen alone was two for 12 with no RBIs in the series.

It was Bowa's opinion that if Rolen had been a better situational hitter with runners on base—a well-placed grounder or fly ball—the Phillies would've swept the series.

From Boston, the Phillies went to St. Petersburg, Florida, to play the Devil Rays, and the losing continued. All the while, their first-place lead over Atlanta continued to diminish.

The Phillies were in the midst of losing nine of 11 games, creating Bowa's first test as a manager—one he perhaps somewhat unwittingly failed because of a miscommunication with a longtime associate in the press.

Bowa has done better over the years dealing with the mentality of the better beat writers, who use the tactic of asking the same question in a number of different forms to elicit the preferred response. In San Diego, Bowa was like a powder keg and easy to set off. Many times he'd remain collected during the first round of questioning. But after the writers left to talk to the players, a return to Bowa's office was almost mandatory. Given time, he wouldn't cool down. Instead, he'd ruminate and percolate like a coffee pot ready to boil over. The result was many a choice quote. While that made for good reading in the next day's newspaper, it would have a detrimental effect on Bowa's relationship with the players.

It was Bill Conlin, a longtime columnist and former Phillies beat writer for the *Philadelphia Daily News*, who acted as the conduit. Conlin covered the Phillies on the field from 1966 to 1986—the entirety of Bowa's career as a player—and had earned the respect of the shortstop, who was nicknamed "Pee Wee." Conlin, still as tough a writer as there is in the business, just happened to be in town for the three-game midweek series.

Seeing a familiar face, Bowa unloaded to Conlin about his feeble offense in a long diatribe that included the killer phrase: "The middle of my lineup is killing me. My cleanup hitter is killing me," Conlin recalled Bowa saying. In any shape or form, the quote was pure Bowa speaking out of frustration.

In Conlin's *Daily News* column the next day about the Phillies' sputtering offense, Bowa's quote read: "If the No. 4 guy even makes contact in either Boston loss, we sweep the series. He's killing us."

Rolen, of course, was then the cleanup (or No. 4) hitter. And the quote created Bowa's first real Philadelphia firestorm since taking over as manager.

"He never mentioned Rolen by name, but it was obvious who the cleanup hitter was, and then we went on to other subjects," Conlin said. "It was funny, just as he was saying it, I looked out his office door and Rolen was standing in this little men's room right across from the manager's office. He was almost, but not quite, within earshot. And then he disappeared."

The next day, Rolen reappeared and confronted Bowa in his office. By all reports, voices were raised. But no one had to be carried out of the clubhouse. Bowa tried, unsuccessfully, to explain his side of the story.

"Our offense was terrible. We just weren't scoring runs," Bowa recalled. "We were catching the ball, we were pitching pretty good, but we just couldn't score. Bill said, 'You guys are going through a tough time now.' I said, 'We're not scoring any runs.' And this is just how he said it: 'Rolen's not swinging very good.' I responded: 'The middle of our lineup is killing us.' He equated that with Rolen not swinging good, and that's what he wrote. I never said Rolen is killing us. I never said that."

But Bowa knew the damage had been done.

"Maybe I had been away from the beat too long to realize how sensitive players had become," Conlin said. "In my mind what Bowa had said was not only very well deserved and merited after that atrocious performance they had in Boston, but the kind of thing that we heard as beat writers in those days all the time and wrote all the time as legitimate criticism of athletes who had produced lousy performances. Apparently, all this sensitivity had passed me by."

Conlin, though, tried to take the heat off Bowa in this case. He said he called Wade and tried to explain the nuances of the situation. Apparently, Conlin wasn't aware before writing his column that there was any friction between Rolen and Bowa.

"He was a new GM at that time. I thought it put him in an uncomfortable position," Conlin said. "He basically told me, 'Don't worry about it. I know what was said.'"

In some quarters, Conlin said, he was even accused of making up the quote, which was highly unlikely. Certainly, sometimes a line or phrase spoken agitatedly in the heat of the moment can be open to interpretation.

"Larry wasn't trying to single Rolen out. He was just talking about the futility of the offense in that Boston series," Conlin said. "He was probably trying to plant a seed against the whole offense without trying to finger Rolen. If I had gotten the drift, I would've generalized it. The column still would've basically said the same thing without pointing out Rolen as the No. 4 hitter. I would've written the column a little differently had I known it was going to be the massive brouhaha that it turned into. I think Larry Bowa and I learned a little bit of a lesson that day."

When Dallas Green, now a Phillies senior adviser, took Rolen to task on a radio show, the debacle was complete. From that juncture on, Bowa tried to mend fences with Rolen, but the relationship remained frosty.

"I just think Scottie and I misunderstood each other," Bowa said. "We came from different backgrounds. We were raised differently. Barring injuries, he might have Hall of Fame numbers when he's done. He's that good."

But the Rolen situation didn't mask all of the good things that happened that season. Bowa developed a love affair with a five-foot, eight-inch, 165-pound rookie shortstop named Jimmy Rollins, who talked a blue streak, had 180 hits that season and was the Phillies' only representative on the NL All-Star team. Rollins, who can be strong-willed and obstinate, reminded Bowa of himself as a young player.

Bowa also sat down with starting left-handed pitcher Randy Wolf after a 10-4 late June loss to Atlanta and gave him the choice of going to the bullpen to work out his problems or accepting an assignment in the minor leagues. The way he handled the situation showed a breadth of depth and compassion that he certainly never exhibited when he was managing the Padres. Back then Bowa probably would have made the decision himself without discussion.

Wolf, then 25 years old, told Bowa he wasn't happy with the situation. "I told him that I didn't expect him to be happy," Bowa said. "'You're a young kid who has been a starter your whole life.' I said he didn't have to give me an answer today. 'Come back tomorrow and think about what you want to do.' I owed it to him. I wanted it to be a mutual decision."

Wolf came back in the next day and told Bowa he wanted to continue starting. "Then I told him flat out I was taking him out of the rotation," Bowa said. "So he said he would go to the bullpen; he wasn't going to the minor leagues."

Wolf made three appearances in long relief, worked on the sidelines with then pitching coach Vern Ruhle and was back in the rotation after the All-Star break. He was 5-2 with a 2.19 ERA the rest of the way.

"There's no doubt it helped," Wolf later told the *Philadelphia Inquirer*. "It shook me up, put things in perspective. At that stage of my career, it was like an epiphany."

The Phillies fell out of first place on July 18 but would flirt with the top spot and remain in second place for the rest of the season, never falling any farther than three and a half games back. Attendance began to increase marginally at the Vet, and certainly baseball interest was again on the rise.

But on September 11, the petty problems between the players and manager received a rough jolt of reality, along with the rest of the country. The Phillies were in Atlanta preparing for a key series against the Braves when they awoke to the terrorist attacks that struck New York City and Washington, D.C. All flights around the country and all sporting events were canceled. The world of fun and games came to an abrupt halt in a hail of smoke, death and smoldering wreckage. The Phillies, like every Major League Baseball team that had reached its destination on the road that day, were stranded. Forget the suddenly insignificant fact that the Phillies were three and a half games behind the Braves with only 19 games to go.

"I think 9/11 basically caused a lot of people to take a step back," Bowa said. "You take for granted just being free. Then something like that happens in the United States of America? That's not supposed to happen. It made a lot of people aware. I remember turning it on and seeing these airplanes going into the side of the World Trade Center. When I first saw it just getting out of bed, I thought it was a promo for a movie. And then they're saying that they had live pictures. Oh, my God! You just forgot about everything. You didn't even think about baseball."

The Phillies remained in Atlanta for the next four days while the country pulled itself together. The baseball season resumed on September 17, and this time the Phillies were at home to face the Braves at the Vet. Like all sporting events played so soon after September 11, the evening had electricity to it, a patriotic fervor. The 27,910 in attendance were rocked by a pregame tribute that included rousing versions of "God Bless America" and "The Star-Spangled Banner." Long into the game, the Philly fans kept chanting, "U-S-A, U-S-A."

Rolen hit two homers that night, giving the Phillies a lead that they never relinquished, and after the second one the fans were so stirred that they called him to the field for a curtain call. Rolen, who usually shuns such attention, was on his way up the runway from the dugout to the Phillies' clubhouse when Bowa called him back.

"I know you're not going to want to do this, but you've got to go out there," *USA Today* reported that Bowa said. "There's something very special about this night."

Rolen jumped back out of the dugout, tipped his cap and disappeared into the clubhouse.

Asked by reporters later about his quick response to Bowa, Rolen said: "We finally agreed on something."

It was an amazing night, Bowa recalled. "The game was different because the crowd was different. It was a crowd I've never seen at a baseball game. The atmosphere was different. They weren't rooting for the Braves. They weren't rooting for the Phillies. They were rooting for America. It was a tough night. But looking back on it, you can say we were part of the healing process. It's something that sticks with you. Even though people never forget, for those few hours they let their minds wander a little bit. It made us all realize that something like September 11 can happen at any time. It made people more aware of other people."

The Phillies won the first three games of the series to pull back within half a game, but that would be the apex. They'd finish Bowa's first season with an 86-76 record only two games out, a remarkable 21-game turnaround from the previous 65-97 season. Rolen finished with a .289 batting average, 25 homers and 107 runs batted in, none of them career highs, but all well within range. Bowa had waved his magic wand; the Phillies, some of them begrudgingly, had responded. And Eddie Wade was almost instantly vindicated for his choice of hiring Bowa to run the team; for the effort, Bowa was named Manager of the Year in the National League.

Wade now agreed with Bowa's assertion during the first phase of his interview process that he had learned from previous mistakes.

"I do think he's changed," Wade said. "When you get to be 54, 55 years old and have different life experiences, you're going to change. At the same time, he would even admit that there have been rough spots and that dealing with today's player is difficult. Sometimes it's the player who doesn't understand. Sometimes it's the manager not making the adjustment that he has to make. And we've had those conversations. Bowa and I have had a lot of conversations, very candid. All designed to help him be the best manager he can possibly be in all areas."

The following spring training, the Phillies made their best pitch to keep Rolen, a reported 10-year $140 million offer. But Rolen turned it down, claiming he was concerned that the Phillies wouldn't be able to keep a competitive team around him for the decade during which he would earn $14 million a year. Instead, he went for one year at $8.6 million and told Wade he'd test free agency. The 2002 season would probably be his last year in a Phillies uniform.

The Rolen situation hung like a shroud over the Phillies all season, and the team returned to the doldrums.

Never playing with the same energy and spark of the previous season, the Phillies sank like a boulder from the beginning, finishing in third place with an 80-81 record, 21 1/2 games behind the Braves, who won the National League East title again.

Not wanting to lose a talent like Rolen in free agency, Wade gauged the marketplace to see if the Phillies could trade him before the July 31 non-waiver deadline.

"At their request, he and his agents did not want us to negotiate during the season," Wade said. "We honored that. He had an opportunity to be a free agent. And we thought rather than put ourselves in that position, we'd go ahead and try and get value for him and move on. And that's what we've done."

On July 29, 2002, the Phillies traded Rolen to the St. Louis Cardinals in a five-player deal that netted them pitchers Bud Smith and Mike Timlin and infielder Placido Polanco, none of them potential Hall of Famers. Timlin, in fact, signed as a free agent with the Red Sox after the season.

The money the Phillies saved on Rolen, though, was put to good use in the free agent market before the 2003 season.

For Rolen, it was a new lease on life. He was told by veteran Cardinals manager Tony La Russa to simply relax and do his best.

"I haven't stopped smiling yet," Rolen said at the news conference upon his arrival in St. Louis. "It feels good to put the Cardinals' uniform on. If you can't be excited about putting this uniform on, you don't have a pulse."

About being away from the Phillies, Rolen said abstractly: "If I try to be somebody I'm not, I'm going to fail. I'm just more comfortable in this situation."

When Bowa found out about the trade, he called Rolen's cell phone. Of course, there was no answer. Bowa said he left this message: "I told him, 'It's been a pleasure managing you. If everybody played the game like you do, there would be no problems. Careers are short; try to be happy wherever you end up.'"

Rolen never returned the call.

17

AND IN THE END...

It was the last season at the Vet, and that fact pervaded every-thing. And so emotions were high all summer leading into the fall as the countdown reached its inevitable conclusion. All sig-nificant events were recorded for posterity, the last hot dog eaten, last hot dog wrapper floating to the spent artificial turf, last loss, last win, and last game. By the time the Phillies got there on September 28, 2003, they had endured the start of the war in Iraq, a hurricane that nearly blew them out of town, a verbal clubhouse flogging from their "Pee Wee" manager that was among the best in his career, the release of their top pinch hitter after a perceived mutiny, and all the vicissi-tudes of ebbing life and then ultimately death.

During the 2003 season, Bowa received more challenges to his job in print than anyone deserved, particularly with the Phillies in the wild-card race until the last weekend of the season. He would be named the "worst manager" in baseball by major league players polled at midseason by *Sports Illustrated*, be suspended twice—each time for one game—and ejected from six others. But then in the end, general manager Ed Wade, who supported him all season, backed up that support by picking up the option on Bowa's contract for 2005, while adding additional options for 2006 and 2007.

This made the message roundly clear: Bowa was the right man for the Phillies. Players who didn't like it could go elsewhere, because the manager was staying. Longtime local writers and columnists who called for his demise would still have Bowa to contend with.

"I think Bo has done an outstanding job handling all these different issues that have come up," Wade said. "Are there rough spots? Yeah, but there's rough spots everywhere. Sometimes you have to figure out which ones are real and which ones aren't. And the bottom line is, our faith—mine, Dave Montgomery's, the partnership—is strong enough that it was a no-brainer to pick up the option."

With Scott Rolen traded to the Cardinals, Wade had an enormous surplus in the budget after the 2002 season. And with Montgomery projecting a large increase in revenue and attendance in the new ballpark, the Phillies could finally be big players in the free agent market. The goal was to have a successful 2003 season and then to charge into 2004 and beyond. To that end, the Phillies had a budget that they didn't want to exceed during the last season at the Vet, but they wanted the team pumped and primed for the anticipated capacity crowds and a possible 3.4 million in attendance that first year in Citizens Bank Park. The Phillies fully expected their local revenue to jump 66 percent in the new ballpark from about $100 million in the last season at the Vet.

"We'll continue to live within our means," Wade said. "But living within our means at the Vet meant being 22nd or 23rd in payroll because we were 22 or 23 in revenue."

Accordingly, during the 2002 free agent season, the Phillies made a big play for Atlanta pitcher Tom Glavine, Cleveland slugger Jim Thome and San Francisco third baseman David Bell. They signed two of the three: Glavine signed with the Mets, but the Phillies got Thome for six years at $85 million and Bell, who played for Bowa when he was a coach in Seattle, for four years at $17 million. To bolster their starting pitching, Wade then made a trade with the Braves for right-hander Kevin Millwood, knowing that after being paid $9.9 million for one season, Millwood could file for free agency. The total contract value of the three new players was $111.9 million, still well under the $140 million the Phillies had reportedly offered Rolen. The Phillies also re-signed two of their own players for big bucks—young left fielder Pat Burrell to a six-year $50 million contract and pitcher Randy Wolf for four years at $22.5 million.

There had never been this kind of spending on players in Philly. But with the new sports palace coming—paid for in part by public funds—the Phillies were duty-bound to polish the product. Among the fans and literati, all of the spending engendered unrealistic expectations for a club that had experienced only four winning seasons since the "Wheeze Kids" played in the 1983 World Series. Inside the organization, though, expectations were more modest. The baseball people knew that the pitching staff was still short one starter and that the bullpen was an injury and an off year away from catastrophe.

A nice run during the season, with fan interest peaking during the final weekend at the Vet against Atlanta, would be acceptable.

The influx of talent gave Bowa peace of mind going into spring training that he didn't have in his first two seasons. But it didn't change his attitude. He knew all season that he had the strong support of management, and he didn't expect that to waver.

"I can't worry about it," Bowa said. "I try to do the best I can. I don't have any control over what player performs well or doesn't. I try to put people into position to be successful, and if they are, they are. And I prepare them. No matter what team we have during spring training, I prepare the same. If I go out there with nine rookies, I expect to win that night. That's just how I approach every game. And if I lose, I'm upset. That's how I was as a player and as a coach. That's how I am as a manager.

"When that changes, when I say, 'Well, if we win, fine; if we lose, fine,' then I'll quit. No one will have to tell me. I'll quit. So as long as that flame is still there and that desire to win is still there, I'm going to keep doing what I do."

Camp opened in Clearwater, Florida, with Bowa making his annual inaugural address to the players. During his first two seasons, that meeting had been filled with fire and brimstone. He sounded more like a "drill sergeant," catcher Mike Lieberthal was quoted as saying in the *Camden Courier-Post*.

This time the talk was upbeat.

"It was different as far as getting his point across," Lieberthal said later in the article. "I don't know if it's fair to say he's in better spirits, but he's more at ease with this team because of the veteran players we have. He talked about this as a team of 25 guys. Last year, one or two of those guys brought the other guys down, and that's not going to work. He pointed out that those guys have been extinguished. We've paved the way now. He showed how excited he was."

One of those guys was obviously Rolen. And from the outset Bowa noticed a real difference in the locker room and the team's chemistry with the arrival of the veterans Thome, Millwood and Bell.

"Not only are they great players, but they have a good word for everybody, whether it's a clubhouse guy or a pretzel vendor," Bowa said early in the season. "There are no egos there. They take care of everything in the clubhouse. The players migrate to them. I don't have to do too much. We lose a tough game, and those guys are as upset as I am. It makes it a lot easier for me.

"[During the 2002 season] I had guys who had their own agendas and couldn't care less about the team. They let other outside interests affect how they played the game. The clubhouse was divided. There was the Scott Rolen camp and someone else's camp. Who needs that?"

The good feeling, though, would soon be overshadowed by outside forces. On March 13 the Phillies received news that Tug McGraw, the reliever who had thrown the last pitches of both the 1980 National League Championship Series and the ensuing World Series, had been taken to a Florida hospital with severe headaches. At the time, McGraw was a special instructor in the Phillies' spring training camp. McGraw, only 58 years old, was one of the most lovable characters in recent Phillies history and a major contributor to the club's only championship.

"It came totally out of the blue; we're all praying for him," said Bowa, his Phillies teammate from 1976 to 1981.

McGraw underwent emergency surgery to remove a malignant brain tumor. At the time, the procedure saved his life. Bowa later called McGraw in the hospital.

"He sounded great," Bowa said. "I asked him how he was feeling, and he said, 'A lot better than I thought I would be.' I told him to hurry up and get back in uniform. If he could walk through the clubhouse, it would be a great lift."

McGraw would do that and more before passing away in early 2004, but it was the first ominous shadow over the season.

On March 20, the United States began bombing Iraq. And for the second time in two seasons, Major League Baseball had to make scheduling changes to accommodate world events. This time, a two-game series in Japan's Tokyo Dome scheduled between Seattle and Oakland was moved back to the United States because of security concerns abroad. The effect this time on the Phillies, though, was more philosophical than practical.

"The war was No. 1 in our mind just like everybody else in the country," Bowa said. "And that's the way it should be."

The Phillies opened playing .500 ball and by the end of April were hanging around the top of the National League East. On April 27, a Sunday afternoon, Millwood threw a no-hitter at the Vet, defeating the Giants 1-0. The Phillies had only four hits and scored their only run on Ricky Ledee's third-inning homer. Meanwhile, Millwood threw 108 pitches, walking three and striking out 10. With little margin for error, he had command of the ballgame all day.

"It was unbelievable," Bowa recalled. "Usually in a no-hitter, you need luck, you need an umpire's call or a guy will make a great play. There was only one ball hit semi-hard to the right side and [center fielder] Ricky Ledee ran it down. Other than that, they were easy outs. He just dominated them with one pitch and very seldom threw anything else. He had an overpowering fastball that he located. He pitched ahead in the count against a good-hitting team. It was well deserved."

It also was the second and last no-hitter thrown on south Broad Street by a Phillies pitcher; Terry Mulholland had crafted the other one on August 15, 1990, also against the Giants in a 6-0 win when Bowa had been the third base coach for the Phillies.

There have been nine no-hitters in Phillies history, and Bowa has been on the field for four of them, including one on June 23, 1971, at Cincinnati when Rick Wise beat the Reds 4-0 and Bowa was a shortstop—it was the only time he played in a no-hitter during his 16-year career.

The Phillies were 15-10 and flew to Los Angeles immediately after the game, tied for first place with the Braves and the Expos.

After a long day's journey into night, Millwood found himself sitting in the lobby of the team's Century City hotel sipping a bottle of Dom Perignon champagne with a few of his closest friends. At Dodger Stadium the next day, he was swamped with national interview requests before the game.

A ball and cap of Millwood's from the no-hitter had already been sent to Cooperstown, New York, and added to the collection of no-hit memorabilia in the National Baseball Hall of Fame. But Millwood said he had kept the ball that center fielder Ricky Ledee caught for the game's last out for himself.

"I don't know what my wife is going to do with it," Millwood said. "I'll leave it up to her. She's the decorator."

The Phillies defeated the Dodgers that night and went into first place by a half a game. But the glow of all that glory quickly wore off. Millwood lasted only six innings in his next outing at San Diego, allowing a single to the first Padres hitter—Ramon Vazquez—and Ledee muffed a 10th-inning line drive to center that cost the Phillies the game. Millwood didn't have his no-hit fastball, and the Phillies didn't play their "A" game.

By the end of the 10-game trip, the Braves had gone right past the 20-15 Phillies, who returned home two and a half games out for a game against the Astros on May 9.

Meanwhile, events unfolding in Miami would provide an interesting subplot to the Phillies' season. With the Marlins floundering at 16-22 on May 10, they fired manager Jeff Torborg. Trader Jack McKeon was back—taken out of mothballs and coaxed out of retirement. Marlins president David Samson thought the now 72-year-old McKeon would be just the elixir for the young Marlins.

"He had a proven track record of turning around young teams," Samson said. "We had every confidence in him that he could do it again."

Another subplot would be the lingering, season-long slump suffered by the new Phillies millionaire, Pat Burrell. Big things were expected from the 26-year-old left fielder, who was in his third full season and in 2002 had hit .282 with 37 homers and 116 RBIs, prompting that fat $50-million contract.

But evidently the pressure of high expectations had weighed heavily on Burrell, who was Bowa's golden boy in 2002 and a perceived outcast in 2003. The more Burrell struggled, the worse he hit, and the worse he hit, the more he was under that harsh Philadelphia microscope.

"Larry was trying to be supportive of the guy," Wade said. "Everybody in the baseball world knows how important Burrell is to our offense. But the guy was hammered every day, the daily Burrell update, "What about Burrell? Is he ever going to come out of his slump?" At some point any response you give was going to be misinterpreted. That's something we frankly have to avoid."

By June 1, Burrell was hitting .207, and Bowa decided to bench him here and there for a few games, a tactic that had worked with the right-swinging hitter in the past. It didn't work this time, and Bowa's relationship with Burrell began to smolder.

"I don't like to see anyone get buried, and he's getting buried right now," Bowa said at the time.

Burrell never snapped out of it. He hit .209 for a lost season with 21 homers and 64 RBIs. And in the end, it was hard for Burrell to shake the illusion that Bowa tried to bury him. Bowa, though, said Burrell's relationship with him was just fine.

"He's not on the outs with me," Bowa said. "I gave him 500-some at-bats [522]. If he was on the outs with me and I didn't like him, I wouldn't have played him. I believe in this kid. But somebody got it in his head that Bo was trying to screw him. I don't know how I was trying to screw him—I played him."

On June 8, the Phillies had dipped to 36-35, were already nine and a half games out of first place and starting to look at the wild-card berth for redemption. For the 12th straight season, the Braves seemed ready to run off and win their division. The boobirds were starting to clamor at the Vet, now in its dying days. And the writers wanted some raw meat.

They were waiting for a trademark Bowa explosion. But Bowa, who had taken a preseason seminar to help him deal with the media, resisted the temptation. Certainly, Bowa continued to vent in private, stinging the ears of his coaches. He had gotten so used to the TV cameras following his every wince that during games at the Vet, he began retreating up the tunnel from the dugout to the clubhouse, out of view of the prying electronic eye.

That day, Dennis Deitch, a writer for the *Delaware County Times*, said in a column that Bowa was an "MIA manager."

"If this team continues its incessant mediocrity and finishes the season at the .500 mark, Larry Bowa should meet the same fate Terry Francona did after 2000," he wrote. "He should be canned without pause."

Deitch went on to say that Bowa had turned into a "shoulder-shrugging manager" and hadn't taken responsibility for the team's lackluster play.

It was the first real salvo from the fourth estate, and the next day, Bowa fired back to the crew of beat writers assembled for their daily pregame meeting.

"I take responsibility for everything out there," Bowa said. "I've never shunned a thing. If something's wrong, it's my fault and that's part of the gig. Not once have you heard me say that's not my fault. It is my fault. For you guys who don't know me, you need to hear this because you don't know me that well to write crap like that."

Ten days later, Eddie Wade issued his first in a season-long series of statements regarding Bowa's job security. Votes of confidence are usually the kiss of death, but coming from Wade, these votes had the ring of truth.

"He's very safe. It's a non-issue," Wade said. "I'm very happy with the job Larry is doing."

"I think we tried hard not to give a vote of confidence," Montgomery said. "When you do that, that engages you in a debate that we were never considering. That was not part of our thought process. And I thought Ed did a nice job of saying that's not where our heads were. I don't believe, personally, in change for the sake of making changes. That's something clubs gravitate to, to take the heat off the current performance, but in reality it just takes you to a new set of problems, a new set of challenges."

Although the Phillies were obviously happy with the job Bowa was doing, evidently, the major league players were not.

From June 13 to July 3, the Phillies went on a nice little tear, winning 13 out of 16 games. At the All-Star break, the Phillies were a healthy 52-40 but couldn't close the gap between them and the 61-32 Braves, who were putting together another mega season and led by eight and a half games. Even in the wild-card race, the Phillies led Arizona only by a game. The Marlins had become competitive since the hiring of McKeon. They were doing it on the strength of rookie sensation left-hander Dontrelle Willis, who came up from the minors just as McKeon joined the team. The Marlins were four and a half games behind the Phillies.

All should have been well in the world of the Phillies and Bowa, but in the demanding world of Philly sports, it never is. During the first week of July, *Sports Illustrated* came out with its 2003 Player Survey, listing the bests and worst in a number of baseball categories. Bowa got the nod as worst manager, with healthy margins over the Reds' Bob Boone (his former Phillies teammate) and the White Sox' Jerry Manuel. Both have since been fired. Cards manager Tony La Russa, one of baseball's most successful managers, was fourth behind

Bowa, Boone and Manuel on the worst skippers list. So take it for what it's worth.

Looking inside their own numbers, *SI* noted that Bowa's highest percentage of negative votes came from players in the American League East, leading Rich Hoffman in the *Philadelphia Daily News* to write that, "Travis Lee, Marlon Anderson, Robert Person, Jeremy Giambi and a couple of other ex-Phillies must be some pretty ardent campaigners."

As a whole, Philadelphia got flogged in the survey. The Vet was listed as the second worst ballpark behind Montreal's Olympic Stadium with the sixth worst playing surface. Philly was considered the third worst city to visit on the road behind Milwaukee and Detroit and to have the third worst fans behind Montreal and New York. Presumably, players will have a different opinion of the new ballpark with its natural turf field. But the fans, the highly underrated city with its top-flight attractions and world-class restaurants— plus Bowa—all still remain.

Bowa, predictably chafing at his poor ranking among the players, said: "If you've never played for me and looked from afar, you might think I was tough to play for. But if you play for me, all I ask is that you play hard."

Wade, too, dismissed the survey as another distraction but said later on that the Phillies are certainly building a team around Bowa that fits his determination and mindset. The weak of heart need not apply.

"He's the right guy for us," Wade said. "We're making the moves, not to put Larry Bowa's team on the field but to put the team together that best handles Larry's personality or exemplifies what he's all about."

The 2003 edition would all be tested during a second half in which the Phillies had the wild card in their grasp. The bullpen, which had its bright moments during the first half, collapsed under the weight of injuries and the failure of closer Jose Mesa, the latest Phillie to be so reviled by the fans that he was useless in any close game down the stretch at the Vet. David Bell, one of their key free agent acquisitions, had been out since mid-June with a serious back injury and wouldn't return until the end of the season.

By the middle of August, the Phillies were 69-54 and about to embark on a 13-game road trip through St. Louis, Milwaukee, Montreal and New York. The Marlins were just half a game back in the wild-card race and had become the Phillies' chief competition for that slot.

At the same juncture, the Marlins went off on a nine-game road trip through Colorado, San Francisco and Pittsburgh. They lost eight of the nine, severely trying the patience of their ancient manager. All the Phillies had to do was play .500 ball and they would've opened up some daylight between themselves and Florida. But the Phillies lost nine of the first 10 games on the trip, their worst losing streak of the season. Instead of daylight, the Phillies were not only in a statistical heat with the Marlins, but both teams had allowed the Expos, Diamondbacks and Dodgers back into the race.

"That trip really cost us the wild card," Bowa recalled. "I mean, we were in it down to the end, but I wish I could have that trip back."

With the Phillies on life support, Bowa tried to keep his calm as the team prepared for the finale of a four-game set at Montreal on August 28.

"If I go crazy, it won't only be in Philadelphia in the papers, it'll go to Japan, it'll go to Istanbul that I snapped again," he told writers before the game. "As bad as things have gone—and they've gone bad, believe me—I'm going to give myself a star because I could go crazy now."

The Expos won again, this time 4-0 behind Javier Vazquez, their best young pitcher, who four-hit the Phillies over eight innings and struck out 10. After the game, Bowa went nuts, matching one of his vintage all-time scream-a-thons from the Padres days. It was his first and only clubhouse meltdown of the year. Reporters covering the game wrote that Bowa was so loud they could hear his words piercing the closed metal doors. It was reminiscent of then-Phillies manager Dallas Green during the 1980 season calling out the manhood of that eventual championship team. The words came from deep inside the motivation that controls Bowa's entire psyche: He still hates to lose.

"Before that I had had a couple of meetings where I tried to build the guys up—you guys are good, we've just got to battle and stick together—never did I undress them the way I did that day," Bowa said in retrospect. "We were playing terrible. Horseshit. It had nothing even to do with Vazquez pitching. It didn't matter who we played that day—the 1927 Yankees—we weren't scoring. Vazquez was on top of his game, but I was thinking that we were getting beat 4-0, but we were never in it.

"So I was thinking about all of the shit that I had been watching the last few weeks, as hard as we worked, and we were throwing it right down the tube. I'm figuring, we worked hard all year and now we're expecting to lose. We played to win every game. So after the game I got everybody in the clubhouse and I just started going off.

"'You guys have dedicated your whole season, but now you're letting it all go down the shitter because you're feeling sorry for yourself. You don't get a break here, and you don't get a break there. You make your breaks. You guys are better than this. Nobody's feeling sorry for us right now. They're kicking us because we're down. I'm sick and tired of watching guys make the same mistakes over and over again. No adjustments at the plate, no two-strike approach. When do we kick it in and say, hey, enough's enough? It was a good one.'"

The skirmish wasn't over. In the background pitcher Brett Myers and pitching coach Joe Kerrigan kept right on jawing, Myers demanded a modicum of respect from his coach and manager. It was that kind of day, ending that kind of week.

Afterward the team took two buses to the airport for the quick trip to New York where they were scheduled to open a three-game series the next night against the Mets, a team that had thrown in the towel not long after the start of the season. Bowa and the coaches boarded one bus while the players boarded the other. On their way to the airport, the players had their own meeting, during which they apparently resolved to win despite Bowa and ignore the histrionics of the manager. Join the crowd. Much better clubs than the Phillies had held those meetings often in the days when managers like Billy Martin and Dick Williams ruled the roost.

The perceived slights included Bowa taking Millwood out of a game for a pinch hitter during the seventh inning, a game the pitcher still thought he had a chance to win; the continued problems being suffered by Burrell; a comment by Bowa that the team wasn't playing with any sense of urgency after the Phillies were swept by lowly Milwaukee earlier on the road trip; and Kerrigan being told to take the pitching staff under tighter control. When had it become so politically correct for a manager to deny himself the pleasure of stating the obvious in public?

Rightly or wrongly, Bowa thought Tyler Houston, the National League's top pinch hitter at that juncture, was the ringleader.

"I guess Tyler Houston got on that second bus and started cursing me out and saying, 'We'll win for ourselves,'" Bowa said. "It was one meeting. If I was browbeating them all year, I could see someone saying, 'We're tired of this.' I had one meeting all year, and it happened in Montreal where there's no press. This story went all the way to Alaska. So Houston is trying to draw a line in the sand. 'It's us against the staff.' That's not how it was all year.

"He was an extra guy. If he was a superstar, I might give merit to it. But a guy who has been with five organizations in five years? You've got to be shitting me. He made more out of it than it really was. It was just a clubhouse meeting when I unleashed."

On August 31, the Phillies' offense erupted as they defeated the last-place Mets, 7-0. Millwood pitched eight innings of three-hit ball to raise his record to 13-9. Millwood, a free agent at the end of year, was one player Bowa wanted back. But Millwood was lukewarm about playing again for Bowa. In the second inning, Burrell hit a two-run homer, his 20th and next to last of the season. When he trotted back to the visitor's dugout on the third base side of Shea Stadium, he seemed to intentionally avoid Bowa, who was high-fiving players at the home plate side of the dugout. Burrell instead went to a break in the railing near the middle of the dugout and stepped inside.

Bowa said he didn't think anything of it at the time. He figured that Burrell was simply trying to avoid the crowd. But after the tumult subsided, one of Bowa's coaches approached and asked: "Did you see what Burrell did?"

"Then I started thinking about it, and I watched because the inning was still going on," Bowa said. "So I see Pat and Houston talking to each other, laughing. I can't prove it, but if I were a betting man, which I'm not, I'd bet that Houston was behind it."

Whether he was or not, Bowa asked Wade after the game to release Houston, calling him a disruptive force on the team, despite the fact that he was 13 for 29 with eight runs batted in as a pinch hitter.

"I told Eddie, 'You've got to get this guy out of here,'" Bowa recalled. "In all fairness to Eddie, he was very diplomatic. He said, 'You know, he's one of our best pinch hitters.' I said, 'I don't care what he is.' He said, 'Sometimes we make rash decisions. Why don't we sleep on it?' I said, 'I have no problem with that.' So in the meantime, Eddie talked to some other people—our PR people, our trainer, talked to our clubhouse person about this guy. It's easy for a manager to say just because he doesn't like a guy that he wants him out. Sometimes you feel that way, and then a week later your feelings change.

"But this time I was really adamant about it, and I knew I wasn't going to change my mind in the morning. I asked my coaches about it. I asked them if I was overreacting or is this guy a bad guy? And to a man they said we had to get rid of him. So Eddie waited, but he did some research, which is what he always does. He's got to be one of the most prepared GMs in the game. And I got a call the next morning in my room at 9 a.m. Eddie said I didn't have to worry about Houston any more. He was out of there."

Houston, of course, took his shots, but in the end, he was the real loser. Life around the Phillies went on without him. He was indeed a journeyman player, a .265 lifetime hitter who has played on six teams in his eight seasons and was certainly disgruntled with the Dodgers for his lack of playing time after the Brewers traded him to Los Angeles late in the 2002 season.

"Everybody feels the same way about Bo," Houston told a pool reporter that weekend. "He doesn't give a crap about anyone in there. He doesn't give a crap about his players. Bo only cares about himself. You see it in the negativity and the disrespect he has toward players, the way he speaks to his players. He's the first one to slam you, embarrass you, throw stuff up in the dugout, throw his hands up in the air."

About the Burrell incident, Houston claimed he played no part in it. "That was kind of a staged thing," he said. "That was more the veteran players endorsing players' doing stuff like that. I had nothing to do with it."

For his part, Burrell eventually said publicly that he was not trying to snub his manager.

But the release of Houston was just another deliberate move by Wade, backing up Bowa and the coaching staff. It sent a message to the players that should have lasted through the off season. Bowa would remain the manager. Unlike a pattern established by some other major sports teams in Philly, management would not allow the players to run the franchise.

"I want people to work together so we can win," Wade said. "Everyone at the big-league level hopefully is an adult. Let's sit down and figure it out and get it resolved. I don't want to get in the middle of it. If I have a conversation with a player about something other than the time of day or the weather, Bo's going to know about it. But I'm going to back the manager because I think he's the right person for our situation. That's the only way for us to get this thing to work, for he and I to be on the same page."

Wade also said that the meeting in Montreal and the release of Houston was appropriate.

"From that point forward, I felt Bo handled himself as well as at any time since he's been back with us," Wade said. "He did his best work under a very high level of scrutiny. Players started talking directly to each other, instead of griping to a writer, talking to a coach or going to me, saying they don't like a teammate, they don't like the way they're being handled, they don't like the manager. All of a sudden we had a lot of people clearing the air, which had been stagnant while we were losing.

"I thought we played better then, people were more open, coaches, manager, front office people, we all agreed to do things a little differently and see things from the other side. I think it worked. But we couldn't get people out. Our bullpen was shot at that point and we couldn't get to the finish line, but it had nothing to do with the volatility of the manager or player-manager relationships. That all got healthier after the meeting took place."

This, of course, was all going on behind the scenes while veteran columnists such as Bill Lyon of the *Philadelphia Inquirer*, Bill Conlin of the *Philadelphia Daily News* and Jason Stark of ESPN.com either called for Bowa's outright dismissal or at least a serious evaluation of his job performance.

At that point, though, only the Marlins really stood in the way of the Phillies getting back to the playoffs for the first time since 1993, and they retooled for the fight. Marlins GM Larry Beinfest filled a real need in the bullpen by acquiring closer Ugueth Urbina, and perhaps that made all the difference. When third baseman Mike Lowell had his hand cracked by a pitch, they added Jeff Conine, a former Marlin and veteran of their run to the 1997 World Series championship.

And Trader Jack still liked to use the media to have a little fun.

With about a month to go in the season, and the Phillies and Marlins neck and neck, McKeon ventured an opinion when asked about the chaos in Philadelphia. The Marlins and Phillies were scheduled to play six times in the final two weeks of the season, and there was no doubt that the wild card would come down to all that.

"This is when you have to temper it," McKeon was reported to have said in response to a question about whether he thought Bowa was panicking. "You can't get excited, you can't panic. That's the thing you see when you get in a situation like this, is the thing you see in Philadelphia, Bowa panicking."

McKeon, the general manager who once hired Bowa to manage the Padres, later said that even though the quote was on tape, he was taken out of context.

"All that I said was that this time of year, you've got to play it cool; you can't panic," McKeon said. "Next thing you know it's all over the place, 'McKeon says Bowa panicked.' The guy finally played the tape back to me, and it wasn't really bad. The writer apologized for putting the thought in my mind. So then I called Larry and apologized. I told him, 'Larry I'm in your corner.' I hired Larry; do you think I'm going to badmouth him?"

With everything Bowa had already gone through, this was just chump change. "Jack called me," Bowa said. "He said, 'I don't remember saying that.' I said, 'Jack, I don't care. You know what I mean? If you think we're panicking, then that's fine.' I wasn't panicking. How was I panicking? I played the same team. Panicking means you're taking a regular out and putting a kid in to try and get something going. I played my same lineup. I did everything the same. I had to go to a different closer. I played Burrell every day. We didn't have David Bell. I don't even know what the panic was. But that's Jack. It didn't bother me."

Bowa has never publicly jousted with McKeon. "I've never taken a shot at Jack. I like him. He gave me an opportunity to get involved in baseball from another end. He did a great job with the Marlins. I know a lot of times he bullshits. If you don't take what he says sometimes real seriously, you're OK. If you dissect everything he says, then I'm sure you'll have problems. But I don't do that."

Thome, who had tried to be the voice of reason in the clubhouse, carried the team on his back for much of September, showing every bit of the residual drive and experience of his two World Series and six playoff appearances with the Indians. And in the end, he finished with 131 runs batted in and a National League-high 47 homers, one short of Mike Schmidt's club record.

In the last crucial series at the Vet, from September 16-18, the Phillies took two of three from the Marlins. The third game had to be rescheduled from the night to early afternoon because of Hurricane Isabel, which was sweeping in on the East Coast. The Phillies won that day and then beat Cincinnati the next night. With an 85-69 record, they led the Marlins by half a game and had eight left to play. It might not have been 1964 all over again, but as another old ballpark was about to close, there were more ominous overtones.

The Phillies lost their next six in a row and seven of the final eight games, including three in Miami to the Marlins, who wrapped up the wild card with an 8-4 victory over Bowa's crew at Pro Player Stadium on September 25. For the second time in Bowa's three seasons, the Phillies had gone down to the wire and failed to qualify. They finished at 86-76, five games behind Florida. The Marlins continued their shocking run in the postseason, upsetting the Giants and Cubs in the first two rounds and the Yankees in the World Series. McKeon, at 72, became the oldest manager in baseball history to take his team to the championship.

In Philadelphia, the finish didn't surprise Tony Gwynn, who played under Bowa in San Diego and is now an ESPN baseball analyst.

"If you ask [Bowa] I think he'd tell you he needed more bodies," Gwynn told the *Philadelphia Inquirer*. "Offensively and pitching-wise, they were a little short."

The only matter remaining was the closing of the Vet, that old dowager decked out for its final weekend, a three-game series against the Braves, a team again preparing for the playoffs.

The last night game was played on September 26. The Phillies' last victory, 7-6, came the next afternoon. Rheal Cormier earned the win to finish the season a perfect 8-0, and Thome hit two home runs. They were the last Phillie homers hit at the Vet. The curtain came down on Sunday, September 28. Greg Maddux, pitching his last game for the Braves, defeated Millwood 5-2. Burrell, with a double, had the last extra-base hit.

The closing ceremonies were emotional, and the 58,554 in attendance for the wake stayed long into the darkening afternoon.

No one knew it at the time, but it would be the last public appearance for two of the franchise cornerstones, Paul Owens and Tug McGraw. McGraw, seemingly in remission from malignant brain cancer, went back to the mound to replicate the scene of perhaps his greatest triumph—leaping, arms stretched skyward in glee just after he struck out the Royals' Willie Wilson to end the 1980 World Series in favor of the Phillies. This time, when he leapt again, the ovation was deafening.

"There were 70 guys on the field, and they all were all waiting," McGraw said, after the event. "Until I headed to the mound, I didn't know exactly what I was going to do. Once I got there, I realized that all I had to do was strike [Willie Wilson] out one more time. It was an exhilarating feeling. That's the last time Willie Wilson will strike out at the Vet. It was louder than anything I've ever heard before."

Owens, nicknamed "The Pope" in the 1960s because of his resemblance to Pope Paul VI, was responsible for the greatest era in Phillies history. As general manager, his teams won NL East titles from 1976 to 1978 and that 1980 World Series. Owens was even brought back to manage the team, replacing Pat Corrales late in the 1983 season and guiding the Phillies into the World Series, where they lost to the Orioles. Bill Giles had been there through all that success, Bowa for most of it as well.

Illness had kept Owens away from the Vet all season until the last game. As the players took their final victory lap around the warning track, Owens, Wade and Dallas Green rode in a golf cart. With the help of Wade and Green, Owens slipped out of the cart to the roar of another standing ovation.

"I thought the defining moment during the closing ceremonies was when the Pope stepped on home plate," Wade said. "Without Paul Owens, there wouldn't be great moments in Vet history. He had a dramatic impact on hundreds of players and millions of fans."

Bowa, too, took his last leap on home plate, his feet together, his arms reaching in the air, his face toward the outfield and back to the stands. His single was the first hit and had come more than 33 years earlier in what was then the spanking new doughnut-shaped ballpark with two decks, the second seemingly reaching toward the moon. There didn't seem to be a dry eye in the house. At the press conference afterward, Bowa choked out a few short words. "Just playing here, winning a world championship, playing with Hall of Famers. The Carpenters. Bill Giles. Paul Owens. Dallas..."

The words stopped coming at that point, and the tears began to flow.

And in the end, another season was over and the era at Vet was complete. A long off season and winter beckoned; Philadelphians, all, were left waiting for the snow.

— Epilogue —

THE AFTERMATH

Winter in Philly usually isn't full of expectation and activity—at least when it comes to baseball. But with the end of the Vet era and the opening of a new ballpark, there is plenty of buzz and excitement. In a way it is like the old giving way to the new: the inevitable cycle of life. The transition is full of hope and optimism.

The holidays were good to the Phillies—full of presents and good cheer. Six days before Christmas, Bowa and a group of past and present Phillies served turkey dinner to about 225 of the homeless, mostly men, who came in from the grey, dank cold. Wearing aprons and shiny red Santa hats, Bowa, John Kruk, Dave Montgomery, Eddie Wade, Ruben Amaro Jr., Milt Thompson, and Dickie Noles stood behind a steam table as the diners passed by collecting edibles along the chatty conga line. Only Bowa shunned the hat. After the turkey and all the trimmings were gone, the Phillies presented a $15,000 donation to the Bethesda Project, the nonprofit organization that runs the shelter.

"You feel good when you do something like this," Bowa said. "It's something small. Maybe it takes an hour or two of your time, but you look back on it and know that it was worth going there. What would you have done otherwise? Sit at home? Go to a mall? I don't think it's asking a lot to help people who are in dire straits."

Earlier that day Bowa and the Phillies had received their own Christmas present. Kevin Millwood opted to forgo free agency, accepted salary arbitration and returned to the Phillies for at least one more season, completing the Phillies' busy holiday shopping season. With a new ballpark ready and starting to generate revenue, the Phillies have attempted to correct the flaws that caused them to fall short in 2003. Wade has rebuilt Bowa's bullpen by acquiring left-handed closer Billy Wagner in a trade with the Houston Astros and by signing free agent Tim Worrell, formerly the Giants' closer. Worrell is expected to set up Wagner, who has amassed 225 saves already in his nine-year career, including 44 in 2003—11 more than the Phillies' entire bullpen that season. In addition, the Phillies picked up another starter from Minnesota, left-hander Eric Milton, who missed most of the 2003 season with an injury, just in case Millwood decided not to come back.

On paper, at least, Bowa's 2004 Phillies seem to have gone right past the Marlins, who lost their first baseman, star catcher, and two closers to trades and free agency and claimed losses of about $20 million despite winning it all in 2003. On the field, all of the pieces are in place.

At the Vet, the catharsis of the last baseball game only a couple of months before has given way to the excitement of expectation. The final stages of letting go are complete. In January, the Phillies moved to their new offices at Citizens Bank Park next door. Books, documents, and photos have been moved to their new homes. The Vet abandoned. The scoreboard stayed dark; the lights remained off. It had been stripped bare of its seats by fans and reporters—a last memento of an era—in the final moments before an old stadium's death.

As the Vet and the era within it closed, death claimed two of the Phillies' own who played such pivotal roles in the old ballyard. After Christmas, Paul Owens, the man who brought the Vet to life, succumbed to a long illness. And just after the start of the new year, Tug McGraw, who was on the mound when the Phillies won it all, lost his eight-month battle with brain cancer. The deaths and ensuing funerals tempered the good cheer of the holidays and all of the positive things accomplished by the Phillies since the end of the season.

At Owens's funeral, Bowa couldn't help but recall the man who had had such an amazing influence on his life by taking a chance on a puny infielder from Sacramento who was short on skill and size but long on hunger and desire. On the word of scout Eddie Bockman and the images of an eight-millimeter film projected on a hotel sheet, Owens signed Bowa to his first professional contract nearly 40 years ago.

"He was probably the most influential person in my baseball career besides my dad as far as his knowledge of the game and his ability to judge the character and makeup of an individual," Bowa said. "He was very observant. He traveled on the road trips. If we had extra hitting at 3:00 p.m. or 3:30, he'd go out in a cab by himself and sit somewhere in the stands. You wouldn't even know where he was, but he'd be watching just to see a guy's work ethic. He'd also do that with opposing teams.

"I mean, Owens had a knack for finding talent and being able to project what a guy could do. To me, of all our Hall of Famers— Robin Roberts, Richie Ashburn, Schmitty, Steve Carlton and if Pete Rose gets in—Paul Owens had a lot more to do with our success than any of those guys."

Bowa has come a long way since that signing, from the sandlots of Sacramento to minor league stops in Spartanburg, Bakersfield, Reading and Eugene as a kid trying to mold himself into a major league player. From Connie Mack Stadium in North Philly to the Vet in the south, where he was a key component in building a team to break the 1964 curse and bring Philadelphia its first world championship. From his first shot at managing in San Diego to his return to Philly, where a now 48-year-old general manager—a kid Bowa remembered as a PR intern who came through the Vet clubhouse and listened to the players boast and grouse—gave him another chance to manage and win.

Drawing on all of his experience and knowledge, Bowa has come full circle and has it made.

"Now you've got a new ballpark coming and an organization willing to make incremental moves up the payroll scale to get there," Eddie Wade said. "All of sudden, instead of your payroll being 23rd in baseball, it's No. 12 or so. These elements create a better working environment for him. Plus he has the level of communication and commitment. He knows he has a 33-year relationship with Dave Montgomery. He could walk into Dave's office any time he wants to talk about anything in the world. He knows what his relationship is with me. He knows that there are people throughout the organization from sales and marketing to the ticket office. A lot of these people grew up with Larry. They were all there when the Vet opened. And they're still there.

"So he's got this great support staff internally within the organization. He's got other people in Philadelphia because he made his home here. There are a lot of positive things. Sometimes you just need to say, 'Hey, pop your head out of the turret for a minute and see that not everybody here is firing at you. We're here to help you out. We're here to cover you. Let us do that.' It's a great situation for him."

In his heart of hearts, Bowa knows that. But his will to win, his "I Still Hate to Lose" mindset is a compulsion and hasn't changed since his San Diego days. He's older and wiser, and at times he has learned not to blow off steam in public. He certainly has made behavioral changes and adjustments. But he can't stand watching his players make the same mistakes over and over again. It isn't a show. He isn't kidding. He really does hate to lose, and he makes no apologies for it. It's a part of the Bowa psyche that has always enticed Wade.

"When we hired him, we didn't want the watered-down version," Wade said. And Bowa appreciates the support.

"I think Eddie believes in what I'm doing," Bowa said. "We talk just about every day. Even during the winter we talk a lot. If he were to fire me tomorrow, I'd have nothing but respect for the way he's handled everything."

Bowa is safe for all the immediate tomorrows, but he knows as well as anyone that the minute a manager is hired the countdown begins toward the day he is fired. Well within his control is the length of the countdown. For the first time in his career as a manager, he has the support of management with money to spend, an improved team on the field, a plan to continue to build a franchise around a new ballpark, and the adoration of the fans in his adopted hometown.

Who better to usher in a new era of baseball in Philly than a man who has been there before and above all desires to be there again?

It is his time.